The Informal Sector
in Francophone Africa

The Informal Sector in Francophone Africa

Firm Size, Productivity, and Institutions

Nancy Benjamin and Ahmadou Aly Mbaye

with Ibrahima Thione Diop, Stephen S. Golub,
Dominique Haughton, and Birahim Bouna Niang

A copublication of the Agence Française de Développement and the World Bank

Library of Congress Cataloging-in-Publication Data
Benjamin, Nancy C., 1956-
    The informal sector in francophone Africa : firm size, productivity and institutions / Nancy Benjamin and Ahmadou Aly Mbaye ; with Ibrahima Thione Diop ... [et al.].
        p. cm.
    Includes bibliographical references and index.
    ISBN 978-0-8213-9537-0 -- ISBN 978-0-8213-9542-4 (electronic)
    1. Informal sector (Economics)--Africa, French-speaking West. 2. Small business--Africa, French-speaking West. 3. Africa, West--Economic conditions--1960- I. Mbaye, Ahmadou Aly. II. Diop, Ibrahima Thione. III. World Bank. IV. Title.
    HD2346.A58B46 2012
    338.70966--dc23

2012011914

Africa Development Forum Series

The **Africa Development Forum** series was created in 2009 to focus on significant issues relevant to Sub-Saharan Africa's economic development. Its aim is both to document the state of the art on specific topics and to contribute to ongoing local, regional, and global policy debates. And it is designed specifically to provide practitioners, scholars, and students with the most up-to-date research results while highlighting the promise, challenges, and opportunities that exist on the continent.

The series is sponsored by the Agence Française de Développement and the World Bank. The manuscripts chosen for publication represent the highest quality research and project activity in each institution and have been selected for their relevance to the development agenda. Working together with a shared sense of mission and interdisciplinary purpose, the two institutions are committed to moving beyond traditional boundaries in a search for new insights and new ways of analyzing the development realities of the Sub-Saharan African Region.

Advisory Committee Members

Agence Française de Développement
Pierre Jacquet, Chief Economist
Robert Peccoud, Director of Research

World Bank
Shantayanan Devarajan, Chief Economist, Africa Region
Célestin Monga, Senior Adviser, Development Economics and Africa Region
Santiago Pombo-Bejarano, Editor-in-Chief, Office of the Publisher

Sub-Saharan Africa

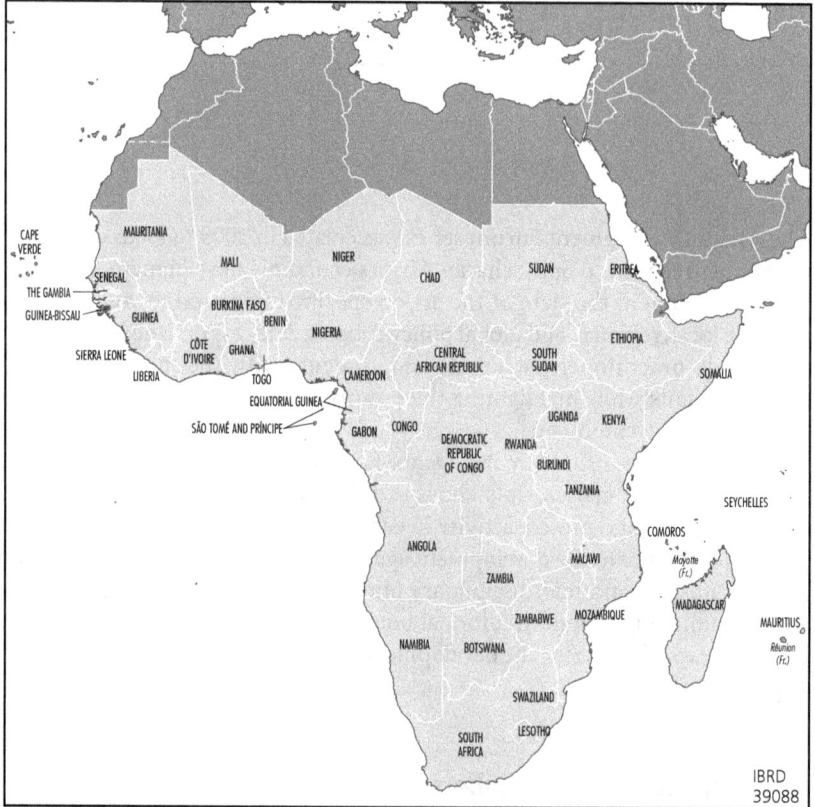

CAPE VERDE	
MAURITANIA	
SENEGAL	MALI	NIGER	CHAD	SUDAN	ERITREA
THE GAMBIA				
GUINEA-BISSAU				
GUINEA	BURKINA FASO			
SIERRA LEONE	CÔTE D'IVOIRE	GHANA	BENIN	NIGERIA	CENTRAL AFRICAN REPUBLIC	SOUTH SUDAN	ETHIOPIA
LIBERIA	TOGO	CAMEROON			SOMALIA
EQUATORIAL GUINEA			
SÃO TOMÉ AND PRÍNCIPE	GABON	CONGO	DEMOCRATIC REPUBLIC OF CONGO	UGANDA	RWANDA	KENYA
	BURUNDI	
	TANZANIA	SEYCHELLES
ANGOLA		COMOROS
	ZAMBIA	MALAWI	Mayotte (Fr.)
	ZIMBABWE	MOZAMBIQUE	MADAGASCAR
NAMIBIA	BOTSWANA		MAURITIUS
		Réunion (Fr.)
	SWAZILAND	
	LESOTHO	
SOUTH AFRICA		

IBRD
39088

Titles in the Africa Development Forum Series

Africa's Infrastructure: A Time for Transformation (2010) edited by Vivien Foster and Cecilia Briceño-Garmendia

Gender Disparities in Africa's Labor Market (2010) edited by Jorge Saba Arbache, Alexandre Kolev, and Ewa Filipiak

Challenges for African Agriculture (2010) edited by Jean-Claude Deveze

Contemporary Migration to South Africa: A Regional Development Issue (2011) edited by Aurelia Segatti and Loren Landau

Light Manufacturing in Africa: Targeted Policies to Enhance Private Investment and Create Jobs (2012) by Hinh T. Dinh, Vincent Palmade, Vandana Chandra, and Frances Cossar

Empowering Women: Legal Rights and Economic Opportunities in Africa (2012) by Mary Hallward-Driemeier and Tazeen Hasan

Financing Africa's Cities: The Imperative of Local Investment (2012) by Thierry Paulais

Structural Transformation and Rural Change Revisited: Challenges for Late Developing Countries in a Globalizing World (2012) by Bruno Losch, Sandrine Fréguin-Gresh, and Eric Thomas White

Contents

6   The Institutional Environment of the Informal Sector in West Africa   123

with Ibrahima Thione Diop and Birahim Bouna Niang

7   Informality and Productivity   145

with Dominique Haughton

Figures

Tables

Foreword

As Africa grows and modernizes, it is crucial to understand how to better translate these positive trends into poverty reduction through productive employment, especially for the 7–10 million young people entering the labor force every year.

Until now, there have been few systematic studies on the informal sector, despite the fact that most Africans work there, and it clearly plays a central role in shaping the continent's growth and social inclusion outlook.

This book is a major step towards improving the understanding of the complex reality of informal sector firms in francophone West Africa. It innovates by concentrating on informal *firms* rather than informal *employment* (as other studies do), and identifying "large informal" sector firms whose sales rival those of large formal-sector firms but operate in ways that are similar to small informal operators. Not only is the regulatory environment facing these two types of informal firms distinct, but policies aimed at improving their productivity need to be differentiated.

The study also breaks new ground with an eclectic methodology and primary data collection. Quantitative and qualitative firm-level data were collected involving a unique and fruitful collaboration among academic researchers, government officials, the West African Economic and Monetary Union Commission, informal and formal sector business associations, and labor unions.

The result is a comprehensive study of the multiple facets of the informal sector—its economic significance, the socio-demographic characteristics of managers and employees, the sector distribution, relationship with government, sources of financing, firm-level productivity, social networks, and the role of culture.

In identifying ways of improving the productivity of informal firms, the book identifies institutional and governance weaknesses, but also highlights social and cultural hurdles to formalization.

This book is not only a window into the workings of the informal sector in West Africa; it is a contribution to understanding how to raise the productivity of these workers. As such, it is more than a compendium of information: it is a useful tool for those who work for an Africa free of poverty.

Makhtar Diop
Vice President
Africa Region
The World Bank

Preface

The informal sector in Africa is poorly understood, having received less systematic attention than the informal sector in other developing countries, particularly in Latin America. In particular, a crucial but little studied characteristic of the informal sector in Africa is the coexistence of large and small informal operators. Usually, the term informal sector connotes very small and precarious firms. While such firms are indeed prevalent in Africa, there are also very large informal firms and powerful ethnic and religious informal networks linking large and small enterprises. One of the main objectives of this work is to provide a detailed understanding of the phenomenon of the informal sector in West Africa through case studies in three countries: Benin, Burkina Faso, and Senegal.

This volume represents the culmination of a long collaboration between the Centre de Recherches Economiques Appliquées (CREA) at the University Cheikh Anta Diop of Dakar and the World Bank. In early 2007, the CREA and the World Bank's Research Department agreed to develop and fund a research proposal developed by Ahmadou Aly Mbaye, then director of the CREA and now dean of the School of Economics and Management at Cheikh Anta Diop University, and Nancy Benjamin, at that time the Senegal economist at the World Bank. For the Bank, this study was the logical continuation of a Country Economic Memorandum on Senegal, drafted and coordinated by Ms. Benjamin, that strongly recommended follow-up investigations of the informal sector as crucial to understanding the business environment in Senegal and West Africa. The CREA has extensive experience with fieldwork in Senegal and other countries of the region.

Most previous economic studies on the informal sector in Africa have focused on the labor market, households, and employment, premised on the idea that informal enterprises are small and household based. Our approach instead centers on surveys of urban enterprises. There are several reasons for this approach. First, we are interested in the role of the business climate and the institutional environment in fostering the informal sector, a topic that is largely outside the purview of previous studies. Second, previous studies have used somewhat different concepts of informality, making cross-country comparisons problematic. Third, previous studies have ignored the role of large informal firms—what we call the "large informal" sector.

Our sampling strategy ensured coverage of the small informal, large informal, and formal sectors. We used data from a variety of sources, including surveys of 300 firms in each of the three countries, less structured interviews with a subset of large informal firms and government officials, as well as various knowledgeable people, and secondary information from the national accounts and other sources. Our results and analysis shed light on multiple facets of the informal sector, including sociodemographic characteristics of actors, the impact of the informal sector on tax collections, the effects of the business climate, the productivity of firms, and more.

The on-site fieldwork involved a unique and fruitful collaboration among academic researchers, government officials in the countries concerned, the West African Economic and Monetary Union (WAEMU) Commission, business associations in the formal and informal sectors, and unions. These individuals and institutions were invaluable sources of information, and without their assistance, gathering the data for this study would have been impossible. We would like to take this opportunity to offer them our deepest gratitude for contributing to our study by obliging our continuing requests for data and explanations. Particular thanks are due to the Department of Tax Policy, Trade, and Customs and the Department of Economic Policy in the WAEMU Commission at that time. Indeed, the WAEMU Commission always dispatched officials to accompany and assist us during meetings with national government agencies and private sector organizations. It also assisted us in obtaining quantitative data, official documents, and reports of all sorts and played a key role in sessions to disseminate the results of this study in Benin, Burkina Faso, and Senegal. We would like to express our deep gratitude to the president of the WAEMU Commission at the time, Soumaila Cissé; commissioners at that time Pape Abdou Sakho and Joseph Marie Dabiré; and their respective chiefs of staff, notably Serigne Mbacké Sougou; as well as the various department heads.

We would also like to thank the governments of the three countries for their generosity in providing data as well as their willingness to speak openly with the team leaders of the study. Officials from customs, tax departments, ministries of commerce, and various informal sector support organizations in the three countries were unfailingly generous and helpful. The national statistical services in the three countries also assisted in sampling and data collection. Their vast expertise and experience in this field have been very useful, and we sincerely thank the Ministry of Sustainable Development, Finance, and Commerce, to which these services are attached in the case of Benin. We would like to particularly express our gratitude to Mr. Antonin Dossou, Chief of Cabinet of the Ministry for Sustainable Development in Benin at that time, for his personal involvement in our project throughout all stages of the process.

This study was implemented with the assistance of the economic research centers of three major universities in each of the three countries: the University of Abomey-Calavi in Benin, the University of Ouagadougou in Burkina Faso, and the University Cheikh Anta Diop in Dakar. These three teams, respectively, were led by professors Fulbert Gero Amoussouga, Kimsey Savadogo, and Ahmadou Aly Mbaye. The researchers and investigators (more than 100) who carried out the fieldwork are too numerous to be thanked individually. However, we would like to take this opportunity to single out and thank Fatou Guèye, Adama Guèye, Léon Akpo, Allé Nar Diop, Bamba Diop, Mbacké Ba, Lassana Cissokho, Sophie Pascaline Faye, and Alain Akanni in Dakar; Michel Soede, Jean-Claude Kaka, Damien Agbodji, and the many other team members in Benin; and Bamory Ouatara, Namaro Yago, Aladari Traoré, and other team members in Burkina Faso. Ndèye Amy Diallo and Germaine Mendes Diaw administratively managed the grant for the CREA side.

Ahmadou Aly Mbaye and Nancy Benjamin were responsible for coordinating all stages of this study, with substantial contributions from other members of the coordinating team in the drafting and editing of certain chapters. These other members of the coordination team are Stephen Golub (Swarthmore College), Dominique Haughton (Bentley University), and Birahim Bouna Niang and Ibrahima Thione Diop (CREA). Ahmadou Aly Mbaye and Nancy Benjamin designed the questionnaire, carried out the sampling, and led the data collection process in the three cities. They were directly responsible for collecting qualitative data through interviews, with the support of Birahim Bouna Niang and Ibrahima Thione Diop. They are also the authors of all chapters in this volume (unless otherwise noted below) and led the dissemination process with government officials and various stakeholders in the three cities, as well as the WAEMU Commission. Stephen Golub is the author of chapters 8 and 9 on cross-border trade and the social networks of the informal sector in West Africa. He was also responsible for translating chapters 1–7 from French into English, with the help of four of his students, Arielle Bernhardt, Peter Davies, Dina Emam, and Zach Schmidt, and participated in the editing of the final document. Dominique Haughton gave advice on sampling strategy and is a coauthor of chapter 7 on productivity and the informal sector. Birahim Bouna Niang and Ibrahima Thione Diop are coauthors of chapter 6, on the institutional environment of the informal sector in West Africa. Ibrahima Thione Diop also codirected the second phase of the surveys carried out in the three countries.

In addition to funding from the World Bank Research Committee, this project received funding from the World Bank Africa Region funds as well as from the Luxemburg Poverty Reduction Partnership (LPRP) Trust Funds. The LPRP was also instrumental in funding both extensive workshops to disseminate the main results in all three countries and in funding the final publication costs. In addition, support for publication and dissemination was provided by the Diagnostic Facility for Shared Growth Trust Fund. The Agence Française de Développement (AFD) also granted some resources to CREA to support fieldwork in the three capital cities.

Finally, we are very grateful to two anonymous referees, as well as to Stephen McGroarty, acquisition editor for this volume, for valuable comments and helpful assistance throughout the manuscript revision process.

Abbreviations

BCEAO	Central Bank of the West African States (Banque Centrale des Etats de l'Afrique de l'Ouest)
BNP	Banque Nationale de Paris (BNP)
CART	classification and regression tree
CET	common external tariff (*tariff exterieur commun*)
CFA	African Financial Community (Communauté Financière Africaine)
CFAF	CFA franc
CREA	Centre de Recherches Economiques Appliquées
DAG	directed acyclic graph
DGE	Division of Large Enterprises (Direction Générale des Entreprises)
DIAL	Développement, Institutions et Ajustement à Long Terme
ECOWAS	Economic Community of West African States
FCI	full conditional independence
GDP	gross domestic product
GIE	*groupements d'intérêts économiques*
HDI	Human Development Indicator (UNDP)
HIPC	Heavily Indebted Poor Countries
ICA	Investment Climate Assessment (World Bank)
ICT	information and communication technology
ILO	International Labour Organisation
IMF	International Monetary Fund
KSB	Keur Serigne Bi
LPRP	Luxembourg Poverty Reduction Partnership
OECD	Organisation for Economic Co-operation and Development

OHADA	Organization for the Harmonization of Business Law (Organisation pour l'Harmonisation du Droit des Affaires en Afrique)
OLS	ordinary least squares
ONATEL	Office National des Télécommunications
ROES	Rassemblement des Opérateurs Economiques du Sénégal
SAR	Special Administrative Region
SME	small and medium enterprises
SONABEL	Société National d'Electricité du Burkina
SONATEL	Société Nationale des Télécommunications
SOPAM	Société d'Outillage de Précision et d'Accessoires Mécaniques
TFP	total factor productivity
TIN	tax identification number
TUTR	road transport tax (*taxe unique sur le transport routier*)
UNDP	United Nations Development Program
USAID	U.S. Agency for International Development
VAT	value added tax
WAEMU	West African Economic and Monetary Union

Overview

Informality usually connotes small and unorganized producers operating on the fringes of the formal economy. In West African countries, however, the normal situation is generally reversed: dynamic informal sectors dominate stagnant formal economies. Moreover, in these countries, small operators coexist with very large and politically well-connected informal enterprises and well-organized networks. This study is the first to describe and analyze large informal firms in a systematic way. In addition to the novel distinction between large and small firms, the originality of this study resides in its eclectic methodology and collection of original data. A key conclusion is that determinants and appropriate policy responses differ between "large" and "small" informal operations.

The informal sector is a central issue for African economic development, yet relatively little is known about it. This volume endeavors to improve our understanding of the complex reality of informal sector firms in West Africa. The book provides detailed description and analysis of the characteristics and functioning of informal sector firms, the causes of the pervasiveness of these firms, the relations between formal and informal firms, the consequences of informality for economic development, and appropriate policy responses.

This study focuses on the urban informal sector in three capital cities: Dakar (Senegal), Cotonou (Benin), and Ouagadougou (Burkina Faso). These three countries have important differences and, as a group, are quite representative of francophone West Africa and, to a lesser extent, West Africa as a whole.

We employ a mix of quantitative and qualitative approaches using data obtained from our own surveys of 900 firms in the three cities, interviews with knowledgeable stakeholders and participants, and all available secondary data. For the surveys, we designed our sampling strategy to include three distinctive categories of firms: formal, small informal, and large informal. In addition, we developed a comprehensive definition of informality to reflect its complexity and heterogeneity. Our definition (chapter 1) covers six components of informality, whereas previous definitions are generally limited to a binary classification based on one or two indicators. Our results for West Africa corroborate many findings from earlier studies, particularly for small informal firms. In addition, we break new ground by shedding light on the large informal sector and the institutional and sociocultural factors shaping it.

Our Approach to Studying the Informal Sector

Understanding the causes and consequences of informality is crucial given that the informal sector plays a dominant role in West African economies, particularly with regard to employment. Chapter 3 describes the informal sector in the three countries and presents their shares of employment and of total and sectoral gross domestic product (GDP) based on national accounts data. Despite the limitations of official estimates, which exclude large informal firms, they reveal that the informal sector accounts for the majority of GDP and 90 percent or more of employment. In fact, formal employment in the private sector is truly scarce, at 1 to 5 percent of the labor force.

The vast majority of previous studies of the informal sector in Africa focuses on very small enterprises, usually individually operated, such as street vendors and craftsmen. While it is certainly true that most informal activities are very small scale, the informal sector is, in fact, far more complex and encompasses some very large operators as well as sophisticated informal networks linking seemingly isolated microenterprises.

The informal sector in Africa differs in particular from that in Latin America. The groundbreaking study of the informal sector in Latin America (Perry et al. 2007) does not include any discussion of large informal firms, although it does note that some large formal firms underreport sales or employees. The evidence from Latin America also indicates that a substantial share of workers voluntarily exit paid employment in the formal sector and form their own small informal businesses, which is rare in West Africa.

The literature's focus on small operators has entailed data collection strategies that focus on household-based enterprises and the labor market. This approach has, by definition, excluded the larger firms. Empirical studies of the informal sector have largely followed the pioneering approach of the International Labour Organization (ILO 1993, 2002). The ILO defines informality by firm size and lack of registration, effectively confining the sample to household and small enterprises. Another strand of the literature uses World Bank Investment Climate Assessment (ICA) data and other similar databases (Gelb et al. 2009; La Porta and Schleifer 2008, 2011). ICA surveys provide much useful information, but they would be better described as private enterprise surveys, in principle covering both formal and informal firms, but in practice excluding much of the informal sector, namely the large informal firms as well as microenterprises. The World Bank also conducts "informal" and "micro" surveys to capture the informal sector. These surveys, however, are limited to small firms, thus excluding the large informal sector.

We argue that informality is a continuum, with even largely formal firms often engaging in some informal practices. Recently, some authors have recognized that informality is a matter of degree, best captured by a range of indicators (Steel and Snodgrass 2008; La Porta and Schleifer 2011; Guha-Khasnobis and Kanbur 2006), but none has proposed or implemented operational definitions. The characteristics of informal firms are indeed rather complex and may be captured best through the use of multiple criteria. Some firms are registered and pay taxes but substantially underreport sales and profits (Dabla-Norris, Gradstein, and Inchauste 2008; La Porta and Shleifer 2011). Our survey results also show that a large number of firms underreport sales.

In chapter 1, we provide a definition of informality using six criteria: size, registration, honesty of accounts, fixity of workplace, access to credit, and tax status. Although these six criteria are more comprehensive than what others have used, they do not capture all dimensions of informality, such as management practices and participation in social security programs. These six criteria are combined to create levels of informality depending on how many of the six a particular firm meets. At the bottom of the ladder are firms that are completely informal—firms that do not fulfill any of the criteria defining formality. The second level consists of firms that fulfill at least one of the criteria defining formality, and so on, with the last level being firms that meet all criteria and are completely formal. The two extremes of purely informal and purely formal are rare.

We further distinguish two categories of informal firms: large and small. Large informal firms are comparable in size to those of the modern sector but behave informally in other respects. These firms satisfy all of the six criteria for formality used here, except for one: their accounts are not accurate. Large informal firms differ from formal firms in less tangible respects not covered in our criteria, such as management structure and personal attributes, as discussed in chapter 4.

Given the complexity of the informal sector and the difficulties of obtaining accurate information, we used three types of data sources. First, we made use of standard national accounts and other public databases, for example, those from customs, fiscal authorities, and national statistical institutes. While useful for cross-checking and providing an overview of the significance of the informal sector, these databases do not enable in-depth analysis of informal sector firms. As a second step, we conducted our own surveys. Third, we also conducted interviews, which allowed us to collect qualitative information to supplement the quantitative data from our surveys. We interviewed key stakeholders and experts on the informal sector from both public and private sectors.

Regarding our surveys, in order to have a mix of formal, large informal, and small informal firms, we used a stratified sampling strategy, described in chapter 2. That is, we sought random samples within three-by-three categories composed of (a) formal, small informal, and large informal enterprises and (b) industry, commerce, and other services. A first set of surveys was conducted in 2007, with a sample of 300 enterprises in Dakar, Ouagadougou, and Cotonou, for a total of 900 units surveyed in the three cities combined. In 2009, follow-up surveys and interviews were conducted with a smaller number of firms in the three cities, focusing on large informal and formal firms.

Characteristics of Informal Businesses in West Africa

We compared the characteristics and functioning of informal and formal firms from a variety of perspectives: size, social and demographic attributes of firm managers, access to credit, participation in global markets, capital investment, access to public services, registration, quality of accounts, fixity of workplace, payment of taxes, and participation in social security systems.

Our most important findings concern the distinction between large and small informal operators. As noted, in West Africa, large informal firms and trading networks coexist with small operators, but little is known about who is involved, the sectors in which they operate, and the nature of their businesses. This study presents factual information on the large and small segments of the informal sector and the formal sector.

Large informal firms are fundamentally different from both formal and small informal firms, while at the same time resembling each of them in some respects. They are discussed in detail in chapter 4, using case studies of firms and sectors where they play a major role. These sectors include import-export trade, domestic wholesale-retail, transportation, and construction. For example, in Senegal, one trader is estimated to control more than a third of the imports of rice, the main food staple in the country. These large informal entrepreneurs often began as small operators with minimal education but became very wealthy and influential thanks to superior entrepreneurial ability and effort, along with assistance from ethnic and religious trading groups. In volume of sales and other measures of activity, these firms do not differ from their formal counterparts. Moreover, they are registered and well known to the authorities. Yet they continue to underreport sales massively and to maintain fraudulent accounts. In their family-based organization and management, they are very much like small informal firms. Typically, a single person (usually a man) controls all major functions (human resources, accounts, finance, and marketing), in contrast to formal firms that have separate departments for each activity. The owners' personal and business assets and liabilities are not clearly separated.

In addition, these enterprises are fragile insofar as the owner may dissolve the business because of a conflict with tax or customs officials or reappear under another name, when identified by the tax authorities.

Large informal firms are very difficult to identify. We were able to identify and understand the operation of these firms through interviews with some of the entrepreneurs as well as with government officials and other knowledgeable people. We also explored the operations of these large firms in Senegal by comparing firm-level imports tabulated by customs with the same firm's level of total turnover, as reported to the fiscal authorities. In many cases, firms' imports far exceeded their reported total turnover, strongly suggesting underreporting of sales.

For small informal firms, our survey results largely confirm the standard findings in the literature (chapter 5). Firm size is tiny and dominated by self-employment. Most firms are registered somewhere, usually with municipalities and the Ministry of Commerce, but rarely with the fiscal authorities. The level of education is generally low, with relatively high (but still low in absolute terms) participation of women. Access to bank credit is almost nonexistent due to insufficient documentation; small informal firms resort to unofficial credit markets with onerous interest rates. Use of information and communication technologies (ICTs) is limited. Small informal firms are concentrated in many of the same sectors as larger informal firms: commerce, handicrafts, transport, and new and used clothes. Small informal firms sell low-quality products to other microenterprises and low-income households in a highly competitive market. They rarely export. Small informal firms also operate in a completely unregulated and competitive labor market, and employees have no social security protection.

Chapter 5 also compares the characteristics of formal, large informal, and small informal firms. Formal firms differ from informal firms in all of the above characteristics; that is, they are considerably larger, are registered with the fiscal authorities, pay regular taxes, have managers and workers who tend to be more highly educated, have greater, although still surprisingly limited, access to formal credit (by international standards), make use of ICT, and are somewhat more export oriented.

Large informal firms' characteristics tend to fall somewhere in the middle, between formal and small informal firms. As noted, the organizational structure of large informal firms differs little from that of smaller informal firms. Volume-of-sales data suggest that large formal firms are generally as big as formal firms, but they have far fewer permanent employees, except in Cotonou. Cotonou is, in general, rather different from the other two cities because of its role as a hub for regional smuggling, as described in chapter 9. Many of the major smuggling enterprises are very large-scale operations, particularly in the used car market, also described in chapter 4.

The literature on the informal sector often notes that a major drawback of informality is lack of access to public services. We largely corroborate this result but also find that formal firms suffer even more than informal firms from the deficiencies of infrastructure; in some cases, formal firms have longer wait times for connections to utilities than small informal firms. Moreover, formal and informal firms share the same highly negative view of the business environment.

Relations between formal and informal firms are complex, with cases of both competition and cooperation. Many formal firms rely on informal distributors. Commerce and construction involve well-developed ties and subcontracting between formal and informal operators. Customs clearance for imports illustrates these interactions. Many unauthorized customs clearance agents work in this sector, in collusion with legally authorized agents. The informal actors clear merchandise from the port at much lower costs, using the authorized agent's seal in exchange for a side payment to the latter. Similarly, in the construction sector, government procurement and other large contracts are usually reserved for formal firms, but these firms then subcontract out most of the work to informal firms.

In other areas, competition from informal firms, particularly importers, undermines formal producers and distributors. A major part of the informal sector revolves around smuggling to evade import barriers designed to protect local manufacturers, for example, in sugar and clothing. Many other goods are smuggled in, notably used cars, used clothes, and pharmaceuticals (including counterfeit drugs), undercutting formal distributors of these products who pay import duties, particularly in Senegal. Chapter 9 describes the operation of smuggling networks, focusing on Benin and Senegal, provides estimates of the magnitude of smuggling, and analyzes the distortionary domestic policies that foster these practices. These smuggling operations are also facilitated by kinship networks of traders that span national borders, as described in chapter 8.

Institutional, Regulatory, and Sociocultural Environment

As detailed in chapter 4, the informal sector dominates the economies of West Africa and is expanding, to the detriment of the formal sector. Our view is that the institutional and social environment plays a crucial two-way role in fostering the pervasiveness of the informal sector. On the one hand, the institutional setting is a major determinant of informality. Weaknesses in the business climate and regulatory framework induce firms to opt for informal sector status. Moreover, traditional African business practices often conflict with largely imported Western rules and norms. On the other hand, the dominance of the informal sector further undermines compliance with rules, regulations, and codes of conduct compatible with a level playing field.

Chapter 6 focuses on the legal and regulatory environment and how it affects the decision of firms to operate in the informal sector. Formal businesses are subject to a proliferation of taxes, including several types of income tax, wage taxes, taxes on equipment and buildings, and various registration and license fees, resulting in numerous duplicative taxes that cumulate to a high incidence and imply onerous compliance costs. Business law in francophone Africa, including the three countries under study, is in principle governed by OHADA,[1] an intergovernmental structure modeled on the French legal system. OHADA imposes a minimal set of recordkeeping for all firms that is feasible even for small firms. Nevertheless, the governments do not enforce these rather minimal regulations, allowing firms to pay the lower lump-sum presumptive taxes without any record-keeping obligations. This reflects weak enforcement capabilities. Another major problem is a lack of cooperation among government agencies, particularly between customs and tax authorities. In fact, as noted earlier, in chapter 4 our own analysis of customs and tax databases indicates massive underreporting of incomes in Senegal. Also, there are a large number of underfunded and ineffective government agencies with overlapping and unclear mandates.

Due largely to these problems, indicators of the business climate are poor. In this regard, our surveys and interview results for the most part corroborate standard rankings and indicators of the business environment, such as the World Bank's Doing Business rankings and the World Economic Forum's Global Competitiveness Report. Waiting times for connection to utilities (water, electricity, telephone) are often very long, and service is expensive and unreliable. Frequent power outages continue to be a major disruption to formal and informal businesses alike.

State failures also include corruption, bureaucracy, and the establishment of state rent-seeking systems, as discussed extensively in chapter 6. Corruption in all rungs of society contributes to the flourishing of large informal firms. Often, such firms are politically well connected, which offers them some impunity. They freely challenge court decisions that go against them, and the press often reports corruption scandals in the courts. Large informal actors are supported by a chain of collusion that involves customs, the administration, and the courts.

The weaknesses of the state are also manifest at the level of tax collection. Fiscal authorities disproportionately target formal firms. Many formal sector managers complain that, once the fiscal authorities identify them as significant taxpayers, they are subject to repeated audits and upward adjustments in payments (chapter 5). Tax officials themselves acknowledge their focus on formal firms. In an environment rampant with corruption, informal firms seem to possess greater flexibility in their relations with the government. Many firm managers also believe that underreporting of income is pervasive and not punished by the government.

The regulatory and state failure issues that emerge clearly from our surveys and interviews are fairly well documented in the literature on African development. Social and cultural settings are less studied by economists, yet also play a prominent role in the spread of the informal sector in West Africa, as we illustrate in chapter 8. In particular, ethnic and religious networks substitute for the state provision of public goods. Ethnic and social networks are a form of "social capital," which can have positive as well as negative effects on economic development. On the plus side, social networks create bonds of trust that enable contract fulfillment, access to financing, and information exchange without documentation or official involvement. Kinship groups play a particularly important part in international trade, helping to overcome transaction costs created by lack of information and differences in business practices across countries. Kinship networks have a major role in informal cross-border trading in West Africa, as described in chapter 9. On the negative side, however, social capital in general and informal networks in particular can be exclusionary, accepting or even promoting antisocial behavior and violation of the rules and norms of the formal economy. Again, this is clearly manifested in West Africa insofar as kinship networks are heavily involved in illegal activities, particularly smuggling and tax evasion. Overall, ethnic and religious networks are particularly significant in West Africa because of the combination of weak formal institutions and the continuing importance of kinship ties dating from the precolonial era and the resistance to colonialism. Chapter 8 notes some common features of the Mouride and Yoruba groups and relates them to the informal sector practices discussed in other chapters of this book.

Chapter 8 also illustrates the effects of kinship groups through case studies of the Mourides in Senegal and the Yoruba in Benin. In both cases, there is a close connection between the informal sector in general and trading in particular. To this day, trading is the foremost activity of the informal sector, as seen in chapter 2, involving both domestic and cross-border dimensions. The trading networks of the Mourides extend to Europe, Asia, and North America in addition to Africa. The Yoruba's trading sphere is confined largely to West Africa. The interplay of historical, cultural, and economic factors is important in understanding the central role of informal trading activities in West African economies. While group solidarity and mutual trust enable the expansion of commercial activities, the political and economic influence of these groups is not entirely benign. Their main markets, such as Touba and Sandaga in Senegal and Dantokpa in Benin, are largely off-limits to the government, enabling these groups to engage in smuggling and tax evasion in plain view of the authorities.

Chapter 9 investigates smuggling in detail, with a focus on trade between Senegal and The Gambia and between Benin and Nigeria. The characteristics and operation of this informal trade are described. The causes of this trade are varied, but the main drivers are policy distortions causing price differentials across borders, combined with long-standing ethnic and religious ties transcending national borders (as described in chapter 8), long porous borders, weak enforcement, and the involvement of influential political actors.

Costs and Benefits of Informality: Productivity, Living Standards, and Tax Revenue

The costs and benefits of informality can be viewed from the perspective of an individual entrepreneur or from the point of view of society as a whole. The former refers to the decision of a firm to formalize or not, whereas the latter concerns the overall economic and social consequences of the informal sector. Regarding the former, as discussed in the previous section, weak state enforcement capabilities, inadequate provision of public goods, and lack of an effective and transparent regulatory framework are critical for firms' decisions. A hostile environment can push an agent into the informal sector. Formalization means greater access to public services but also requires compliance with regulations and payment of taxes. Participation in the formal sector engenders both fixed costs (related to registration and normalization of formerly informal activities) and variable costs (taxes and contributions for social security), as pointed out by Levenson and Maloney (1998). Our results show that these institutional factors are very important for explaining the expansion of the informal sector (especially chapters 4 and 6).

The remainder of this section examines the larger question of the social effects of informality. Among the outcomes of informality, the productivity issue is critical. As many other studies have found, the productivity gap between formal and informal firms is large. Our results unambiguously corroborate this fact in the three cities, as reported in chapter 7. In addition, when informality is broken down into six levels, as described previously, formality and productivity are strongly and positively correlated. This finding is robust with respect to alternative definitions and correlates of informality and is confirmed using alternative multiple regression specifications.

The correlation between productivity and informality may reflect two-way causation. Low productivity may lead to informal sector status through self-selection of firms by quality of management. The most talented managers choose to formalize because they reap greater benefits from access to public services, provided government has the necessary enforcement capabilities and the business environment is sufficiently favorable (Gelb et al. 2009). Reverse causation running from firm status to productivity could be due to the reduced access to public services that informality entails. Informality also prevents companies from acquiring modern management skills and worker training, further reducing productivity, although Grimm, Knorringa, and Lay (2012), using West African survey data, are able to distinguish some informal firms with better management capabilities. Lack of finance in particular means that firms are unable to invest, resulting in lower capital intensity and hence lower labor productivity.

This study examines total factor productivity (TFP) in addition to labor productivity. TFP controls for capital intensity, yet we find the same positive correlation between TFP and formality as we do for labor productivity. This shows that capital intensity alone cannot explain differences in labor productivity and, in turn, provides further evidence that access to credit is not the ultimate source of the productivity gap between formal and informal firms.

We also investigate productivity differentials between large and small informal firms. Our results indicate that large informal firms also have lower productivity than formal firms, but the differential is minor, whereas the productivity gap between large and small informal firms is much greater. Thus, with regard to productivity, large informal firms resemble formal firms much more than their smaller informal counterparts.

The effects of informality on poverty are also important. The literature from various African countries indicates that small informal firms offer returns that can attract workers out of agriculture, but these firms are far more fragile and less likely to grow than formal or large informal firms (Calvès and Schoumaker 2004). They tend to proliferate when economic growth is poor, consistent with the view that such firms are a survival activity of last resort when other employment fails. An implication of this hypothesis is that incomes tend to be much lower in the informal sector than in the formal sector. In chapter 3, we use two measures of poverty—monetary and nonmonetary—and the Living Standards Measurement Survey datasets in the three countries and confirm that poverty is much more prevalent among employees in the informal sector. Overall, the informal sector is a source of income for individuals with limited options, but it cannot be a sustainable source of long-term growth and income generation.

Tax evasion is another well-recognized social cost of informality, and we examine the tax implications of informality on fiscal systems in the three countries. There is a gaping disparity in the respective shares of GDP of the formal and informal sectors and their contributions to fiscal revenue. Indeed, the informal sector provides almost no government revenue, despite accounting for more than half of GDP. We estimate that the loss of fiscal revenue due to tax avoidance of the informal sector amounts to between 3 and 10 percent of GDP. Governments have attempted to impose taxes on small informal firms, mainly through the lump-sum presumptive tax, but outcomes so far have been very disappointing. Large informal firms are capable of paying far more than they do but are able to evade their responsibilities due to underreporting and political clout.

Main Conclusions and Recommendations

Our results confirm the heterogeneity of the informal sector. Specifically, they confirm the importance of the large informal firms in West Africa and the importance of distinguishing the large from the small informal firms in describing behavior and identifying obstacles in the investment climate. While the vast majority of informal firms are very small, large informal firms play a major role in some sectors, notably commerce, and provide important role models, good or bad, for how different governments structure and enforce their regulatory frameworks.

Policy recommendations are likely to differ between large and small informal enterprises. For large informal firms, the goal must be to bring them under the formal regulation net and register them for formal tax regimes. For small informal firms, the policy implications are already quite well known: programs that seek to reduce poverty by improving the capacity of microenterprises, often by supplying training, credit, and business development services, must be instituted or expanded.

The informal sector is in part a symptom of institutional deficiencies, and the large informal sector, in particular, is a symptom of government failure to enforce regulations that should apply to these firms as well as of the burdensome nature of regulations and taxation that inhibits compliance.

For the large informal firms with a genuine choice, policy should be oriented toward a more systematically enforced and enforceable regulatory regime. Governments should systematically test regulations for their social-benefit content and explicitly consider the cost of compliance for firms and the requirements of systematic enforcement for government, along with the cost to credibility of irregular enforcement.

The informal sector is concentrated in nontradable industries, mainly services, commerce, distribution, construction, or locally sourced food products or raw materials. Although the informal sector provides a large share of employment and incomes, these activities lack the growth potential of more globally traded goods.

In order to reach national growth targets, governments cannot rely on the growth of informal businesses, and policy will need to promote the international competitiveness of formal firms, including foreign investors, which have greater potential to boost exports and productivity growth.

The informal sector contributes to an inimical investment climate for formal firms, particularly foreign investors. Thus the dualistic nature of West African economies, characterized by a large unregulated and untaxed informal sector, is an obstacle to sustained growth. The small formal sector—substantially consisting of foreign investment—must shoulder a disproportionate tax burden, severely hampering its competitiveness. These higher taxes and fees lead to further disadvantages for formal firms—and advantages for the informal sector—and reduce foreign direct investment.

It seems impossible for an economy to develop when the bulk of economic activity operates outside of the regulatory and tax regime, so formalization of the informal sector must be a long-term objective.

The informal sector relies on practices that hinder productivity growth. Their lower productivity may be influenced by the fragility noted earlier, lack of transparency or lack of knowledge of their own accounts, long-established traditions based on well-entrenched control of territory and rents, and suboptimal allocation of productive factors (including reliance on family sources for credit). Informality also prevents companies from acquiring modern management skills and worker training, limiting growth potential and access to the world market.

The issue of productivity is also connected to export competitiveness. Given Africa's small and declining share in global trade, improving competitiveness is a key factor for stimulating growth and raising incomes. Informality makes exporting difficult. Further, survey results indicate that lack of demand is a key constraint facing informal firms. In this context, remaining cut off from world markets through low competitiveness is a devastating obstacle. Finally, the motivation for improving competitiveness and growth may provide a useful entry point for addressing the political economy and governance problems indicated earlier, which have high economywide costs.

Improving the coordination among the diverse registration and tax authorities and the enforcement of a single taxpayer identification system, especially between customs and tax offices, would help to improve the investment climate and address the governance issues giving rise to the large informal sector. However, such reforms will undoubtedly encounter much resistance, given the rents that arise from the current systems.

The informal sector in general—and large informal firms in particular—is responsible for a substantial loss of fiscal revenues and narrowing of the tax base. In addition to numerous difficulties in paying taxes, these informal firms frequently say they do not pay formal taxes because public money is poorly spent.

Business and government should collaborate on an effort to improve both the business environment and tax compliance, in recognition that each side can take actions that will improve the circumstances of the other. Government can and should move independently to improve public expenditure management and promote results-based management. And firms can gain in productivity and access to bank credit if they maintain sincere and transparent accounts and pay formal taxes. However, firms prefer to pay taxes when they know others like themselves will also pay, and the business climate especially needs a systematic enforcement of regulations, which requires public intervention. This mutual interest in reforms should be exploited, and such collaboration is more likely to succeed than a unilateral push for new tax revenues from the informal sector.

The main positive contribution of the small informal sector is that it provides employment and incomes and thereby alleviates poverty. But the incomes in the informal sector are generally low, and low productivity of the small informal sector suggests a limited scope for improvement. Government and donor programs intended to assist small informal firms have had limited effectiveness.

The goal of policies overall is to assist small informal sector firms while inducing them to move toward formal sector status in the long run through a combination of carrots and sticks. However, efforts to promote growth should not focus on small informal enterprises, as their potential is limited. At the same time, enforcement should focus on larger informal firms rather than small firms so as to avoid worsening poverty and unemployment.

In addition to state failures, sociocultural traditions, particularly ethnic and religious trading networks, underpin the informal sector. Understanding the latter may be helpful in fostering the transition toward a stronger formal sector. For example, many people accord far more authority to kinship chiefs than to government. Also, traditional education systems are in some respects far more practical and conducive to building entrepreneurial skills than the Western-style schools, which are oriented toward preparing future civil servants. There is much that is positive in the informal sector, and policy can build on this to foster development.

Further research on the sociological basis of economic behavior in West Africa could enhance policies in a wide range of areas, from education to regulation.

Note

1. Organisation pour l'Harmonisation du Droit des Affaires en Afrique (Organization for the Harmonisation of Business Law in Africa).

References

Calvès, Anne-Emmanuele, and Bruno Schoumaker. 2004. "Deteriorating Economic Context and Changing Patterns of Youth Employment in Urban Burkina Faso: 1980–2000." *World Development* 32 (8): 1341–54.

Dabla-Norris, Era, Mark Gradstein, and Gabriela Inchauste. 2008. "What Causes Firms to Hide Output? The Determinant of Informality." *Journal of Development Economics* 85 (1-2): 1–27.

Gelb, Alan, Taye Mengistae, Vijaya Ramachanran, and Manju Kedia Shah. 2009. "To Formalize or Not to Formalize? Comparison of Microenterprise Data from Southern and East Africa." Working Paper 175, Center for Global Development, Washington, DC.

Grimm, Michael, Peter Knorringa, and Jann Lay. 2012. "Constrained gazelles: High potentials in West Africa's informal economy." *World Development* 40(7): 1352–68.

Guha-Khasnobis, Basudeb, and Ravi Kanbur, eds. 2006. *Informal Labour Markets and Development*. Studies in Development Economics and Policy. New York: Palgrave Macmillan.

ILO (International Labour Organization). 1993. "Development Policies and Institutional Environment for Employment Promotion in the Informal Sector in Ghana." Jobs and Skills Program for Africa, ILO, Geneva.

———. 2002. *Decent Work and the Informal Economy: Sixth Item on the Agenda*. Report VI, ninetieth session of the International Labour Conference, Geneva, June 20.

La Porta, Rafael, and Andrei Shleifer. 2008. "The Unofficial Economy and Economic Development." *Brookings Papers on Economic Activity* 2: 275–364.

———. 2011. "The Unofficial Economy in Africa." NBER Working Paper 16821, National Bureau of Economic Research, Cambridge, MA.

Levenson, Alec R., and William F. Maloney. 1998. "The Informal Sector, Firm Dynamics, and Institutional Participation, Volume 1." Policy Research Working Paper 1988, World Bank, Washington, DC.

Perry, Guillermo E., William F. Maloney, Omar S. Arias, Pablo Fajnzylber, Andrew Mason, and Jaime Saavedra-Chanduvi. 2007. *Informality: Exit and Exclusion*. Washington, DC: World Bank.

Steel, William F., and Don Snodgrass. 2008. "World Bank Region Analysis on the Informal Economy." In *Raising Productivity and Reducing Risk of Household Enterprises*. Annex 1, "Diagnostic Methodology Framework." Washington, DC: World Bank.

Chapter 1

The Informal Sector in West Africa: Definition

Researchers studying the informal sector must first confront the lack of a widely accepted definition of informality. Since the groundbreaking 1972 report of the International Labour Organization (ILO) on informal activity in Kenya (Hart 1972), researchers have proposed numerous definitions of informality. A researcher's chosen definition of informality largely determines the sampling method used to gather data on the informal sector as well as the conclusions obtained and the policy recommendations that follow.

The informal sector has become the subject of renewed interest from researchers, as its importance for development has been increasingly recognized. Most definitions of informality are binary and limited to just a few criteria, notably firm size, registration, and honesty of accounts. Our approach differs in two ways. First, we examine firms rather than employees because our focus is on the business climate and economic growth rather than poverty alleviation. Second, we argue that the complexity and heterogeneity of informality cannot be captured by a single criterion. We instead combine several criteria to distinguish various levels of informality. In this chapter, we review the rationale for using these criteria and present our method of computing measures of informality based on multiple criteria. Informality is more of a continuum than a binary variable, depending on how many criteria a firm fulfills.

Informality versus Illegality

Informal activities are commonly associated with illicit activities such as drug trafficking, the underground economy, and black markets. In most cases in West Africa, informal activities, while often undeclared and thus illegal in a narrow sense, are not otherwise criminal in nature. In fact, the informal sector produces ordinary goods and services not much different from those produced by the modern sector. An activity is not deemed informal as a function of its illicit or licit nature. Rather, informality is determined according to the type of organization carrying out the activity. Both criminal activities and informal activities are hidden, but not to the same extent, and they clearly are not viewed with the same degree of disapprobation or exposed to the same risk of prosecution.

The Organisation for Economic Co-operation and Development (OECD) distinguishes the informal economy from the hidden, household, and illegal economies:

- The hidden economy includes all activities that are hidden to evade taxation and the payment of other legal obligations.
- The illegal economy includes all illicit activities such as drug trafficking and counterfeiting.
- The household economy includes activities for personal use, such as paid domestic services.
- The informal economy includes all activities that are not registered or are registered poorly.

In practice, however, these distinctions are rather hazy, to say the least. Perhaps this reflects the OECD's desire to encompass the realities of both developed and developing countries in a single set of definitions. Overall, the activities in which informal firms engage usually are not illegal in themselves, but the practices of informal firms are often illegal insofar as they involve tax avoidance and lack of compliance with regulations.

In West Africa, many formal firms engage in informal activities, so informality is a matter of degree. Many formal firms hide or underreport their revenues and subcontract with informal firms. For instance, in the construction sector, only formal firms can obtain official contracts; as a consequence, the rate of subcontracting to informal firms is especially high in this sector. Most work in the construction sector in the region, even on projects funded by the state or international donor agencies, is carried out by informal subcontractors. Even at the ports and airports, informal firms operate under the cover of modern firms.

West African authorities are well aware of the activities of the informal sector. In fact, most often these activities are clearly identified and even benefit from special tax and regulatory status. The fiscal regime has several provisions specifically targeting the informal sector. In particular, informal firms, on account of their supposed small size and limited capabilities to comply with business income taxes, are subject to a presumptive tax in lieu of ordinary business income taxes. This method of taxation is considered appropriate because it requires a minimal amount of paperwork and information. The tax is based on limited and often inaccurate estimates of the volume of the firm's sales. Another method of taxing informal activities is to require formal firms subcontracting out to informal firms to withhold estimated taxes and remit them to the treasury. These payments are refunded to the subcontractor if it can provide evidence that it is in compliance with its tax obligations. Many other methods of taxing informal activities exist in West Africa, clearly indicating that the authorities are aware of the widespread existence of informal firms. Rather, informal firms are simply categorized as a specific type of firm that is organizationally weak and unable to supply certain accounting documents. Such a strategy can be justified as promoting small enterprises for which it is prohibitively costly to comply with ordinary business income taxation. In West Africa, however, this situation is sometimes abused by what we call the "large informal sector."

How, then, should informality be defined? Various criteria are used in the literature to define informal enterprises: the size of enterprise, absence of registration, nonpayment of taxes or type of taxes paid, existence of honest accounting statements, level of access to bank credit, and mobility of the workplace. In the following sections, we argue that all of these criteria capture some aspects of informality, but can be misleading when used alone. We propose instead to use a combination of these criteria and view informality as a continuum based on the number of criteria that a firm fulfills. Based on several of these criteria, we define three categories of firms: formal, large informal, and small informal, as described in detail below.

A Critical Review of the Criteria Used to Define Informality in Africa

There are a number of possible definitions of informality, and various studies have adopted different concepts. The most commonly used criteria are the size of the business, registration with the government, and maintenance of honest and complete accounts. Because of the differing definitions of informality, data on the informal sector are collected in various ways, and international comparability is difficult. Adams (2008) reviews survey methods used by studies on the informal sector. He confirms that one of the greatest challenges faced by analysts of the informal sector is a lack of consensus on the definition of the phenomenon. Kanbur (2009) rightly argues that any researcher studying the informal sector should begin by defining informality. In this section, we review the main criteria for informality and show that each captures a part of the phenomenon. We then suggest that a composite definition is more appropriate.

Below we suggest and implement six criteria for informality. While more comprehensive than previous measures that are limited to one or two of these criteria, our six criteria do not cover all aspects of informality. Other possible aspects include management practices and participation in social security.

Size

The most widely used criterion for defining informality in the literature is small size of the firm, measured by number of employees, derived from the ILO's approach (ILO 2002), which defines an informal firm as an unregistered firm with no clear line separating business activities from household activities. A further qualifier is a lack of registration, a lack of honest accounting that fully reports the firm's operations, or both. The only firms that fit these criteria are family enterprises, classified as households in the United Nations' System of National Accounts (UN 1993). According to this definition, the informal sector encompasses small enterprises that employ fewer than 10 employees and are not registered with a given administration. The Nairobi report, which first used the "informal sector" terminology in its analysis of development in the early 1970s (Hart 1972), emphasized two criteria in its definition of informality: the size of activity and the lack of registration.

Since the fifteenth conference for labor market statisticians in 1993, the ILO has drawn a distinction between the informal sector and informal employment. While the informal sector refers to all enterprises meeting the size and registration criteria, informal employment includes not only informal sector employees, but also uncompensated family workers, workers with a precarious status in formal firms, and uncompensated household workers.

The ILO's approach is problematic in two respects (see AFRISTAT 1997):

- The recommended upper limit for number of employees is set at 10, but individual countries have leeway to set a different upper limit in their statistical definition of informal firms. Certain countries choose an upper limit of five employees, whereas others choose either lower or higher limits.

- Countries are able to choose whether to include agriculture in informal activities, along with unpaid domestic help, individuals with a second job in the informal sector, rural zones, minimum age, and so forth.

The reasoning behind the size criterion is that small-scale activities tend to be informal because they lack the institutional and organizational capacity needed to obtain the accounting and financial documents required by the tax authorities, the statistical agency, and other public services. Most proponents of this approach consider informal activities to be survival strategies, providing income to poor households with little marketable skills. The informal sector is understood here as a social safety net in countries where formal employment is rare and poverty is widespread. In their study of informal activity in Burkina Faso, Calvès and Schoumaker (2004) consider the informal sector to be small-scale survival activities. In the countries of the West African subregion, this view is substantiated by the proliferation of small-scale trading activities that are largely a form of hidden unemployment. Vehicle repairmen, street hawkers, as well as many other small tradesmen crowd the streets of big urban centers, barely making incomes necessary for survival. A large part of the labor for this segment of the informal sector derives from an exodus from villages to the cities, where lack of skills and opportunities confine workers to informal activities.

This point of view is similar to the conclusions of Fields (1990) and Hart (1972) in their studies of Kenya. Galli and Kucera (2004) seem to have a similar perspective: according to them, informality is essentially characterized by the size of endeavor, defined by a maximum of five to 10 people. In contrast, firms in the formal sector are defined as having more than 10 employees. The OECD (1997) opts for a similar definition, characterizing the informal sector as enterprises that (a) do not have a legal worksite, instead usually working out of private residencies, (b) have a low level of capital investment, or (c) are managed by family members either in total or in part.

While retaining the focus on micro and small businesses, Maloney's (2004) study of Latin America provides a more optimistic perspective on the informal sector, with individuals freely choosing to leave the formal sector to reap the benefits of informality. In an earlier study, Maloney (1998) defines informal actors in Mexico as individual businesses with a maximum of six employees who are not covered by a program of social protection and who have at most a secondary level of education.

Even analysts who do not consider size a defining feature of informal firms note a strong correlation between size and informality. Such is the case with Steel and Snodgrass (2008), who do not differentiate between individual household enterprises and informal or small enterprises. According to them, the criteria that define household enterprises would define informal enterprises as well. They include in their definition of individual enterprises those with self-employed workers and those with unpaid household workers, an inclusion that corresponds to the ILO's definition of the informal sector. In the same vein, using a general equilibrium model, Dabla-Norris, Gradstein, and Inchauste (2008) find a strong positive association between the size of a firm and its formal or informal status in a sample of 41 developed and developing countries. Similarly, Charmes (1993) uses three criteria when defining informal activities. Size of the activity is listed as the most important criterion, along with the keeping of accounts and registration and legal status.

An important implication arising from the understanding of informality as a small-scale family activity is that survey data on the informal sector are retrieved mostly from household data. For the most part, these studies measure the well-being of households, with a focus on the household's economic activities and whether these activities are part of the formal or informal sector. Based on these data, researchers can infer output and employment in the informal sector. This approach is very useful for understanding the dynamics of poverty and the labor market and for understanding the dynamics of the informal labor market in particular. However, studies on informal sector firms rather than employment may lead to overrepresentation of employees relative to entrepreneurs. To avoid this problem, when constructing a sample of informal firms (and not households), we use a hybrid sample, which consolidates data on households and data on firms.

More important, equating informality with small size is not always valid in West Africa. Large informal firms are quite common and constitute what we call the "large informal sector." This is not to deny that a large majority of informal firms are small-scale, even miniscule, enterprises. However, a minority of larger informal firms also exists, accounting for a sizable share of the informal sector's output. Conversely, some formal firms are small. Gelb et al. (2009) analyze firms in seven South and East African countries where formal microenterprises coexist with informal microenterprises. They distinguish between three types of enterprises: formal microenterprises (five or fewer employees), formal small enterprises (five to ten employees), and informal microenterprises (five or fewer employees). Among the seven countries studied, the number of formal small and micro firms as a proportion of all firms surveyed varies between a low of 28 percent in Namibia and Kenya and a high of 54 percent in Uganda. This study ignores the existence of larger informal firms, however.

In summary, the size and formal or informal status of the enterprise are indeed correlated in West Africa, but the idea that the size criterion can in and of itself be used to define informality is not entirely valid. In this region, many large firms are informal. Consequently, while size should be considered in categorizing informal activity, it should be used in conjunction with other criteria to form a complete understanding of the phenomenon.

Registration

Another commonly used criterion for defining informality is registration with a government agency. In our view, this criterion is superior to the one based on small firm size. Nevertheless, multiple government agencies oversee the private sector (central or local administration, tax authorities, or others), and firms may register with some but not others.

La Porta and Shleifer (2008) use the registration criterion. According to them, a distinction should be made between two categories of informal firms: (a) those that fail to register with tax authorities and other regulators and (b) those that are registered but understate revenues. They therefore observe that the registration criterion alone is not sufficient to qualify a firm as formal. The authors propose additional criteria as necessary for defining informality and determining its weight in the economy: the proportion of small and microenterprises in the economy, the total participation of men in the workforce, the proportion of self-employed workers in the nonagriculture sector, the proportion of workers who benefit from social security, the amount of electricity consumed, and, finally, the total amount of money in circulation. The problem is that, while these criteria are useful for comparing national economies, they are much less applicable when studying survey data. Sinha and Adams (2006) apply India's official definition of informality and define the informal sector as the unorganized sector of the economy. The authors also opt for the completeness of accounts and registration criteria when categorizing a firm as informal. In the same vein, OECD (1997) states, "The informal economy could be defined as the output of production units not registered with fiscal or social security authorities." The registration criterion is given priority in this definition as well.

In Senegal, Benin, and Burkina Faso, the second phase of the 123 study developed by DIAL (Développement, Institution et Ajustement à Long Term) and conducted by national statistics institutes (INSAE 2002; INSD 2003; DPS 2004) applies the lack of registration or the absence of written accounting criteria to define informality. The firm's tax identification number (TIN) is used as the sole criterion for registration. Furthermore, the informal sector is defined as "the units of production lacking identification numbers and/or formal written accounting."

It is unusual for firms not to be registered with at least one government agency, however, casting doubt on the registration criterion. Most of the firms studied by Gelb et al. (2009) were registered with at least one of the government agencies whose responsibility is (a) approval of firm names, (b) granting of operating licenses, (c) registration at the municipal level, or (d) registration with tax authorities. Only the last criterion is considered when defining informality, which allows the authors to distinguish between informal and formal microenterprises.

Likewise, Steel and Snodgrass (2008) refute the notion that the informal sector is unknown to fiscal authorities. According to them, informal activities are well identified and taxed by public authorities; these authorities often go so far as to distribute the market stalls that informal businesses use for their own commerce in urban markets. As discussed in more detail below, in francophone West Africa, firms can be separated by whether they pay the regular business income tax or a presumptive tax that applies to firms deemed informal. Indeed, virtually all firms considered informal are recognized explicitly by at least one government agency. Most likely, it is this difficulty of applying the registration criterion that led Steel and Snodgrass (2008) to conclude that only street hawkers and household-based firms could be classified as unregistered and hence informal. They observe that, while informal firms may not be registered with central authorities, they are often registered and pay taxes at the local level.

In fact, in West Africa, there are generally as many identification numbers as there are agencies dealing with enterprises:

- The fiscal authorities use a TIN as the identification number of firms. Firms identified by this number are taxed according to a specific fiscal regime. The fiscal service is under the control of the Finance Ministry.

- Enterprises engaged in commerce have to be registered with the commerce registry and have a commerce registration number, issued by the minister of commerce.
- Enterprises that participate in importing and exporting require an import-export card, also issued by the minister of commerce.
- All enterprises are required by law to submit a copy of their books to the national statistical agency. Many firms do not abide by this law, and among firms that do, many do not submit their finances on a regular basis. This irregularity and lack of submissions greatly lessen the reliability of the collected data.
- Municipal authorities tax merchants, including street vendors, on site.

Because of the many departments that register firms, multiple databases exist, and one firm can be registered with one administration and not with others. Even within government agencies, inconsistent recording systems coexist. Within the tax authorities, internal services are either specialized according to the geographic locality of specific enterprises or according to the type of operations of specific firms. Each internal department manages a particular database, and these databases are not always appropriately consolidated. In all three countries, a division of tax authorities oversees large firms: the Division des Grandes Entreprises (DGE) within the tax authority.[1] In general, this division collects the bulk of taxes, while departments collect taxes in the capital cities. Each department oversees a given set of taxpayers, yet the consolidated records of the tax authorities diverge from summing the records of the individual departments!

Tax Status

There are two types of fiscal regimes in West African Economic and Monetary Union (WAEMU) countries: regular business income tax and presumptive lump-sum tax. The presumptive tax is intended for small informal firms that are viewed as unable to provide detailed documentation and precise estimates of revenues. In Senegal and Burkina Faso, enterprises with annual sales of less than or equal to CFAF 50 million (US$100,000) are, in principle, subject to the presumptive tax.[2] In other countries of the subregion, the threshold is fixed at similar, but not always identical, levels. Firms with revenues above the threshold are supposed to be taxed under the regular regime, with the presumption that such firms maintain documents that allow fiscal authorities to determine objectively the amount of the firm's tax and the tax bracket under which the firm belongs. In practice, however, many small firms do not pay any tax, and most are not registered with the tax authority at all. Conversely, some large informal firms with sales far above the threshold massively understate their incomes and pay the presumptive tax.

Thus in WAEMU countries, the important distinction is not so much whether firms are registered with the fiscal authorities but rather the type of tax they are subject to and whether or not they pay any taxes. Businesses can be split into two main categories: (a) the vast majority of firms that are subject to the presumptive tax or pay no tax at all and (b) the small number of firms that pay regular business income taxes.

Honest Accounting

The lack of accurate and complete books is also a fundamental distinguishing feature of informality. Indeed, a characteristic of the informal sector is a lack of visibility about the operations of the firm. The majority of informal firms in West Africa lack regular and up-to-date books, which makes monitoring and taxation of these firms very difficult. In practice, however, this definition is difficult to implement. How does one decide which types of financial statements to use and whether or not they are accurate? Normally, the statements required by tax authorities and the statistical agency would be considered relevant. However, in WAEMU countries, this definition is inadequate. In fact, the financial statements required of formal firms differ, with large enterprises reporting to the DGE having to provide much more detailed financial statements than smaller enterprises.

The honest-financial-statements criterion follows the same underlying logic as the criterion of regular business income tax. Only enterprises that are capable of providing satisfactory financial statements are taxed under the regular business income tax; others are taxed a presumptive tax or escape taxation.

The problem is that it is difficult to ascertain the honesty of a firm's books. Many enterprises, especially the large informal operators, are highly skilled at producing false financial statements. These firms are aided by accounting firms that specialize in producing misleading accounting certificates. Many informal actors admitted anonymously to us that they retain several versions of their accounts: one for themselves, one for loan requests from a bank, one for tax authorities, and so forth. Each version is created with a specific use in mind, and these firms have no trouble getting them all certified by accounting firms complicit in this elaborate hoax.

This criterion is related to the government's capacity to establish rules governing business and society in general. Kanbur (2009) calls attention to the crucial role of state failures and argues that the quality of the state is the greatest determinant of the size of the informal sector. However, because of the wide range of regulations that apply to enterprises in each country, there are as many criteria defining informality as there are regulations considered. Kanbur identifies four possible options for economic actors in response to regulations:

- Stay within the ambit of the regulation and comply.
- Stay within the ambit of the regulation but do not comply.

- Adjust activity to move out of the ambit of the regulation.
- Stay outside the ambit of the regulation in the first place and avoid the need to adjust.

According to Kanbur, only firms that choose the first option are part of the formal sector, while those that choose one of the other three options represent the informal sector. He argues that the government's capacity to enforce its laws determines in large part the decision of economic actors to remain in the informal sector.

Mobility of Workplace

In West Africa, many informal actors are highly mobile and without a fixed workplace. This applies not only to traveling salesmen and street hawkers but also to mechanics, carpenters, and small business owners. In general, these actors do not own or rent their workplace. Instead, they occupy an unused space and vacate when the space is needed by its owner. Given this situation, some researchers identify the informal sector with a lack of fixed workplace. While it is true that many informal firms are highly mobile, many more informal firms do have a fixed workplace, so this criterion identifies only a limited part of the informal sector.

Access to Bank Credit

Limited access to credit is also a characteristic of informality. Bank credit is largely an option only for the formal sector, while most small enterprises are confined to informal loans from friends, family, or tontines, which generally demand high interest rates (Johnson 2004; Akoten, Sawada, and Otsuka 2006). La Porta and Shleifer (2008) argue that informal actors' limited access to credit can be explained by their relatively low level of education.

The criterion of access to bank credit is very relevant to African countries. Banks demand several financial and administrative documents before even examining a loan application. It is practically impossible for informal actors to assemble the required documents. Nevertheless, this criterion too has its limitations because many formal firms are also credit constrained in Africa. This is because lack of documentation is not the only constraint to obtaining credit. Collateral requirements are also a major impediment, and even some large firms are discouraged from obtaining bank credit due to the onerous collateral requirements as well as the general reticence of banks to lend to all but the largest and best-known businesses. Many formal enterprises, notably small and medium enterprises, finance their investments with internal funds or through informal financing at high, even exorbitant, interest rates. Indeed, governments, in collaboration with donor agencies, have repeatedly extended lines of credit to the private sector because of the dysfunctional banking system (Mbaye, Diarisso, and Diop 2011). As a consequence, the access-to-bank-credit criterion

Figure 1.1 Share of Firms Satisfying Various Criteria of Informality in Three West African Cities

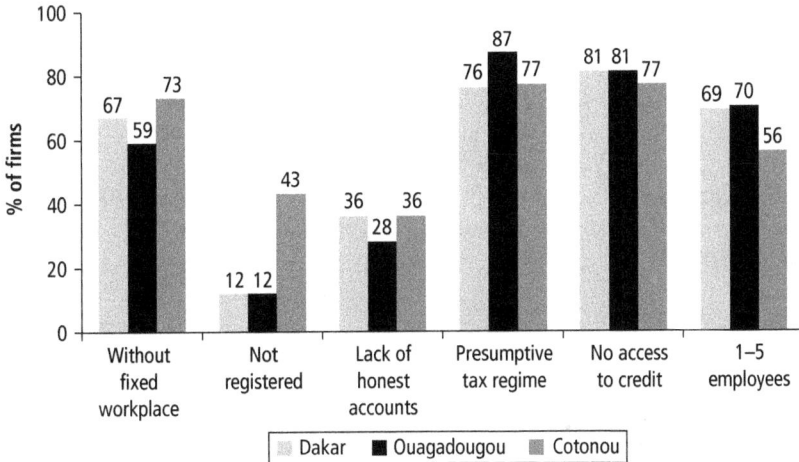

Source: Based on authors' firm survey data.

does not necessarily help to discriminate between the informal and formal sectors. What is more, certain informal firms, with the complicity of accounting firms, create fake administrative and financial documents with which they fraudulently access bank credit. The access-to-bank-credit criterion, just like all preceding criteria, captures some aspects of informality, but with limitations.

Figure 1.1 shows the proportions of firms in the sample that fulfill the various criteria of informality. Most of the criteria suggest that most firms are informal. For example, more than 75 percent of firms in all three cities do not pay regular income taxes and do not have access to credit. Similarly, but to a lesser extent, most firms fulfill the criteria of small number of employees and lack of a fixed workplace. Maintaining honest accounts and especially registration are exceptions: most firms are registered and maintain reasonably honest accounting.

A New Approach to Informality

In this study, we define informality as a continuum rather than in a dichotomous way.

Informality as a Continuum

As suggested in the previous discussion, no single criterion fully captures informality. Each one reflects some dimensions of the informal sector but ignores others. The registration criterion is difficult to apply because almost all firms are registered with at least one of the many government agencies overseeing the private sector. Even if one limits the focus to registration with particular agencies, the issue then becomes choosing which one(s) to select. The small-size criterion applies to most informal firms, but it does not cover large informal sector firms, or what we call "the large informal sector." Moreover, it does not take into account the fact that some small firms may be formal. The honesty-of-accounts criterion is difficult to operationalize because many accounting statements are of dubious accuracy and many firms produce different books with different figures for different audiences. Both formal and informal firms have difficulty gaining access to bank credit, and so this criterion does not fully distinguish between the two sectors. Finally, the mobility-of-workplace criterion is deficient because it applies to only a limited part of the informal sector.

Each of these criteria covers only one aspect of the informal sector, ignoring the larger picture of the phenomenon, suggesting that informality is better described as a continuum defined by a combination of criteria. As Steel and Snodgrass (2008) note, "There is a continuum of different degrees of formality (in terms of different characteristics such as nature of registration, payment of taxes, management structure, contractual arrangements with employees, market orientation, etc.)" The multiple-criteria approach is also used by Guha-Khasnobis and Kanbur (2006), who, when defining informal employment, give prominence to the absence of social security coverage, rights to vacation, written contracts, low levels of revenue, lack of affiliation to a workers organization, unstable work conditions, and the illegal or quasi-illegal nature of the firm's activity. Although our focus is on informal businesses and not informal employment, we retain some of the same criteria. Informality in the subregion is a complex reality that varies enormously among different economic actors. Very few firms fit all of the criteria of formality.

Table 1.1 presents correlation tests among the six indicators. The correlation coefficients are always positive, with nine out of 15 being statistically significant. The correlation between maintaining honest accounts and each of the other five indicators are all statistically significant. The informality variables, however, are discrete variables, making it difficult to calculate the correlation matrix between them. Instead, we have used Cramer's V, which is a measure of correlation based on the Chi-squared test.

Therefore, we can distinguish between several levels of informality:

- At the bottom of the ladder are firms that are completely informal—firms that do not fulfill any of the criteria defining formality. These firms are unknown to fiscal authorities and all other administrations. They are small, do not have access to bank credit, are not subject to the regular business income tax, and are itinerant. These firms are at level zero of informality. Very few businesses are completely informal in this sense, other than the large number of street traders and individuals engaged in other petty activities.

Table 1.1 Statistical Significance of Correlations between Criteria of Informality in Three West African Cities, Using Chi-Squared Test

	Maintaining accounts	Registration	Fixed workplace	Access to credit	Number of employees	Mode of taxation
Maintaining accounts	1.000					
Registration	0.131*	1.000				
Fixed workplace	0.120*	0.213*	1.000			
Access to credit	0.202*	0.020	0.018	1.000		
Number of employees	0.192*	0.092	0.133*	0.037	1.000	
Mode of taxation	0.357*	0.258*	0.292*	0.148	0.225	1.000

Source: Based on authors' firm survey data.
* = statistically significant at the 5% level.

- Level one of informality consists of firms that fulfill at least one of the criteria defining formality. This level includes firms that are registered with an administration dealing with enterprises, have more than five employees (or sales of more than CFAF 50 million, or US$100,000), or have received a bank loan within the previous five years.
- Level two of informality consists of firms that fulfill at least two of the six criteria defining formality.
- Level three consists of firms that fulfill three of the six criteria, and so on.
- The last level (six) consists of formal firms that fulfill all six criteria of formality. These firms are registered with at least one administration, employ more than five people or have sales of more than CFAF 50 million, are taxed through the regular business income tax, have had access to bank credit within the past five years, and have a fixed workplace.

These categories provide six levels of informality. However, in most of the subsequent analysis, we compress these into three main categories of firms: formal, large informal, small informal.

Large and Small Informal Firms

We further distinguish two categories of informal firms: large and small. Large informal firms are comparable in size to firms in the modern sector, but they behave informally in other respects. These firms satisfy all of the criteria for formality except one: their accounts are inaccurate and deliberately misleading. The large informal sector is discussed throughout this book, particularly in chapter 4.

Table 1.2 Characteristics of Formal, Large Informal, and Small Informal Firms

Characteristic	Formal	Large informal	Small informal
Pay regular business income tax	Yes	Sometimes	Rarely
Maintain honest accounts	Yes	No	Rarely
Are registered	Yes	Yes	Sometimes
Have sales in excess of CFAF 50 million	Yes	Yes	Rarely
Have a fixed workplace	Yes	Yes	Sometimes
Are eligible for bank loans	Yes	Yes	Rarely
Level of informality (number of criteria of formality fulfilled)	6	4–5	0–3

Source: Authors.

Thus we separate firms into three categories: formal, large informal, and small informal, as shown in table 1.2. Formal firms, in principle, satisfy all six criteria of formality.[3] Large informal firms satisfy most of the criteria, but generally do not maintain honest accounts and thus very often understate income so much that they qualify for the presumptive tax. Small informal firms may have a fixed workplace and be registered, but they rarely satisfy any of the other criteria of formality.

Large informal firms are difficult to identify with official data because such firms massively underreport their sales to the authorities. We have adopted several strategies for identifying these firms:

- For the 900 firms surveyed in the first phase of this study in 2007, we compared sales reported to us in confidential surveys to sales reported by the tax authorities.
- For a smaller subset of formal and large informal firms surveyed again in 2009, we repeated this procedure.
- We interviewed stakeholders, including managers of firms, government officials, and others.
- We cross-checked firm-level data collected at customs against data reported to the tax authorities.

Conclusions

In this chapter, we proposed a definition of informality using six criteria: size, registration, honesty of accounts, fixity of workplace, access to credit, and tax status. These six criteria were combined to create levels of informality, depending on how many of the six a particular firm meets. Among these criteria, three were particularly significant: firm size, the tax regime to which a firm is subject, and honesty of accounting. We further distinguished between large and small informal firms, an important feature of West African economies that has not been widely studied. Large informal firms are comparable in size to firms in the modern sector, but they behave informally in other respects. These firms satisfy all of the criteria for formality except one: their accounts are falsified.

Notes

1. This is the tax division to which big firms, with a turnover exceeding a threshold of about CFAF 1 billion, have to file.
2. Important variations in thresholds are evident across countries and over time.
3. In practice, almost all firms engage in some fraudulent behavior, so purely formal firms are rare in West Africa.

References

Adams, Arvil V. 2008. "Skills Development in the Informal Sector of Sub-Saharan Africa." World Bank, Washington, DC.

AFRISTAT (Economic and Statistical Observatory of Sub-Saharan Africa). 1997. *Proceedings of the Seminar on the Informal Sector and Economic Policy in Sub-Saharan Africa.* Bamako: AFRISTAT.

Akoten, John E., Yasuyuki Sawada, and Keijiro Otsuka. 2006. "The Determinant of Credit Access and Its Impacts on Micro and Small Enterprises: The Cases of Garment Producers in Kenya." *Economic Development and Cultural Change* 54 (4): 927–44.

Calvès, Anne-Emmanuele, and Bruno Schoumaker. 2004. "Deteriorating Economic Context and Changing Patterns of Youth Employment in Urban Burkina Faso: 1980–2000." *World Development* 32 (8): 1341–54.

Charmes, Jacques. 1993. "Estimation and Survey Methods for the Informal Sector." Centre of Economics and Ethics for Environment and Development, University of Versailles-St. Quentin en Yvelines. Paper prepared for an ILO international seminar.

Dabla-Norris, Era, Mark Gradstein, and Gabriela Inchauste. 2008. "What Causes Firms to Hide Output? The Determinant of Informality." *Journal of Development Economics* 85 (1–2): 1–27.

DPS (Direction de la Prévision et de la Statistique). 2004. "Le secteur informel dans l'agglomération de Dakar: Performances, insertion, perspectives; Résultats de la phase II de l'enquête 1-2-3 de 2003." DPS, Senegal, June.

Fields, Gary S. 1990. "Labour Market Modelling and the Urban Informal Sector: Theory and Evidence." In *The Informal Sector Revisited*, ed. David Turnham, Bernard Salomé, and Antoine Schwarz. Paris: OECD.

Galli, Rossana, and David Kucera. 2004. "Labor Standards and Informal Employment in Latin America." *World Development* 32 (5): 809–28.

Gelb, Alan, Taye Mengistae, Vijaya Ramachandran, and Manju Kedia Shah. 2009. "To Formalize or Not to Formalize? Comparisons of Microenterprise Data from Southern and East Africa." Working Paper 175, Center for Global Development, Washington, DC.

Guha-Khasnobis, Basudeb, and Ravi Kanbur, eds. 2006. *Informal Labour Markets and Development.* Studies in Development Economics and Policy. New York: Palgrave Macmillan.

Hart, Keith. 1972. "Employment, Income, and Inequality: A Strategy for Increasing Productivity and Employment in Kenya." ILO, Geneva.

ILO (International Labour Organization). 2002. *Decent Work and the Informal Economy: Sixth Item on the Agenda*. Report VI, 90th session of the International Labour Conference. Geneva: ILO.

INSAE (Institut National de la Statistique et de l'Analyse Economique). 2002. "Le secteur informel dans l'agglomération de Cotonou: Performances, insertion, perspectives; Enquête 1-2-3, premiers résultats de la phase 2, 2001." INSAE, Bénin, September.

INSD (Institut National de la Statistique et de la Démographie). 2003. "Le secteur informel dans l'agglomération de Ouagadougou: Performances, insertion, perspectives; Enquête 1-2-3, premiers résultats de la phase II, 2001." INSD, Burkina Faso, September.

Johnson, Susan. 2004. "Gender Norms in Financial Markets: Evidence from Kenya." *World Development* 32 (8): 1355–74.

Kanbur, Ravi. 2009. "Conceptualizing Informality: Regulation and Enforcement." Working Paper 09-11, Department of Applied Economics and Management, Cornell University, Ithaca, NY.

La Porta, Rafael, and Andrei Shleifer. 2008. "The Unofficial Economy and Economic Development." *Brookings Papers on Economic Activity* 2: 275–364.

Maloney, William. 1998. "Are LDCs Markets Dualistic?" Policy Research Working Paper 1941, World Bank, Washington, DC.

———. 2004. "Informality Revisited." *World Development* 32 (7): 1159–78.

Mbaye, Ahmadou Aly, Sogué Diarisso, and IbrahimaThione Diop. 2011. *Quel système bancaire pour le financement des économies de l'UEMOA?* Paris: Harmattan France.

OECD (Organisation for Economic Co-operation and Development). 1997. "Framework for the Measurement of Unrecorded Economic Activities in Transition Economies." OECD, Paris.

Sinha, Anushree, and Christopher Adams. 2006. "Reforms and Informalization: What Lies behind Jobless Growth in India?" In *Informal Labour Markets and Development*, ed. Basudeb Guha-Khasnobis and Ravi Kanbur. New York: Palgrave Macmillan.

Steel, William F., and Don Snodgrass. 2008. "World Bank Region Analysis on the Informal Economy." In *Raising Productivity and Reducing Risk of Household Enterprises*. Annex 1, "Diagnostic Methodology Framework." Washington, DC: World Bank.

UN (United Nations). 1993. System of National Accounts. New York: UN.

Chapter 2

Data Sources and Methods

This chapter presents the methodology and sources of the data used in this book. We used three main sources:

- Survey data collected from the three cities (Cotonou, Dakar, and Ouagadougou)
- Secondary data from the national accounts and other relevant survey data
- Qualitative information collected from semistructured interviews with stakeholders in the informal and formal sectors, government agencies that are responsible for overseeing the informal sector, and others who are involved with the informal sector in one way or another.

Data collection is a major challenge facing researchers on the informal economy. This difficulty arises for two reasons. First, informality must be defined, as discussed in detail in chapter 1. The definition obviously determines the approach to data collection. Second, the question needs to be settled of whether to approach informality using household-level or firm-level data. The sampling methods used in previous studies are strongly influenced by the national income accounting system of the United Nations (UN 1993), which identifies the informal sector with the production of goods and services in the household sector. This makes some sense because informal producers often operate from within households and is appropriate when the goal is to study informal employment. Our study focuses on the structure of informal enterprises rather than informal workers, so the question is whether to develop a survey focused on households, firms, or both.

Later in this chapter, we review previous approaches to gathering data on the informal sector, noting their strengths and weaknesses. We then outline the sources and methods used in our investigations.

Data Collection Methods on the Informal Sector in Africa

The Implications of Alternative Definitions of the Informal Sector
Various international organizations and conferences have been held to discuss the collection of data on the informal sector based on different definitions of

informality. Consequently, different methods have been adopted in different countries.

The approach that has incontestably had the greatest impact on data collection in the informal sector in Africa is that of the fifteenth International Conference of Labor Statisticians (ILO 1993). This approach is centered on the criteria of small size and lack of registration, largely corresponding to household enterprises. An implicit assumption in this definition is that the production units in question operate on a relatively small scale and at a low level of organization.

An important feature of individual companies is that they have assets and operations that overlap with those of their owners, unlike companies with formal legal status and financial autonomy. Individual firms within the informal sector rarely have reliable accounting mechanisms for isolating the financial activities of firms from those of their owners. This lack of consistent and accurate accounts on the part of individual enterprises is an integral part of the two criteria mentioned above.

As seen in chapter 1, various criteria are used to define informal sector enterprises and employment and to develop corresponding sampling strategies. For example, some countries apply a threshold of five employees in defining informal firms, while others apply higher or lower numbers. This process leads to inconsistencies, which makes comparisons across countries difficult. In some surveys, the size criterion for number of employees is omitted. For example, the 123 study developed by DIAL (Développement, Institutions et Ajustement à Long Terme), and conducted by national African statistics offices (INSAE 2002; INSD 2003; DPS 2004), defines informal firms solely as firms lacking formal accounting. Furthermore, some countries define informal firms as firms with no fixed location. Some countries include agriculture in the informal sector, whereas most countries exclude it (UN Economic and Social Council 2007). With regard to informal employment, the threshold for minimum age of employees is subject to differential treatment in national surveys. In some countries, the minimum age threshold is five years (Tanzania), while in others, it is seven (Zambia), 10 (Madagascar), 15 (South Africa), or more.

Employment-Based versus Firm-Based Sampling Strategies

Data on the informal sector are collected from a variety of surveys focusing either on employment or on production. Employment surveys have commonly been used to collect data on the informal sector. The sampling group in this instance is the labor force. Analysis of these data enables the researcher to sort employment into formal and informal and to determine the main characteristics of informal employment and its share of total employment. These data can also be used to identify owners of informal businesses, which in turn can be a way of identifying informal businesses in a given locality. In this case, firms are identified indirectly through the analysis of employment (Verma 2007).

Much data collection has focused on informal employment rather than informal enterprises. The fifteenth International Conference of Labor Statisticians (ILO 1993) distinguishes informal employment from informal firms. Informal employment consists of all informal occupations, including informal work within formal firms or in households. This distinction implies that the unit to be investigated is the employee rather than the individual, who may have more than one job in the informal sector.

The 123 study, which is used by many countries in Africa and elsewhere, focuses on employment.[1] It proceeds in several stages, beginning with households and working up to informal production units. Phase 1 of the study involves a household survey consisting of a questionnaire on the sociodemographic characteristics of the household, followed by a survey dealing specifically with employment. The surveyed individuals are then classified as either in or out of the labor force. The former are then divided into two categories: those involved in formal production units and those involved in informal production units; informality is defined as firms that are not registered or that fail to maintain regularly updated formal accounting records. One of the major limitations of this survey method is the difficulty of accurately determining whether the companies are registered or keep regular formal accounts. It is difficult to obtain this information, and employees may not know whether or not their employers fulfill the conditions of formality, which can impair the classification of firms into formal and informal sectors. Even managers may not correctly report this information. Indeed, during our interviews, we observed numerous instances in which owners and employees claimed to be working in the formal sector but were actually working in the informal sector, often due to honest misunderstanding rather than deception.

Another type of survey focuses on firms rather than employees. The problem is that there are no comprehensive sample frames of informal firms on which to base a representative sample. Consequently, this approach is less widely used by government statistical agencies, which opt instead to use mixed household-enterprise surveys.

Surveys on consumption spending of households also provide a good avenue for studying informal sector activities. In this case too, the individual household is the starting point for the survey. Household consumption is decomposed according to whether the good originates in the formal or informal sector.[2] The main limitation of this approach is that informality is equated with small size, ignoring large informal firms as well as small formal ones.

Our Data Collection Strategy

Most of the available surveys in developing countries, particularly in Africa, are surveys of households. The main strength of such surveys is their comprehensive coverage of the various segments of the informal sector, with the notable exception of large informal firms. However, this method is subject to several limitations. First, household-based surveys use small size as a criterion for informality, thus excluding the large informal economy, which is important in Africa, as noted in chapter 1 and discussed in detail in chapter 4. These large informal firms are a minority, but they are very important for formulating growth strategies as well as understanding the deep connections between the formal and informal sectors. Small informal operators are limited to survival strategies, which is important for analyzing poverty and employment, but less so for understanding the causes and consequences of informality for growth. Very often in Africa, these large informal businesses are as big as formal enterprises. Charmes (2007) notes, "There will be no possible transition from the informal to the formal sector, when no companies of intermediate status are observed in the survey." Another limitation of this approach is that whether or not a firm is categorized as informal is based on the responses to the survey questions. Interviewees are asked several questions regarding criteria such as the keeping of accounts, registration, as well as other criteria for informality. However, one cannot always be certain that the employees are knowledgeable about these aspects of their employer's operations.

We are more interested in informal businesses than in informal employment or household information, given our focus on the implications of informality for economic growth and the business climate. We are also particularly interested in how the informal sector in these countries is conditioned by the institutional environment, as discussed in chapter 6. This particular focus greatly influenced our sampling strategy approach, which involved targeting both households (to identify small informal operators) and businesses. Moreover, we included the formal sector in our sample, which enabled us to compare formal and informal firms.

Data Sources

Our survey of formal and informal sectors targeted a sample of 300 enterprises each in Dakar, Ouagadougou, and Cotonou, for a total of 900 units surveyed.

A major difficulty was to identify a representative sample of informal and formal enterprises in these cities. Directories of companies in the formal and informal sectors are available from various government agencies in each country, but these agencies typically do not coordinate their definitions and methods. They also use different identification numbers, further impeding a consolidated database. Even worse, sometimes even within the same organization, different departments compile different subdirectories of companies, using different identifiers. This applies, for example, to fiscal authorities where different tax collection centers often manage various directories independently and inconsistently.

The following directories were identified in each of the three countries:

1. The census of the National Statistical Office on formal enterprises. This directory contains a database of formal enterprises, which is compiled from information supplied by businesses to the tax collection and national statistical agencies.

2. The list of formal enterprises compiled by the fiscal authorities. This database is generated from financial statements that companies provide at the end of each fiscal year. Only those businesses that pay formal income taxes are included in this database.

3. The directory of informal firms of the tax collection agencies. This covers all firms that are subject to the presumptive tax rather than the regular income tax (see chapter 1).

4. The registries of the Ministry of Commerce, customs, and the Chamber of Commerce. These directories include both formal and informal businesses, which are identified on the basis of the importer license or professional identification card.

Our database was formed by combining three different sources of information:

1. For the formal sector, we consolidated the business records maintained by the national statistics and tax bureaus.

2. For the large informal sector, we used the directory of companies recorded by the tax department, restricted to firms that are subject to the presumptive tax and that also have annual turnover exceeding the threshold of CFAF 20 million per year. Subsequently, during the survey and interview phase, we obtained information about actual sales used to determine which of these firms should have been subject to regular business income taxes. In many cases, actual sales were much greater than sales reported to the tax authorities.

3. For small informal businesses, we used the 123 survey for each country, restricted to businesses with annual turnover below CFAF 20 million. In this case, we identified the main locations for particular informal activities (for example, Sandaga market in Dakar and Dantokpa market in Cotonou for commerce), and the enumerators randomly selected the units to survey within these areas.

Sampling Method

We opted for a stratified sampling strategy. That is, we sought random samples within each of two three-by-three categories composed of (a) formal, small informal, and large informal enterprises and (b) industry, commerce, and other services. With regard to the modern sector, given that official statistics on output are available, we used the share of the various sectors to determine the size of the formal sector strata by industry. For the informal sectors, the sectoral distribution of firms and employment was determined from the results of the 123 survey (tables 2.1 and 2.2).

Because we base our analysis on a logistic regression, it is difficult to find a simple formula to determine the standard errors associated with the coefficients of our model. A rough approximation is $1\sqrt{n}$, where n is the number of observations. This approximation depends on the assumption that we have a random sample of the parent population of firms (which is not strictly valid because we adopted a stratified sampling method). This means that improvements in the precision of estimators associated with an increase in sample size are small when sample size is on the order of 300 units.[3] This consideration, in addition to the fact that a sample size of 300 is practical, led us to choose 300 observations per city. Within each stratum, firms were randomly sampled. However, the stratified sampling approach means that the overall sample is not representative of the parent population of firms, with an overrepresentation of formal and large informal firms.

A potential problem is that the responses of firms to sensitive questions may not always be accurate. Nevertheless, while underreporting of income is pervasive in the statements of informal sector firms to government officials, it is likely to be much less so in statements to our interviewers. Informal actors were made to understand that we were collecting data for research purposes and that we would not provide any information to tax officials. Furthermore, during our interviews, we randomly cross-checked survey data against our interview findings and confirmed that misreporting in the former is rare, as discussed in the next section.

Table 2.1 Breakdown of GDP in the Three West African Countries, 2003 and 2004

	Benin		Burkina Faso		Senegal	
Indicator	2003	2004	2003	2004	2003	2004
Total value added						
Amount (CFAF billions)	1,900	19,610	2,583	2,713	3,500	3,715
% of total	100	100	100	100	100	100
Formal sector value added						
Amount (CFAF billions)	510	519	1,308	1,379	1,578	1,730
% of total	26.8	26.5	50.7	50.8	45.1	46.6
Informal sector value added						
Amount (CFAF billions)	1,390	1,442	1,274	1,334	1,922	1,984
% of total	73.7	73.5	49.3	49.2	54.9	53.4

Source: For Senegal, DPEE 2008; for Benin, INSAE 2007; for Burkina Faso, INSD 2005.

Table 2.2 Distribution of Nonagricultural Informal Firms in the Three West African Countries, by Sector

Sector	Benin		Burkina Faso		Senegal	
	Number of firms	% of total	Number of firms	% of total	Number of firms	% of total
Industry	45,080	21.86	56,520	34.20	86,200	30.62
Clothing industry	18,900	9.17	12,395	7.50	21,100	7.50
Construction	16,740	8.12	9,255	5.60	21,100	7.50
Other industries	9,440	4.58	34,870	21.10	44,000	15.63
Commerce	102,040	49.49	84,449	51.10	131,000	46.54
Out-of-store retail trade	28,440	13.79	61,643	37.30	308,000	10.94
In-store wholesale or retail trade	73,600	35.70	22,806	13.80	100,300	35.63
Services	59,060	28.64	24,293	14.70	64,300	22.84
Repair	6,630	3.22	4,131	2.50	5,700	2.02
Food service	21,640	10.50	7,932	4.80	11,500	4.09
Transport	10,800	5.24	1,653	1.00	11,900	4.23
Other services	19,990	9.70	10,577	6.40	35,200	12.50
Total	206,180	100	165,262	100	281,500	100

Source: DPS 2004; INSAE 2002; INSD 2003.

Other Data Sources

In addition to the survey data, we used interviews, which allowed us to collect qualitative information to supplement the quantitative data from our surveys. We also made use of secondary data, including official statistics and other results from previous surveys.

Qualitative Data from Interviews

Besides the survey and secondary data used throughout the work, results from semistructured interviews with various key stakeholders in the informal sector were also important sources of information. We used a set of predetermined questions, but also allowed the interviewees some flexibility to discuss their views as openly as possible. The usual duration of an interview was an hour and a half. One of the major challenges we faced throughout the interviewing process was to avoid being perceived as fiscal agents, a concern of traders, or as independent researchers who might reveal sensitive or embarrassing information, a concern especially of government employees. We sought to reassure our interviewees that the aim of our work was mainly academic, without denying that the results would be made available to policy makers. We stressed the fact that no individual identifying information would be disclosed without expressed consent of the respondent and that we were interested in general trends and opinions that we would report anonymously.

We made efforts to identify well-informed organizations and individuals. In the case of the government, we relied on our team's prior contacts with a number of ministries and the West African Economic and Monetary Union (WAEMU) Commission, which enabled us to get interviews with well-informed officials. To obtain interviews with entrepreneurs in the formal and informal sectors, we made contacts through the chambers of commerce, employer organizations, and private accountants, generally informally.

The aim of the interviews was to collect qualitative information to complement the mainly quantitative data obtained through our surveys and secondary data collection. The questions covered the same topics as those included in the surveys. In the case of private firms, we probed to identify whether a firm was truly formal or informal, beyond what the interviewee asserted. For example, we discussed the registration of the company with various government agencies (tax authorities, Ministry of Commerce), the type and magnitude of tax payments, access to bank credit, the size of the enterprise measured by turnover or the number of employees in the firm, and so forth. Taken together, responses to these questions and related discussions enabled us to obtain an accurate picture of the extent of formality or informality of the firm. While the same questions were asked in the survey questionnaires, the give and take of the interviews provided additional information. Indeed, comparing the results of the semi-structured interviews with the survey data from the same firms revealed many inconsistencies in the answers given by respondents regarding their formal or informal status. Some operators claimed to be taxed as formal firms, yet they did not meet certain minimum requirements to be taxed at that level, such as keeping regular accounts or even sometimes having a fixed employment location. Aberrant responses were identified and corrected in the process of sifting through the survey database, but the filtering methods used in these cases were sometimes ad hoc and imprecise. The interviews enabled a more reliable determination of inconsistencies.

The interviews also covered the business environment, relations with the government, the interactions between actors in the formal and informal sectors, social relationships in the business world, and sociodemographic trends within the company and its employees (such as age, education level, parental education levels). All of these factors were included in the survey questionnaire, but because of the binary nature of responses (that is, yes or no), the respondent had no opportunity to elaborate, nuance, or clarify his or her thoughts.

Finally, the interviews enabled us to obtain the perspective of knowledgeable stakeholders rather than relying only on respondents within private firms, particularly officials in the tax and customs offices responsible for overseeing the informal sector, WAEMU officials, and representatives from business associations. In addition, the interviews focused on the large informal sector, which is very difficult to identify from the surveys alone. Overall, the interviews were complements to, rather than substitutes for, the surveys, as they provided additional information, larger perspectives, and alternative points of view.

Secondary Data

We also made extensive use of secondary data from the national accounts of the three countries and previous surveys of companies and households.

The national accounts contain estimates of gross domestic product (GDP) for both the formal and informal sectors, listed by industry. Estimates of informal sector GDP is extrapolated from the results of the 123 survey. Thus for each sector, we have the overall value added and its breakdown between the formal and informal sectors, as presented in chapter 3. These estimates are only as good as the 123 survey results and the assumptions on which the extrapolation is based. In our view, the official estimates understate the size of the informal economy. The large informal sector is not included in the estimates. In addition, the survey approach accepted the firm's self-described status as informal or formal. As noted above, many informal individuals are confused about their status or prefer to present themselves as formal even though they behave informally. Nevertheless, even if understated, official data still indicate a very large share of output attributable to the informal sector.

Previous survey data on households and businesses for the three countries complemented our own in the areas of social welfare, the labor market, and the business environment.

Conclusion

Given the complexity of the informal sector and the difficulties of obtaining accurate information, we used three sources of data: national accounts and other secondary databases, our own surveys, and qualitative information from interviews. Regarding our surveys, in order to have a mix of formal, large informal, and small informal firms, we used a stratified sampling strategy. This enabled us to obtain information on the three categories of firms. More detailed interviews with managers of firms and other stakeholders provided an important way to check findings from the surveys and develop a greater understanding of the informal sector, particularly large informal firms.

Notes

1. The countries using this survey in Africa are Cameroon, Madagascar, Morocco, Benin, Burkina Faso, Côte d'Ivoire, Mali, Nigeria, Senegal, Togo, the Democratic Republic of Congo, and Burundi. Developing countries outside Africa also use this survey, including China, Bangladesh, Guatemala, Peru, and Mexico (UN Economic and Social Council 2007).
2. It is generally assumed that goods produced in the informal sector are of lower quality than goods produced in the formal sector (Gautier 2002).
3. For example, $1\sqrt{n}$ falls from 0.058 to 0.05 when the sample size goes from 300 to 400.

References

Charmes, Jacques. 2007. "Estimation and Survey Methods for the Informal Sector." Centre of Economics and Ethics for Environment and Development, University of Versailles-St Quentin en Yvelines. Paper prepared for an ILO international seminar.

DPEE (Direction de la Prévision et des Études Economiques). 2008. Les comptes nationaux du Sénégal. DPEE, Dakar.

DPS (Direction de la Prévision et de la Statistique). 2004. "Le secteur informel dans l'agglomération de Dakar: Performances, insertion, perspectives; Résultats de la phase II de l'enquête 1-2-3 de 2003." DPS, Senegal, June.

Gautier, Jean-Francois. 2002. "Taxation optimale de la consommation et biens informels." Revue Economique 53 (3, May): 599–610.

ILO (International Labour Organization). 1993. "Conference Report of the Sixteenth Conference of Labor Market Statisticians." ILO, Geneva, January 19–28.

INSAE (Institut National de la Statistique et de l'Analyse Economique). 2002. "Le secteur informel dans l'agglomération de Cotonou: Performances, insertion, perspectives; Enquête 1-2-3, premiers résultats de la phase 2, 2001." INSAE, Bénin, September.

———. 2007. Les comptes nationaux du Bénin. INSAE, Cotonou.

INSD (Institut National de la Statistique et de la Démographie). 2003. "Le secteur informel dans l'agglomération de Ouagadougou: Performances, insertion, perspectives; Enquête 1-2-3, premiers résultats de la phase II, 2001." INSD, Burkina Faso, September.

———. 2005. Les comptes nationaux du Burkina Faso. INSD, Ouagadougou.

UN (United Nations). 1993. System of National Accounts. New York: UN.

UN (United Nations) Economic and Social Council. 2007. "Étude sur la mesure du secteur informel et de l'emploi informel en Afrique." African Center for Statistics, Economic Commission for Africa, December.

Verma, Vijay. 2007. "Sample Design Consideration for Informal Sector Survey." University of Essex, Colchester, U.K.

Chapter **3**

The Informal Sector in West Africa: Overview of Economic Significance and Welfare Effects

This study focuses on the informal sector in three West African Economic and Monetary Union (WAEMU) countries: Benin, Burkina Faso, and Senegal. We use these three countries because they are quite typical of the rest of WAEMU and West Africa in general. They are small, with populations ranging from 8 million to 14 million people in 2008, very low per capita incomes and human development indicators, and generally poor rankings on standard investment climate indicators such as the World Economic Forum and the World Bank Doing Business measures (table 3.1). Like most African countries, their small formal economies depend on a few primary products, with most output and employment contained in the informal sector. Tables 3.2 and 3.3 display the shares of WAEMU countries in WAEMU and Sub-Saharan African gross domestic product (GDP).

Senegal is a coastal state, relatively industrialized and developed by West African standards, but still very poor. It was the capital of colonial French West Africa from which it inherited decent infrastructure (for example, the harbor and airport) as well as close trade relations with the other francophone countries. Senegal completely surrounds The Gambia, an English-speaking country with markedly different traditions in economic policy and whose economy essentially relies on often-fraudulent trade with Senegal. Benin is a coastal state in the Gulf of Guinea whose geography (climate, vegetation, and proximity to Central Africa) is quite different from that of Senegal. In addition, it is heavily influenced by its long border with Nigeria, the economic heavyweight of the region. Burkina Faso is an arid landlocked Sahelian country with much more limited productive potential than the other two.

In this chapter, we provide an overview of the significance and consequences of the informal sector in the three countries. Following a brief description of the three economies, the contribution of the informal sector to fiscal revenues is shown to be far below its share of GDP. We also analyze the effects of informality

Table 3.1 Economic Indicators in the Three West African Countries, 2006–08

Indicator	Benin			Burkina Faso			Senegal		
	2006	2007	2008	2006	2007	2008	2006	2007	2008
Economy									
Population (millions)	7.6	7.9	8.1	13.4	13.7	14.0	11.9	12.2	12.5
GDP (US$ billions, PPP)	11.3	12.2	13.0	15.6	16.6	17.8	19.3	20.8	21.8
GDP per capita (US$, PPP)	1,484.0	1,548.0	1,608.0	1,161.0	1,209.0	1,268.0	1,617.0	1,701.0	1,739.0
GDP growth rate (%)	3.8	4.7	5.0	5.5	3.6	5.0	2.3	4.7	2.5
GDP per capita growth (%)	4.1	4.3	3.9	6.5	4.2	4.8	3.3	5.2	2.2
Exports as % of GDP	30.7	31.2	31.5	10.8	10.4	10.5	25.4	23.7	27.1
Competitiveness									
World Economic Forum ranking	—	107	—	—	119	127	—	—	—
Doing Business ranking	—	137	151	—	163	161	—	146	162
Informal sector as % of GDP	70.3	70.1	70.3	49.0	49.0	—	46.7	45.5	46.8
Quality of life									
Incidence of poverty	36.8	33.3	—	13.9	42.6	42.8	—	—	—
Severity of poverty	0.07	0.04	—	6.0	—	—	—	—	—
Human Development Index ranking	161	161	163	173	177	176	153	166	156
Education									
Elementary education rate (%)	95.9	—	—	66.5	65.3	—	81.8	86.0	—
Illiteracy rate (%)	65.3	54.7	—	78.2	69.6	—	60.7	56.0	—
Health									
AIDS prevalence (%)	2.0	—	—	2.0	—	—	1.5	—	0.7
Malaria prevalence (%)	39.7	—	—	—	—	—	30.0	—	—

Sources: World Bank 2009; for Senegal, ANSD 2009; for Benin, INSAE 2009; for Burkina Faso, INSD 2009.
Note: — = Not available.

on social welfare by comparing indicators of living standards of households engaged in formal versus informal activities.

An Overview of the Three Economies

As is typical in most of Sub-Saharan Africa, Senegal, Benin, and Burkina Faso are all very poor countries, with formal sectors revolving around a few primary products and much of the rest of the economy dominated by the informal

Table 3.2 Shares of WAEMU GDP of West African Countries, 1990–2008
% of WAEMU GDP, unless otherwise noted

Country	1990	1995	2000	2001	2002	2003	2004	2005	2006	2007	2008
Benin	6.5	8.2	9.3	9.3	9.4	9.6	9.6	9.6	9.6	9.7	10.1
Burkina Faso	10.9	9.0	10.1	10.5	11.0	11.6	11.9	11.8	11.7	11.8	11.8
Côte d'Ivoire	37.9	41.6	40.5	39.2	38.6	36.9	36.5	35.7	35.3	34.6	34.1
Mali	9.7	10.7	10.4	11.2	11.2	11.9	11.8	12.0	12.4	12.5	12.7
Niger	8.7	6.6	6.5	6.7	7.0	7.1	6.8	7.4	7.4	7.4	7.8
Senegal	20.1	18.5	18.2	18.1	17.9	18.4	18.9	19.0	19.0	19.7	19.4
Togo	6.3	5.5	5.0	4.9	4.9	4.5	4.6	4.6	4.5	4.4	4.2
WAEMU GDP (US$ millions)	28.5	26.5	25.8	26.9	29.9	37.3	42.5	45.9	49.3	57.4	69.0

Sources: World Bank 2009; for Senegal, ANSD 2009; for Benin, INSAE 2009; for Burkina Faso, INSD 2009.

Table 3.3 Shares of Sub-Saharan GDP of West African Countries, 1990–2008
% of Sub-Saharan GDP, unless otherwise noted

Country	1990	1995	2000	2001	2002	2003	2004	2005	2006	2007	2008
Benin	0.6	0.7	0.7	0.8	0.8	0.8	0.7	0.7	0.6	0.7	0.7
Burkina Faso	1.1	0.7	0.8	0.9	1.0	1.0	0.9	0.9	0.8	0.8	0.8
Côte d'Ivoire	3.7	3.4	3.1	3.3	3.4	3.2	2.8	2.6	2.3	2.3	2.4
Mali	1.0	0.9	0.8	0.9	1.0	1.0	0.9	0.9	0.8	0.8	0.9
Niger	0.9	0.5	0.5	0.6	0.6	0.6	0.5	0.5	0.5	0.5	0.5
Senegal	2.0	1.5	1.4	1.5	1.6	1.6	1.5	1.4	1.3	1.3	1.4
Togo	0.6	0.4	0.4	0.4	0.4	0.4	0.4	0.3	0.3	0.3	0.3
WAEMU	9.8	8.1	7.7	8.4	8.8	8.5	7.8	7.2	6.6	6.7	7.0
Sub-Saharan Africa GDP (US$ millions)	291.1	325.7	333.6	320.9	340.7	436.5	545.0	640.6	743.4	856.1	991.5

Sources: World Bank 2009; for Senegal, ANSD 2009; for Benin, INSAE 2009; for Burkina Faso, INSD 2009.

sector. Here we provide a brief description of the three economies (table 3.1 provides some basic data).

Benin

A small country with a coast on the Gulf of Guinea, Benin has a rather favorable geographic position, with borders on the north with the landlocked Sahelian countries Burkina Faso and Niger, on the east with Nigeria, and on the west with Togo. Benin has the shape of a long north-south strip of land measuring about 700 kilometers between the Gulf of Benin and the Niger River. The country has a relatively flat terrain and an ample water supply. About 65 percent of the land is covered by arborous vegetation, but this proportion is shrinking steadily.

After the shift from a socialist to a market-oriented economy in 1990 and the devaluation of the CFA franc in 1994, economic growth has picked up substantially. The GDP growth rate has risen to around 5 percent in recent years—from 2.5 percent in 2005 to 4.7 percent in 2007 and to 5.0 percent in 2008. The economy is dominated by the primary and tertiary sectors, with a very small secondary sector. The primary sector has long contributed a large, albeit declining, portion of Benin's GDP, averaging 37.1 percent between 1994 and 1999 and 30 percent between 2000 and 2008; it still accounts for about 60 percent of employment. Agriculture is dominated by the cultivation of food crops (cassava root, beans, yam, corn, millet, rice) and cotton, the main cash crop. Benin's formal economy is highly dependent on cotton, of which it is the largest exporter in West Africa. Cotton is the main source of income for more than half of Benin's farmers. As a result of low world prices and, more importantly, of mismanagement of the liberalization of the sector, cotton production has fallen sharply, from 350,000 tons in the 2005–06 season to 240,000 tons in 2006–07. A partial recovery of cotton production has occurred in the last few crop years. Efforts are under way to promote diversification of crops (cashew nuts, cassava, pineapples, shea) in order to ensure food security and boost exports of domestically produced goods.

Benin derives only 13 percent of GDP from the industrial sector, much of which revolves around cotton processing, particularly ginning. Industrial development is hindered by an unfavorable institutional environment, the pervasiveness of smuggling, and low education levels. In cooperation with the private sector, the government has instituted a five-point plan to promote investment: legal and judicial system reforms to strengthen the protection of property rights, financial system reforms, improvements in industrial competitiveness, deeper integration within the Economic Community of West African States (ECOWAS), and improvements in basic infrastructure, particularly communication networks and industrial parks. The practical significance of these plans is doubtful, as is the case with so many similar plans in Benin and other countries of the region, past and present.

Services represent the largest share of GDP, at about 42 percent. Regional trade, mostly via smuggling with the landlocked countries to the north and especially Nigeria, is Benin's main industry, along with exporting cotton. Transport, banking, insurance, and other services are highly dependent on this mostly unrecorded cross-border trade. The informal sector plays a major role in smuggling, as described in detail in chapter 9. Wholesale-retail trade accounted for an average of about 19 percent of GDP between 1990 and 2008, while transport contributed another 9 percent during the same period.

Like many African countries, Benin runs very large trade deficits, on the order of 20–25 percent of GDP. The current account deficits are smaller in view of official transfers and exports of services, notably related to the informal cross-border trade. Cotton dominates official exports and ships mainly to countries like France, China, Indonesia, India, and Nigeria. Official imports originate primarily from developed countries, with France (45 percent of imports) leading, followed by the United States, Japan, China, WAEMU member states, and Nigeria. Recorded trade with WAEMU and Nigeria is thus quite small, but official statistics are misleading. Vast volumes of unrecorded trade flow in both directions between Benin and Nigeria.

Despite the global economic turmoil since 2008, Benin has maintained relative macroeconomic stability, due largely to the CFA franc's peg to the euro. Inflation has been kept at around 3 percent, conforming to WAEMU's convergence criteria. Inflation rose temporarily to about 7.9 percent in 2008, due to rising global food and petrol prices. The budget deficit deteriorated from 5.2 percent of GDP in 2005 to 10.4 percent in 2008. However, the cancellation of debt under the Highly Indebted Poor Countries (HIPC) Initiative and the Multilateral Debt Relief Initiative and prudent foreign borrowing helped to reduce external public debt from 58.3 percent to about 12.6 percent of GDP in 2008.

Benin, like many other Sub-Saharan African nations, experiences high population growth rates, averaging 3.25 percent in 1992–2002 and falling slightly to 3 percent in 2007. Given the high population growth rates, the government has recognized the need for increased investment and improved public services such as education and training and sanitation and food safety, but the effectiveness of its policies remains to be seen. Despite some improvement in social indicators, Benin remains a very poor country, with GDP per capita of US$600, life expectancy of 54 years, a literacy rate of 45.3 percent, a United Nations Development Program (UNDP) Human Development Indicator (HDI) ranking of 163 out of 177 countries, and monetary and nonmonetary poverty rates of about 40 percent.

Burkina Faso

Benin's neighbor, Burkina Faso faces one of the harshest geographic situations of any country in the world. A landlocked and arid Sahelian country, it is bordered on the north and west by Mali, on the northeast by Niger, on the southeast by Benin, and on the south by Togo, Ghana, and Côte d'Ivoire. The slight decline in the terrain guides the water flow of the three rivers—Mouhoun, Nayinon, and Nakambé—that cross the country. Economic growth averaged a solid 5.9 percent between 1997 and 2006 and fell to a still respectable 5.0 percent in 2008.

Burkina Faso is highly dependent on the primary sector, whose share of GDP rose from about 40 percent in the 1990s to 51 percent in 2007. Agriculture and livestock represent about 36 percent of GDP and are the source of employment and income for 80 percent of the population. The government aims to lift agricultural output growth from 5 to 10 percent and to increase income per person of farmers and stockbreeders by at least 3 percent annually. Burkina Faso has considerable agricultural potential: only a third of total farmland and 12 percent of irrigable land is used. Fruits and vegetables remain a promising, but largely untapped, source of export diversification.

Industry accounts for a relatively sizable 26 percent of GDP, reflecting the importance of mining, which has substantial potential for growth. The government's industrial strategy is based on 12 industries: cotton, cereals, fruits and vegetables, oil products, milk, meat, leather, metalwork, rubber and plastic, quarries, construction materials, and chemical products (fertilizer and phytosanitary products and pharmaceuticals). Manufacturing remains underdeveloped, however, with factories concentrated around Ouagadougou and Bobo Dioulasso.

Burkina Faso's service sector is dominated by trade and tourism. The tertiary sector represented about 32 percent of GDP between 1990 and 2007. Wholesale-retail trade is a major but declining activity, accounting for 22 percent of GDP between 1990 and 2000 and 11 percent in 2007. Burkina Faso is a focal point for trade in WAEMU, given its location at the center of the group. With its two commercial centers—Ouagadougou and Bobo Dioulasso— Burkina Faso has the best network of road connections among WAEMU countries. Tourism also plays an important role, thanks in part to the country's well-known handicrafts. The handicraft industry employs about 900,000 people and accounts for nearly 30 percent of GDP. Burkina Faso promotes itself as the showcase for African artifacts, hosting the biannual International Handicrafts Fair of Ouagadougou.

Despite regional instability since 1998, caused by the crisis in Côte d'Ivoire, international trade has increased steadily, accelerating to an annual average of 12.7 percent between 2005 and 2007. Burkina's exports cover only a third of imports, and exports are dominated by primary products, mainly agricultural goods, with cotton being by far the largest export (55.4 percent of total exports), followed by livestock (15.9 percent), a variety of other agricultural products like green beans, sesame, and shea (together, 15.4 percent), and gold (5.2 percent).

Since 1997, Burkina Faso has benefited from debt reduction under the HIPC Initiative, with external debt of 34.5 percent of GDP in 2007. The country ranked second to last in the 2007 HDI index, and its income per capita of US$430 in 2008 is well below the Sub-Saharan average of US$592. The poverty rate fell from 55 percent in 1998 to about 42.6 percent in 2007. Official unemployment in 2007 was estimated at 7.8 percent in rural areas and 17.7 percent in urban areas, but these figures ignore massive underemployment.

Senegal

Senegal has a favorable location. It is bordered by the Atlantic Ocean to the west, Mauritania to the north, Mali to the east, and Guinea and Guinea-Bissau to the south. The Gambia forms a virtual enclave within Senegal, penetrating more than 300 kilometers inland, and the islands of Cape Verde are located 560 kilometers from the coast of Senegal. GDP growth has averaged around 5 percent since the 1994 devaluation, but declined significantly to 4.7 percent in 2007 and 2.5 percent in 2008, due largely to the global economic crisis and erratic economic policies.

The primary sector accounts for a relatively small and declining share of GDP, falling from 16.9 percent in 2000 to 13.2 percent of GDP in 2008. Slow growth in agriculture can be attributed largely to low rainfall levels and mismanagement, resulting in a spectacular decline in groundnut production, the country's main cash crop. In recent years, the Senegalese government has introduced several new programs to promote agricultural development, but, as in the past, lack of consistency makes it difficult to put these initiatives into practice. The government's proclivity for launching multiple initiatives without fully articulating their content or identifying the resources necessary to support them dooms these grandiose plans from their inception.

Fishing employs around 600,000 people, the majority of the coastal population, but its overall share of GDP is still low, hovering at around 1.7 percent over the period between 2000 and 2008. The fishing industry has been affected adversely by overfishing, with the government seemingly unable to control the problem.

Industrial output in Senegal has also experienced sluggish growth since the phosphate industry crisis in 2005. Its share in GDP has remained at around 20 percent over the period between 2000 and 2008. The construction industry is an exception, benefiting from ambitious infrastructure projects, mainly in Dakar, undertaken by the Senegalese government in recent years, and thriving residential construction, funded in part by remittances. The construction sector's share of GDP rose from 4.1 percent in 2000 to 4.7 percent of GDP in 2008. Manufacturing accounted for 12.8 percent of GDP in 2008, a relatively large portion by African standards, but the sector exhibits little dynamism, particularly in labor-intensive sectors such as textiles and apparel.

Services account for approximately 45 percent of GDP. Wholesale-retail trade is the largest subsector, accounting for around 16 percent of GDP. Commerce in Senegal is also marked by the proliferation of street vendors, who account for the majority of retail trade operations. Trade in Senegal has long been dominated by the Mouride Islamic brotherhood, with a worldwide trading diaspora, as described in chapter 8. There has also been a massive installation of Chinese shops, which compete strongly with Lebanese and Mouride vendors in the region. Retail trade is controlled largely by the informal sector. Telecommunications have also witnessed substantial growth and now account for 11 percent of GDP. There are three major mobile operators alongside the nation's main fixed-service operator, SONATEL (Société Nationale des Télécommunications).

Like the other countries of the region, Senegal has a high level of trade in relation to output and a large trade deficit, funded by remittances and foreign aid. France is Senegal's largest bilateral trading partner, but China's share has been rising rapidly. Senegal's main exports are phosphates, salt, peanuts, and fish products. The share of the traditional cash crop, peanuts, has declined sharply due to structural problems, including desertification, soil erosion, and aflotoxin contamination (Mbaye 2005), resulting in poor product quality and loss of market share. Aside from the capital-intensive phosphate factories, Senegal has had little success in export diversification, particularly in labor-intensive manufacturing. Horticulture has recently emerged as a promising export, but is still small.

The Significance of Informality in West Africa

In Africa, although informal activities are undeclared, attempts have been made to estimate their magnitude. Our estimates, as well as those of others, indicate that more than 80 percent, perhaps even 90 percent, of total employment is informal. Official statistics from West African countries indicate that up to 60 percent of the GDP of these countries is produced by informal activities.[1]

Other studies provide somewhat different estimates, depending on the definition of informality adopted, but all of them agree that the informal sector occupies an important position in African economies. According to Schneider and Enste (2002), the informal sector represents 10 to 20 percent of GDP in developed countries, more than a third of GDP in developing countries, and well above that in Africa. Schneider (2000) reports that the informal sector accounts for 42.3 percent of GDP in Africa and 60 percent of GDP in Nigeria. The International Labour Organization's estimates are of the same magnitude: 48 percent of nonagricultural employment in North Africa, 51 percent in Latin America, 65 percent in Asia, and 72 percent in Sub-Saharan Africa (ILO 2002). Chen (2001) estimates that 93 percent of new jobs created in Africa during the 1990s were created by the informal sector. Xaba, Horn, and Motala (2002) find that, while formal sector employment is stagnant at best, both employment and share of GDP are steadily increasing in the informal sector. Focusing on the rural economy, Otsuka and Yamano (2006) report that the informal sector accounts for 13 percent of nonfarm income in Ethiopia, 30 percent in Kenya, and 38 percent in Uganda. Steel and Snodgrass (2008) report that the informal economy in Africa accounts for 50 to 80 percent of GDP and as much as 90 percent of employment. A Botswana Central Statistics Office report finds that the number of informal firms in Botswana rose 28.7 percent between 1999 and 2007 (CSO 2008). According to one estimate, the informal sector accounts for three quarters of Ghana's national income; in rural areas, this proportion reaches 90 percent (Canagarajah and Mazumdar 1999). In Burkina Faso, researchers have found that 80 percent of total employment is attributed to the informal sector (Calvès and Schoumaker 2004).

Some of the largest and fastest-growing sectors of West African economies are dominated by informal firms: wholesale and retail trade, transportation, restaurants, reproduction of compact discs and tapes, carpentry, construction, and real estate, among others. This tendency for informal firms to dominate in certain sectors, notably retail, construction, and other services, also occurs in other developing countries (Adams 2008; Lund and Skinner 2004; Haan 2006). Verick (2006) also finds that the retail sector is the largest locus of informal activities in African economies. Similarly, Charmes (1993) finds that 80.7 percent of firms in Benin's urban zones are street vendors. The CSO's 2008 study finds that 39.6 percent of informal firms in Botswana are involved with retail trade. Other sectors with significant proportions of informal activity in Botswana are real estate (20.7 percent), manufacturing (11.3 percent), and hospitality (10.3 percent). According to a 1988 survey by the U.S. Agency for International Development (USAID), 72 percent of informal activity in Senegal consists of wholesale and retail trade, with very small firms averaging just 1.1 employees per firm (ILO 1995). The results from the second phase of the 123 study in Senegal (DPS 2004) show that the size of informal firms had barely changed as of 2003: average employment per firm had edged up to only 1.5. However, the sectoral distribution among informal sectors had evolved substantially: trade fell to 46.5 percent of informal activity in 2003, while industry accounted for 30.6 percent, services for 21.3 percent, and fishing for 1.6 percent.

A Sectoral Analysis of Informality Based on National Accounts Data

In this section, we report the official estimates of the share of the informal sector in GDP and employment based on national accounts data. These estimates are derived from surveys that are extrapolated to other years. The definition of the informal sector in the national accounts is based on household-level surveys that identify small household enterprises as informal. While this captures an important part of the informal economy, it neglects large informal firms, so the national accounts estimates are likely to underestimate the size of the informal sector. Nevertheless, they are a good starting point.

The informal sector accounts for half or more of GDP in all WAEMU countries. For our three countries, the informal sector's share has averaged 74, 49, and 54 percent, respectively, for Benin, Burkina Faso, and Senegal since 2000.

Figures 3.1, 3.2, and 3.3 show the growth rates of total GDP and that part of GDP attributable to formal and informal sectors in the three countries between 1991 and 2007. Until 2000, informal sector growth outpaced formal sector growth in most years, but since 2000, growth rates of formal and informal sectors are fairly similar, except in Senegal where growth of the formal sector has picked up markedly.

Figure 3.4 displays the share of GDP attributable to the informal sector, by major industry group. The primary sector is dominated by the informal sector in the three countries. For the secondary sector, the distributions are more variable. In Senegal, the informal sector accounts for a little more than half of the value added in both secondary and tertiary sectors; in Burkina Faso and Benin, the informal sector accounts for about three quarters of tertiary output, but in Benin, the formal sector produces the majority of value added, whereas in Burkina it produces about half.

Figure 3.1 Growth Rate of Value Added in the Formal and Informal Sectors in Benin, 1991–2007

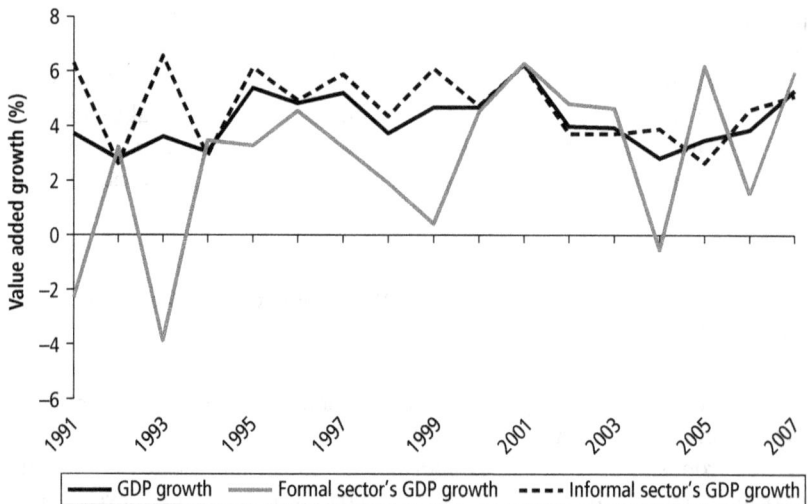

Source: INSAE 2009.

Figure 3.2 Growth Rate of Value Added in the Formal and Informal Sectors in Burkina Faso, 1991–2007

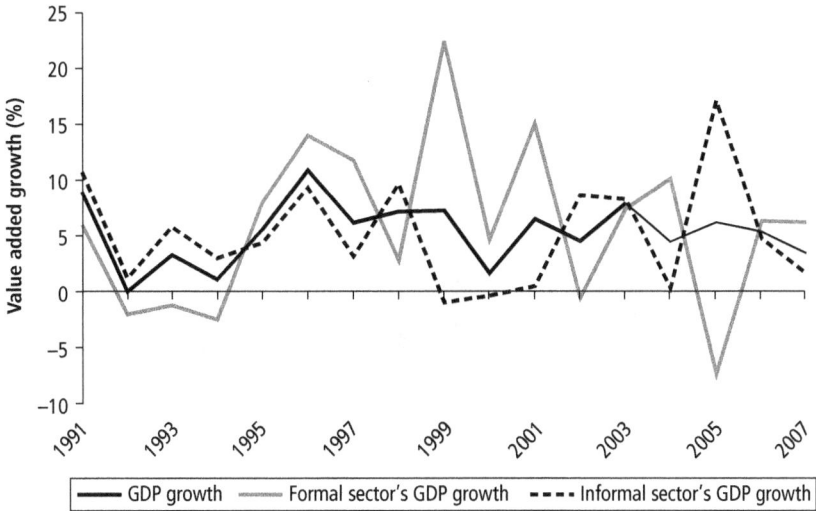

Source: INSD 2009.

Figure 3.3 Growth Rate of Value Added in the Formal and Informal Sectors in Senegal, 1991–2007

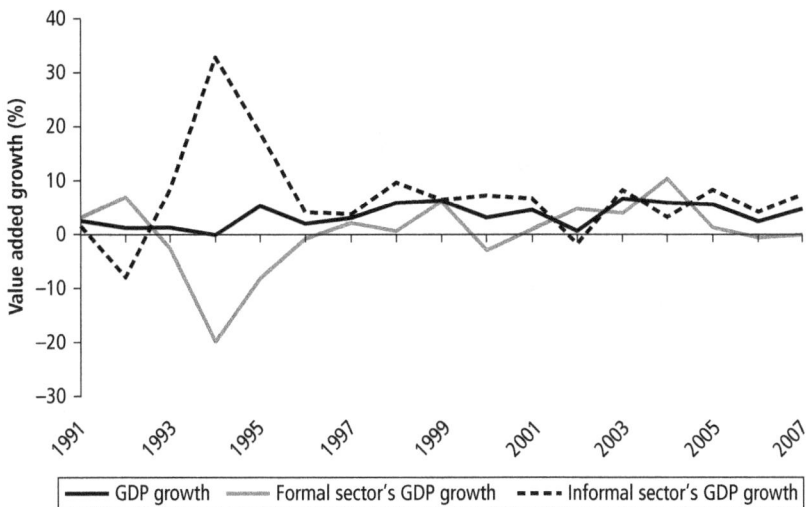

Source: ANSD 2009.

Figure 3.4 Proportion of GDP Attributed to the Informal Sector in the Three West African Countries, by Industrial Sector, 2007

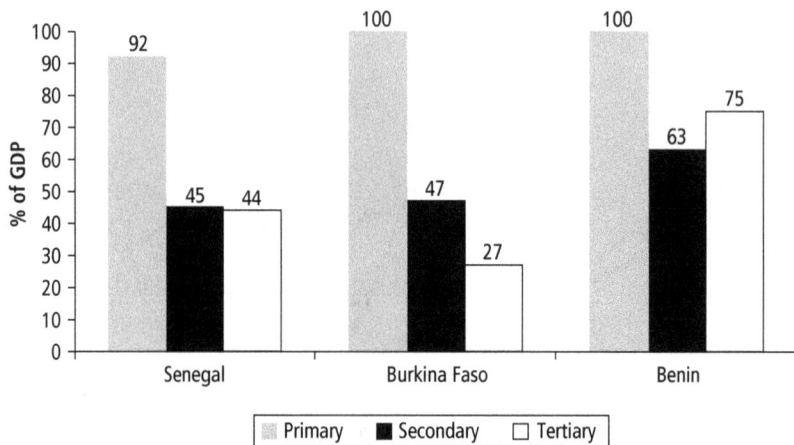

Sources: ANSD 2009; INSAE 2009; INSD 2009.

Figures 3.5–3.13 display a more detailed sectoral distribution of the informal sector in the three countries over time. All primary industries (agriculture, livestock, fishing) are entirely or heavily dominated by informal production (figures 3.5–3.7). The shares of formal and informal firms differ considerably within subsectors in the secondary (figures 3.8–3.10) and tertiary (figures 3.11–3.13)

Figure 3.5 Share of Value Added Contributed by Informal Businesses in the Primary Sector in Senegal, 1990–2007

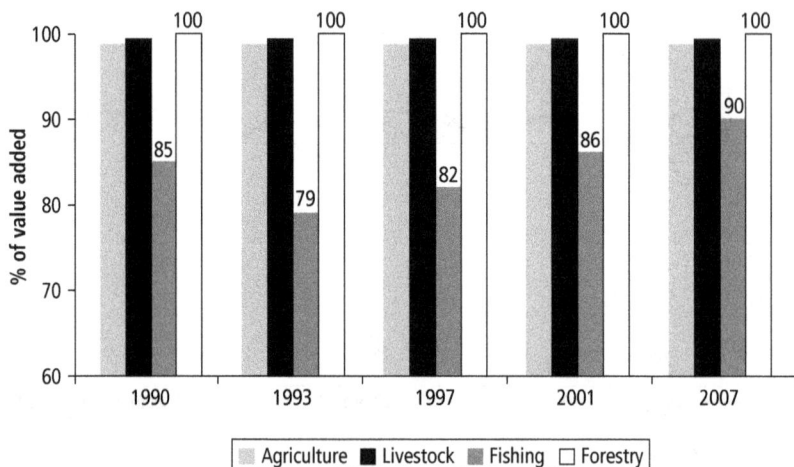

Source: ANSD 2009.

Figure 3.6 Share of Value Added Contributed by Informal Businesses in the Primary Sector in Burkina Faso, 1990–2007

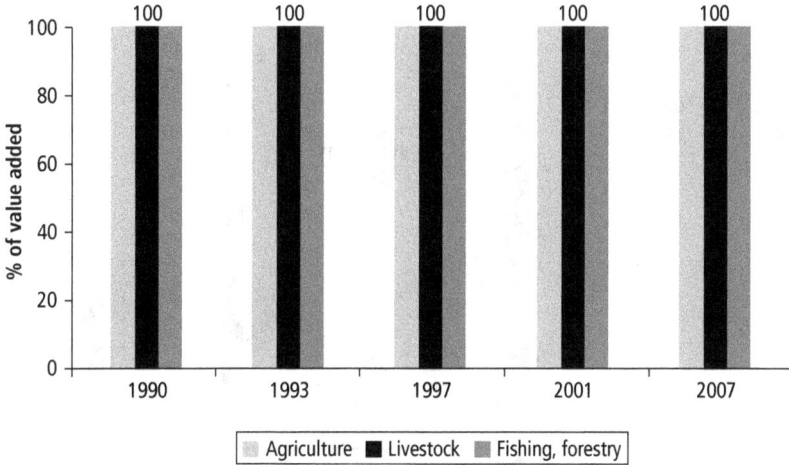

Source: INSD 2009.

Figure 3.7 Share of Value Added Contributed by Informal Businesses in the Primary Sector in Benin, 1990–2007

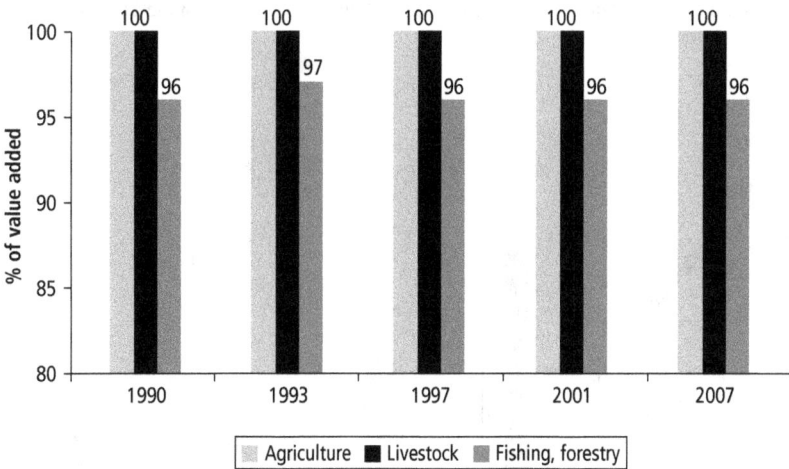

Source: INSAE 2009.

sectors, however. Mining has become increasingly informal in Benin and Burkina Faso, but the opposite is true in Senegal.

The construction industry is heavily informal in Benin and Burkina Faso but more evenly divided between formal and informal sectors in Senegal. Construction is an interesting example of how the informal and formal firms interact.

Figure 3.8 Share of Value Added Contributed by Informal Businesses in the Secondary Sector in Senegal, 1990–2007

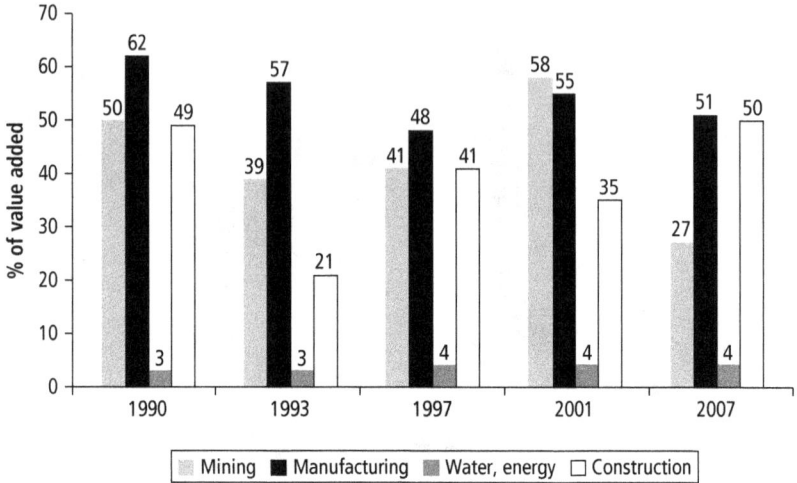

Source: ANSD 2009.

Figure 3.9 Share of Value Added Contributed by Informal Businesses in the Secondary Sector in Burkina Faso, 1990–2007

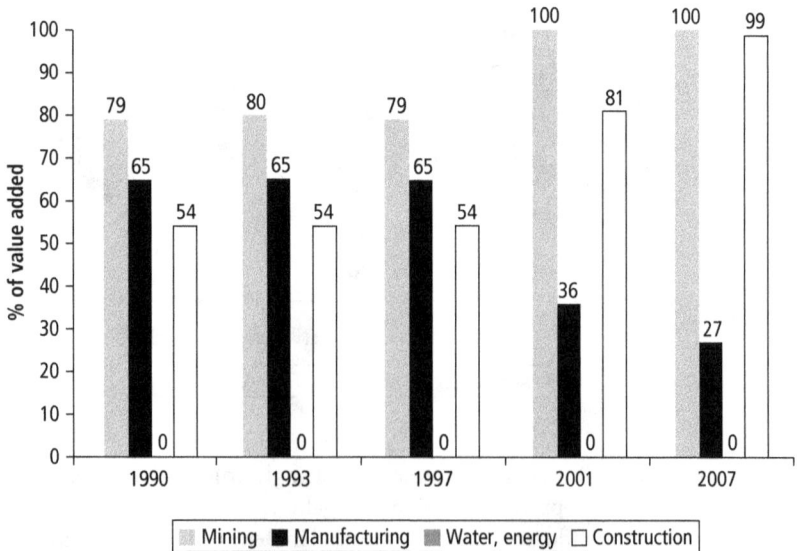

Source: INSD 2009.

Figure 3.10 Share of Value Added Contributed by Informal Businesses in the Secondary Sector in Benin, 1990–2007

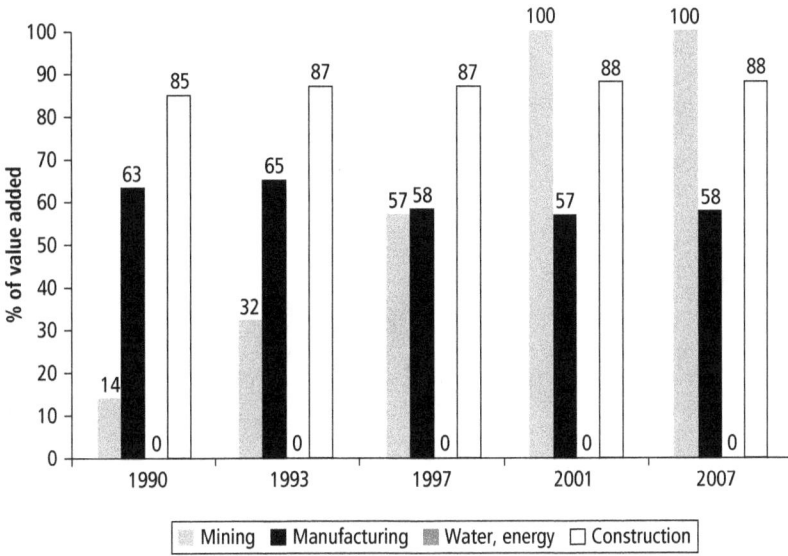

Source: INSAE 2009.

Figure 3.11 Share of Value Added Contributed by Informal Businesses in the Tertiary Sector in Senegal, 1990–2007

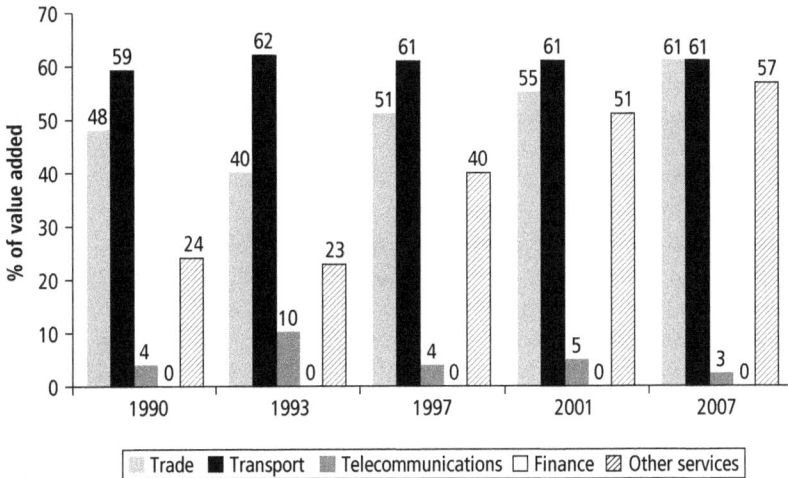

Source: ANSD 2009.

Figure 3.12 Share of Value Added Contributed by Informal Businesses in the Tertiary Sector in Burkina Faso, 1990–2007

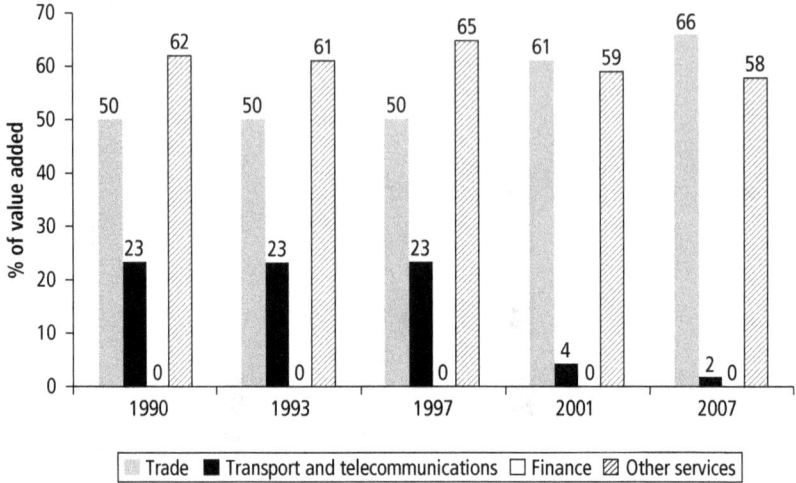

Source: INSD 2009.

In residential housing, small informal operators predominate. In public works (roads, bridges), the government finances construction through its investment budget or with funds supplied by donors. Informal firms do not have the funds or the legitimacy to participate in the bidding process. Formal companies always obtain the contracts, but they usually subcontract the projects to informal building firms. Manufacturing is split more evenly between the formal and informal sectors, with the informal sector's share having shrunk since 2001.

Parastatals with monopoly status usually provide energy and water, explaining why almost 100 percent of the value added of these sectors can be attributed to formal activities. In the case of transport, private and public providers share the market. The formal sector also predominates in telecommunications and financial services. For example, the official Senegalese transport company (Dakar Dem Dikk) coexists with a variety of informal urban and interurban transport enterprises, which belong to individuals, to professional groups called *groupements d'intérêts économiques* (GIE), or to others of a more informal nature. Telecommunications, in contrast, tends to be dominated by one or a few large formal firms, often partially foreign owned, such as SONATEL in Senegal, ONATEL (Office National des Télécommunications) in Burkina Faso, or Benin Telecom, which had, until recently, exercised a monopoly over fixed-line telecommunications, but now competes in the mobile market with a few other firms. In most countries, there are plans to open competition in fixed

Figure 3.13 Share of Value Added Contributed by Informal Businesses in the Tertiary Sector in Benin, 1990–2007

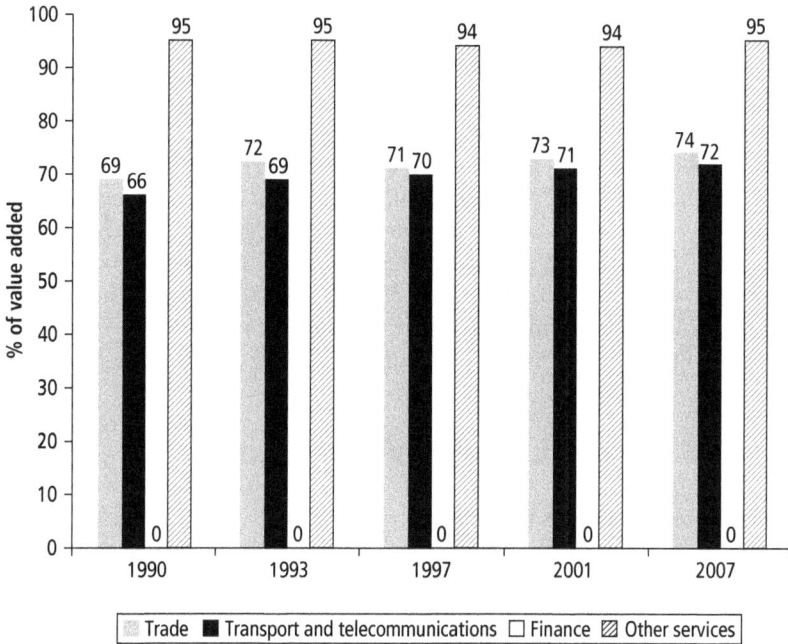

Source: INSAE 2009.

lines, and this is progressively being implemented. Major providers of fixed and mobile telecommunications services in the subregion are all formal. Nevertheless, informal operators function on the fringes of the market. For example, most mobile operators rely on informal street vendors in urban centers to sell a certain number of products, including SIM cards and refill cards. Telecenters, which sell fixed-line calling services, and Internet cafés are often informal.

The banking and financial services in WAEMU countries are subject to strong regulation by the regional central bank, Banque Centrale des Etats de l'Afrique de l'Ouest (BCEAO). Entry and prudential regulations are quite strict. Although access to banking services is still low, with fewer than 5 percent of economic agents having a bank account, the number of banks and financial institutions, including microfinance, is increasing (Mbaye, Diarisso, and Diop 2011). These institutions are almost all in the formal sector, but more informal forms of tontine and other traditional credit mechanisms remain active. Many actors in the informal sector who are shut out of bank credit rely on these informal networks and family ties. These informal financial networks do not seem to be included in the national accounts estimates, which incorrectly attribute all of value added in the financial industry to the formal sector.

We have seen that the informal sector accounts for a very large share of GDP; it accounts for an even greater, indeed overwhelming, share of employment, reflecting low productivity (see chapter 7). Formal sector jobs in government and the private sector are very scarce in African economies, and our three countries are typical in this regard. As shown in table 3.4, the formal sector accounts for about 5 percent of employment in Benin and Burkina Faso and 8 percent in Senegal. In Benin and Burkina Faso, private sector formal employment is lower than public sector employment. Senegal has been somewhat more successful in creating formal private sector jobs, with some 6 percent of the labor force engaged in the formal private sector in 2003. Overall, however, in all three countries, the informal sector accounts for more than 90 percent of employment.

Tax Burdens on Formal and Informal Sectors

Data on tax revenues for the three governments indicate a remarkable imbalance in the share of the informal sector in national income relative to its contribution to government revenue. The tax institutions of the three countries are also discussed in chapter 6. In this section, we examine the loss of fiscal revenue associated with lack of tax receipts from the informal sector.

Overview of Tax Collection in the Three Countries

An analysis of contributions stemming from different categories of firms reveals a strong imbalance in favor of big businesses and against the informal sector. In the three countries, large enterprises contribute more than 95 percent of tax

Table 3.4 Employment in the Formal and Informal Sectors in the Three West African Countries, Various Years, 2003–05

	Benin (2005)		Burkina Faso (2005)		Senegal (2003)	
Sector	Number of workers	% of labor force	Number of workers	% of labor force	Number of workers	% of labor force
Labor force	2,811,753	100.0	5,077,926	100.0	3,513,104	100.0
Public sector, including state-owned enterprises	73,106	2.6	218,351	4.3	62,885	1.8
Formal private sector	59,047	2.1	50,779	1.0	214,651	6.1
Informal sector	2,668,354	94.9	4,808,796	94.7	3,235,217	92.1

Sources: For Senegal, DPS 2003; for Benin, INSAE 2005; for Burkina Faso, INSD 2003.

revenue, while firms in the informal sector contribute less than 3 percent—completely out of proportion to the informal sector's 50 percent or greater share of total value added. The shares of total domestic tax revenue (that is, excluding customs duties) levied on the informal sector are very low. In Senegal, the informal sector contributed a tiny 2.4–3.5 percent of domestic tax revenue over 2004–07; in Benin and Burkina Faso, it contributed even less.[2] Data on informal sector contributions to customs revenue are particularly scarce because the customs regimes of the three states largely fail to distinguish between the imports of the formal and informal sectors. Some data distinguishing the two categories of importers are available for Burkina Faso, indicating that the informal sector contributes minimally to customs duty collections. These figures, however, may understate the informal sector's payments insofar as informal firms present themselves as formal to the customs authorities and pay indirect taxes.

In all three countries, revenues as a share of GDP have increased but remain low (table 3.5). In the 2000–05 period, only Senegal (barely) met the WAEMU convergence criterion of a minimum revenue-to-GDP ratio of 17 percent. In all three countries, indirect taxes account for a very large proportion of revenues (around 70 percent), making for rather regressive tax systems. The informal sector's low contribution to direct tax revenues is a big part of this problem. The harmonization of fiscal regulations and the implementation of a common external tariff (CET) and a value added tax (VAT) among countries in WAEMU at the end of the 1990s involved substantial fiscal and customs changes. Indeed, in 2001–05, after implementation of the CET, the proportion of fiscal revenue from taxes on domestic goods and services was higher than in 1990–95, before implementation, while taxes on external trade (customs duties) were substantially lower in all three countries.

Senegal   Although Senegal had the highest ratio of tax revenue to GDP in WAEMU—17 percent during the period 2000–05—the Senegalese fiscal system is quite regressive due to its high dependence on indirect taxes. Indeed, indirect taxes represented 72 percent of total taxes in the mid-2000s, an increase of 2 percentage points since the late 1980s (table 3.6).

Table 3.5 Tax Revenues as a Percentage of GDP in the Three West African Countries, 1980–2005

Country	1980–85	1985–90	1990–95	1995–2000	2000–05
Senegal	14.8	13.4	14.3	14.8	17.0
Benin	—	8.4	9.6	12.5	14.4
Burkina Faso	—	—	9.1	10.5	11.1

Sources: For Senegal, ANSD 2006; for Benin, INSAE 2006; for Burkina Faso, INSD 2006.
Note: — = not available.

Table 3.6 Tax Revenues in Senegal, by Type of Tax, 1996–2005
% of total

Type of tax	1986–90	1991–95	1996–2000	2001–05
Direct taxes	24.6	23.4	21.8	22.7
Indirect taxes	69.9	69.6	73.1	72.2
Domestic	29.1	24.9	31.8	33.4
Foreign trade	40.8	44.7	41.3	38.7
Other taxes	5.5	7.0	5.1	5.1

Source: DGID 2008.

Over 2004–07, the informal sector accounted for less than 3 percent of direct tax receipts in Senegal (table 3.7). Informal sector tax receipts as a share of total Senegalese business income taxes vary by sector: 1.1 percent in the secondary sector (0.9 percent in industry and 3.2 percent in construction) and 3.2 percent in the services sector as a whole. The informal sector's contribution to total taxes is greatest in retail trade, where it amounts to 16.4 percent of total direct taxes. Even in retailing, however, the informal sector's contribution to direct taxes is very low in relation to its share of value added in that sector, estimated at 60 percent in 2002.

The Senegalese administration has undertaken several initiatives to increase the informal sector's contribution to fiscal revenue. Agencies established in the early 1990s to assist the informal sector had little effect. The *contribution générale unique* (CGU), set up in 2004, is the most recent major attempt to collect more taxes from the informal sector. The CGU is a single comprehensive tax that substitutes for all other direct taxes for eligible firms. As shown in table 3.8, the CGU has had a very limited effect. A very small number of informal firms (a few thousand out of hundreds of thousands of existing firms) have been

Table 3.7 Share of Informal Sector in Business Income Taxes in Senegal, by Sector, 2004–07
% of total

Sector	2004	2005	2006	2007	Average, 2004–07
Secondary sector	0.9	1.0	1.5	1.0	1.1
Industry	0.7	0.8	1.3	0.9	0.9
Construction	3.0	3.0	4.1	2.7	3.2
Service sector	3.0	3.0	4.1	2.7	3.2
Retail	17.0	15.1	19.9	13.6	16.4
Services	1.1	1.0	1.4	1.1	1.2
Total	2.4	2.5	3.5	2.4	2.7

Source: ANSD 2009.

Table 3.8 Estimated Evasion of Informal Sector Sales Taxes in Senegal, 2004–07

Indicator	2004	2005	2006	2007
Number of firms subject to CGU	2663	3498	5166	4970
Total sales (CFAF millions)	21,635.4	31,420.0	42,383.2	51,237.8
Tax due (CFAF millions)	1,525.1	2,210.3	2,931.4	1,939.8
Average CGU (tax per unit)	0.573	0.632	0.567	0.39
Collections (CFAF millions)	793.8	1,319.8	1,504.9	1,463.9
Recovery rate	51.9%	59.7%	51.3%	75.4%
Loss to fiscal revenue (theoretical tax—collection, CFAF millions)	732.2	890.4	1,426.4	476.0
Rate of loss to fiscal revenue	48.0%	40.3%	48.7%	24.5%

Sources: DGID 2008; authors' estimates.

subject to the CGU. Moreover, for those firms that have been subject to the CGU, collections never reached 5 percent of total sales, representing a recovery rate of about 50 percent of tax due in 2004–06. Although the recovery rate rose sharply in 2007 to 75.5 percent, average tax collection per firm subject to the CGU fell to about CFAF 400,000, down from more than CFAF 600,000 in 2005, as tax due fell. Consequently, the total amount recovered in 2007 was less than CFAF 1.5 billion—a paltry 0.6 percent of total direct taxes and 1.9 percent of total business taxes in that same year.

Benin   Benin has substantially increased its tax collections, albeit from a low level, with the ratio of tax revenue to GDP rising from 8.4 percent in 1985–90 to 14.4 percent in 2000–05, still well below the 17 percent threshold set by the WAEMU convergence criteria (table 3.5). The share contributed by direct taxes fell 5 percentage points, from 31 percent of total revenue during 1990–95 to 26 percent during 2000–05 (table 3.9). Taxes on domestic goods and services as a portion of total fiscal revenue jumped from 33.9 percent in the early 1990s to 51.7 percent in 1995–2000, before falling back to 46.5 percent in 2000–05.

Table 3.9 Tax Revenues in Benin, by Type of Tax, 1990–2005
% of total

Type of tax	1990–95	1995–2000	2000–05
Direct taxes	30.9	28.2	25.9
Indirect taxes	68.5	66.1	65.6
Domestic	33.9	51.7	46.5
Foreign trade	34.5	14.3	19.1
Other taxes	0.6	5.7	8.4

Sources: INSAE 2006; authors' estimates.

Taxes on external trade, in contrast, fell during the same period, dropping sharply from 34.5 percent of total fiscal revenue in 1990–95 to 14.3 percent in 1995–2000, before partially recovering to 19.1 percent in the early 2000s. Other taxes rose sharply, from 0.6 percent of total revenue in 1990–95 to 8.4 percent in 2000–05.

Burkina Faso   In Burkina Faso, the share of tax revenue to GDP rose more modestly than in Benin, from 9 percent in 1990–95 to 11 percent in 2000–05, among the lowest in the region (table 3.5). Shares of indirect and direct taxes as a portion of total taxes have remained stable. Direct taxes have held steady at about one quarter of total revenue, while indirect taxes have remained at around 71 percent of total revenue (table 3.10). As is the case with the other economies in WAEMU, the application of the CET and the introduction of the VAT engendered a restructuring of indirect taxes, with an increase in taxes on domestic sales of goods and services and a decrease in taxes on external trade. Taxes on domestic goods and services, which amounted to less than 40 percent of fiscal revenue during 1990–95, rose to above 50 percent during 2000–05. Taxes on external trade decreased from one-third of total revenue to less than 18 percent over the same period. Burkina's fiscal system is thus doubly weak: on the one hand, it suffers from a relatively low level of tax collection; on the other hand, it is strongly regressive.

Estimates of Revenue Loss Due to Tax Evasion in the Informal Sector

In this section, we examine the loss of fiscal revenue associated with tax evasion in the informal sector in the three economies. To measure the amount of fiscal evasion, we estimate the hypothetical level of fiscal revenue under full taxation of the informal sector. These estimates do not take into account the costs of collecting revenue from the informal sector, which are likely to be substantial, particularly for smaller firms. Therefore, our estimates are biased upward for net revenue obtained from taxing the informal sector.

Table 3.10 Tax Revenues in Burkina Faso, by Type of Tax, 1990–2005
% of total

Type of tax	1990–95	1995–2000	2000–05
Direct taxes	25.5	25.4	25.9
Indirect taxes	70.9	70.1	70.9
Domestic	38.1	43.5	53.3
Foreign trade	32.7	26.6	17.5
Other taxes	3.7	4.5	3.2

Sources: INSD 2006; authors' estimates.

We estimate the loss to fiscal revenue caused by the informal sector's evasion of taxes over 2000–05 using fiscal data from the three countries and the shares of the informal sector in GDP (table 3.11). We assume that informal sector enterprises currently pay indirect taxes at the same rate as the formal sector but do not pay any direct taxes, and we estimate the increase in direct tax payments under the assumption that direct tax payments in the informal sector have the same ratio of value added as in the formal sector. These assumptions are not completely realistic but roughly reflect the actual situation, and possible biases are likely to be roughly offsetting. As we have seen in the case of Senegal, formal direct tax payments are negligible. Regarding indirect taxes, informal sector firms do not remit value added taxes to the government on sales, but they also are not eligible for VAT rebates on inputs. Informal firms are generally subject to VAT on imported goods, although not when the goods are smuggled into the country. To the extent that value added is low relative to the value of gross sales, as is the case for most industries (particularly commerce), formal firms face a higher effective tax rate on domestic sales than informal firms, but only by the share of value added in total sales. Overall, therefore, informal firms pay indirect taxes to a greater extent than direct taxes, but our assumption that informal firms pay their "fair share" of indirect taxes likely overestimates indirect tax payments by informal firms. Our method is likely to be an upper bound on the potential increases in revenue from direct taxation of the informal sector because it is unlikely that informal enterprises can ever be taxed at these levels, particularly small informal firms. Using this method, table 3.11 suggests that the potential revenue gains are particularly significant for Benin, resulting in an increase of 10.6 percent in the share of tax receipts to GDP, from 14.4 to 25.0 percent. The large effect reflects Benin's very high share of the informal sector in GDP (74 percent). For Senegal and Burkina Faso, the potential gains

Table 3.11 Estimates of the Potential Gain from Taxing the Informal Sector's Business Income in the Three West African Countries, 2000–05
% of GDP, unless otherwise noted

Activity sector	Benin	Senegal	Burkina Faso
Direct taxes as % of total tax revenue	25.9	25.9	22.7
% of GDP			
Informal sector	74.0	50.0	55.0
Total tax receipts	14.4	11.1	17.0
Direct tax revenue	3.7	2.9	3.9
Hypothetical informal direct tax	10.6	2.9	4.7
Hypothetical total tax	25.0	14.0	21.7

Sources: Authors' calculations, based on tables 3.4–3.7 in this volume.

in revenue are not as large, but they are still significant: 2.9 and 4.7 percent of GDP, respectively.

Informality, Employment, and Living Standards

In this section, we discuss the controversies regarding whether or not the informal sector contributes to poverty alleviation and improved social welfare. The perspectives and results of previous studies concerning the impact of informality on economic well-being are mixed. Some authors consider the informal sector as a last resort for employment, providing meager incomes, while others argue that informal sector work can be relatively lucrative. To provide more information on these issues, in this chapter, we compare the living standards of people engaged in formal and informal activities.

Maloney (2004) is the leading proponent of the view that the informal sector can be a source of improved well-being. He argues that when workers leave the formal sector to set up their businesses in the informal sector, they typically are better off for several reasons. First, these entrepreneurs are often relatively talented, educated, and hardworking, contrary to the general view that the informal sector is the repository of the least capable people. Second, they benefit from more freedom and flexibility. Levenson and Maloney (1998) acknowledge, however, that informal sector actors are excluded from certain public services such as legal protection, with resulting weak property rights, diminished credibility with formal sector customers, and reduced access to credit, which diminishes their incomes. Informal sector workers have a much higher incidence of poverty than formal sector workers.

The majority opinion, overall, is that the informal sector is primarily a last-resort source of employment for those who have few opportunities in the formal sector. The greater flexibility of product and labor markets in the informal sector allows employment in informal firms to absorb the surplus labor created by contraction of the formal sector during structural adjustment. Various authors note that informal business creation and employment swell during downturns. The wave of trade liberalization in Africa led to the contraction of many previously protected industries, resulting in losses of formal sector jobs. Verick (2006) finds that trade liberalization contributed to the development of the informal sector. In Kenya, liberalization associated with structural adjustment programs was followed by a rise in employment in the informal sector from 4.2 percent of total employment in 1972 to 53.4 percent in 1994! Similarly, Gelb et al. (2009) find that development of the informal sector is strongly correlated with unemployment and that the informal sector acts as a safety valve. Calvès and Schoumaker (2004) also argue that the informal sector develops in the markets that are most highly exposed to international competition and structural adjustment. Based on data from a study in Burkina Faso, they find a large increase in informal enterprises following structural adjustment programs. This increase in employment in the informal sector occurs not only among unskilled workers but also among university-educated workers. Golub and Mbaye (2002) and Lindauer and Velenchik (2002), using data from Senegal, also note that the formal sector has lost international competitiveness, while the informal sector is thriving. Notwithstanding steady growth of aggregate GDP at around 5 percent, formal manufacturing has seen huge losses in employment, which have been absorbed largely by the rapidly growing informal sector. Lindauer and Velenchik estimate that employment in the industrial sector as a percentage of total employment fell from 12.3 percent to 8.6 percent between 1994 and 2001.

Our findings generally support the view that living standards are lower in the informal sector. We compare levels of monetary and nonmonetary poverty among households engaged in formal and informal activities and find that poverty is much higher among those working in the informal sector.

Monetary and nonmonetary poverty affect different segments of the population to varying degrees, depending on factors such as place of residence, gender, social and professional status. Household surveys show that a high proportion of workers derive their income from the informal sector, with 85 percent of heads of household in Benin, 79 percent in Senegal, and 91 percent in Burkina Faso engaging in informal activities on their own behalf or as part of a household enterprise. Informal activities by heads of household in Benin are concentrated in agriculture and services (table 3.12). The respective shares of agriculture and services are 52.7 and 36.8 percent in Benin, 48.1 and 39.0 percent in Senegal, and 81.1 and 12.8 percent in Burkina Faso. In West Africa, poverty is concentrated in agriculture and the rural economy in general. In urban areas,

Table 3.12 Informal Employment in the Three West African Countries, by Sector
% of firms in the sector

Activity sector	Benin	Senegal	Burkina Faso
Agriculture	52.7	48.1	81.1
Mining	0.3	0.6	0.6
Manufacturing	6.7	6.0	2.8
Construction	2.8	5.3	1.8
Transport	4.6	3.4	1.1
Commerce	17.4	23.7	9.4
Other services	12.2	7.4	1.2
Education and health	0.5	0.8	0.5
Government	0.1	0.0	0.1
Other	2.6	4.5	1.3

Sources: For Benin, INSAE 2005; for Senegal, DPS 2002; for Burkina Faso, INSD 2003; authors' calculations.

the poor work largely in petty services, particularly retail, that is, in the informal sector. Formal employment is minimal in these sectors.

Formal and Informal Activities and Income Poverty

The income measure of poverty is based on a utilitarian approach that focuses on the effect of purchasing power on the consumption of goods and services (Ravallion 1994). Since utility is not directly observable, we used resources (revenue and spending) to approximate well-being.

Labor compensation is much lower in the informal sector. According to Poapongsakorn (1991), businesses within the informal sector pay their workers 13 to 22 percent less in wages, due to evasion of labor market regulations. Lower taxes and labor costs are clear advantages for informal firms. Pay scales and benefits in the formal sectors in francophone West Africa are influenced by those in France. In the government and large private firms, labor compensation is established, European style, in negotiations between the government, unions, and employers. In the informal sector, worker pay is by agreement between the employer and the individual employee, with resulting much lower pay levels and minimal benefits.

Our surveys confirm large salary differentials (table 3.13). In Dakar, 41 percent of small informal employees, but only 2 percent of formal employees, are paid at or below the minimum wage of CFAF 35,000 per month (US$70). In Ouagadougou, the proportion of formal and small informal workers with wages below the minimum is high, at 40 and 66 percent, respectively; in Cotonou, the respective figures are 24 and 66 percent. Employees of the large informal sector are paid somewhere between employees of the formal and small informal sectors. Among employees of the large informal sector, 77 percent of those in Dakar, 7 percent of those in Cotonou, and 22 percent of those in Ouagadougou are paid monthly salaries above CFAF 200,000. Among employees of the formal sector, 91 percent of those in Dakar, 29 percent of those in Cotonou, and 27 percent of those in Ouagadougou are paid that much per month.

Labor costs are considerably higher in Dakar than in Ouagadougou and Cotonou, reflecting a somewhat higher level of development originating in the colonial period. Dakar was the capital of French West Africa and, therefore, had higher levels of investment in infrastructure and industry.

Table 3.14 shows that in all three countries per capita expenditures of informal actors are well below those of formal actors; in Benin, for example, each sector averages CFAF 172,000 and CFAF 289,000, respectively. The difference between the two averages is statistically significant (*t*-statistic of 17.3). In Burkina Faso, the gap is the largest, with formal sector workers spending nearly four times the amount of informal sector workers; the differential in favor of formal sector workers is more than 100 percent in Senegal and 60 percent in Benin. Consequently, income-based poverty is much more prevalent among

Table 3.13 Monthly Salary per Person in the Three West African Cities, by Formal or Informal
Status

% of persons in the sector in the salary range

City and status	Less than CFAF 35,000	CFAF 35,000 to CFAF 200,000	More than CFAF 200,000	Total
Cotonou				
Formal	24	47	29	100
Large informal	44	48	7	100
Small informal	66	25	9	100
Total	51	35	14	100
Dakar				
Formal	2	7	91	100
Large informal	6	16	77	100
Small informal	41	41	18	100
Total	21	25	54	100
Ouagadougou				
Formal	40	33	27	100
Large informal	28	50	22	100
Small informal	66	24	10	100
Total	53	31	16	100

Source: Calculations based on authors' survey data.

Table 3.14 Average Monthly Expenditure per Person and Proportion of People in Poverty in
the Three West African Countries, by Formal or Informal Status of the Household Head

Country and variable	Formal sector	Informal sector	All
Benin			
Standard of living indicator (CFA francs)	289,443	172,126	194,045
Proportion of persons in poverty (%)	16.0	26.0	24.5
Senegal			
Standard of living indicator (CFA francs)	492,142	232,956	286,543
Proportion of persons in poverty (%)	—	—	48.5
Burkina Faso			
Standard of living indicator (CFA francs)	580,935	155,913	192,778
Proportion of persons in poverty (%)	3.1	39.5	36.3

Sources: For Benin, INSAE 2005; for Senegal, DPS 2002; for Burkina Faso, INSD 2003; authors' calculations.
Note: — = Not available.

informal than formal actors: in Benin, it reaches 26 percent among informal actors versus 16 percent among formal actors; in Burkina Faso, average spending per person by households in the informal sector is equivalent to slightly more than one-quarter of spending per person by households in the formal sector. This explains the high incidence of poverty in the informal sector (39.5 percent) compared to the formal sector (3.1 percent). Formal sector households in Senegal spend slightly more than double per person what informal sector households spend: CFAF 492,000 versus CFAF 233,000, respectively.

The gap between formal and informal spending per capita occurs in all sectors of activity, although to varying extents. In Benin, for example, disparities are less significant in agriculture, manufacturing, and transport and larger in construction and retail (table 3.15). In the construction and retail sectors, disparities are much greater: formal actors spend almost double what informal actors spend.

Across all sectors, average spending per person among formal sector households in Senegal is higher than spending per person among informal sector households. Formal sector households' spending per person in different activity areas is as follows: CFAF 252,000 in agriculture, CFAF 356,000 in manufacturing, CFAF 500,000 in transport, CFAF 593,000 in retail, and CFAF 531,000 in the service industry. These averages can be compared to spending per person in the informal sector (see table 3.15): CFAF 145,000 in agriculture, CFAF 261,000 in manufacturing, CFAF 295,000 in transport, CFAF 316,000 in retail, and CFAF 420,000 in the service industry. Formal sector spending is, on average, almost double informal sector spending per person, which confirms the argument that informal sector households have a relatively low standard of living when compared to formal sector households.

Similar to the two other cities, spending per person in the informal sector in Burkina Faso is lower than spending per person in the formal sector, in all

Table 3.15 Average Monthly Expenditure per Person in the Three West African Countries, by Formal or Informal Status of the Household Head and Sector of Activity
CFA francs

Area of activity	Benin		Senegal		Burkina Faso	
	Formal	Informal	Formal	Informal	Formal	Informal
Agriculture	194,200	144,648	251,822	145,855	377,844	123,712
Manufacturing	239,778	195,664	356,498	261,770	347,462	273,136
Construction	296,835	155,262	562,881	237,131	528,733	298,686
Transport	264,320	187,753	499,678	295,728	766,189	315,015
Retail	379,364	220,542	593,752	316,356	455,534	289,326
Services	308,968	197,326	531,313	420,604	664,489	422,388

Sources: For Benin, INSAE 2005; for Senegal, DPS 2002; for Burkina Faso, INSD 2003; authors' calculations.

sectors of activity. Significant disparities exist in the agricultural and transport sectors.

Formal and Informal Activities and Nonmonetary Poverty

In contrast to the income-based approach to poverty, which measures well-being by looking at household resources, the nonincome-based approach uses freedom and accomplishments as measures of well-being. The nonincome-based approach evaluates an individual's living situation by looking at factors such as the ability to nourish and clothe oneself. The approach places little emphasis, if any, on measures of utility. Nonincome-based approaches have enabled the identification of specific forms of deprivation and are frequently used in studies on both developing and developed countries. Classifications range from "total deprivation of goods" (this classification is used in studies based on nutrition or other fundamental necessities and is more common in studies of developing countries) to "relative deprivation of goods."

Nonutilitarian approaches are more diverse, but one can distinguish two subgroups: Sen's (1985) capabilities approach and the basic necessities approach. Sen's capabilities approach measures well-being through freedom and empowerment of individuals. The individual must retain certain fundamental capabilities that are necessary to attain a certain standard of living. To this effect, the individual must be adequately nourished, be educated, be in good health, have adequate accommodation, take part in community life, appear in public without feeling shame, and so forth. Nonmonetary poverty focuses on basic needs for attaining a minimum standard of living and human dignity (Sen 1985). These basic necessities include education, health, hygiene, waste management, drinking water, housing, and access to basic infrastructure, among others. Non-income poverty is proxied here by access to electricity, water, and cooking fuel.

Lighting Source   Table 3.16 shows that formal sector households in Senegal have greater access to electricity (76.9 percent of households) than informal sector households (26.2 percent of households). Informal sector households rely instead on traditional forms of lighting: 36.3 percent use kerosene lamps, compared with only 12.5 percent of formal sector households. Similarly, artisanal oil lamps and wood-burning lamps are more common in informal than in formal sector households (among informal sector households, 25.7 percent use oil lamps and 2.7 percent use wood-burning lamps; only 3 percent of formal households use oil lamps). Electricity usage in Benin follows a similar pattern: informal sector households have less access to electricity (19.8 percent) than formal sector households (63.6 percent). In Burkina Faso, only 7.8 percent of informal sector households have access to electricity compared with 70.6 percent of formal sector households. Almost three out of four informal sector households use gas lamps, compared with only one out of four in the formal sector.

Table 3.16 Indicators of Nonmonetary Poverty in the Three West African Countries, by Formal or Informal Status of the Household Head
% of households

Indicator	Benin		Senegal		Burkina Faso	
	Formal	Informal	Formal	Informal	Formal	Informal
Cooking fuel						
Wood	42.7	84.6	13.4	61.6	54.5	93.1
Coal	41.4	11.1	8.7	9.9	15.5	3.7
Petroleum	8.7	3.2	—	—	0.1	0.2
Gas	6.0	0.6	76.9	26.5	28.2	1.5
Lighting						
Lamps	35.4	79.3	15.5	62.0	28.1	74.1
Electricity	63.6	19.8	76.9	26.2	70.6	7.8
Water source						
Private	24.5	6.2	66.1	24.0	37.6	2.5
Public	35.2	19.3	24.0	24.0	32.3	15.6
Wells	17.6	33.6	37.6	13.7	13.8	48.3
Streams and rivers	16.5	28.4	2.5	30.4	3.8	32.1

Sources: For Benin, INSAE 2005; for Senegal, DPS 2002; for Burkina Faso, INSD 2003; authors' calculations.
Note: — = Not available.

Water Sources   Likewise, most formal sector households (66.1 percent) in Senegal have running water in their home, compared to only 24 percent of informal sector households. In Benin, these proportions are 24.5 and 6.2 percent, respectively. In both Senegal and Benin, informal sector households use public water taps (24 and 19.3 percent, respectively) or wells (13.7 and 33.6 percent, respectively). Meanwhile, in Burkina Faso, 37.6 percent of formal sector households and 2.5 percent of informal sector households have a water tap installed in their homes. Informal sector households resort to wells (48.3 percent) and protected boreholes (32.1 percent).

Home Energy Sources   In Senegal, informal sector households make greater use of traditional combustibles, such as wood (61.6 percent) and wood coal (9.9 percent), than formal sector households (13.4 and 8.7 percent, respectively). Formal sector households, conversely, use butane gas much more often (76.9 percent) than informal sector households (26.5 percent). In Benin, more than four out of five informal sector households use wood as a combustible, while only two out of five formal sector households do so. Differences in usage are more marked in Burkina Faso, where more than 90 percent of informal sector households use wood versus only slightly more than half of formal sector households (table 3.16).

Conclusion

In recent years, Benin, Burkina Faso, and Senegal have registered respectable growth rates in the context of general macroeconomic stability. Poverty remains endemic, but social indicators have improved somewhat. In this regard, these three countries are quite typical of West Africa and Africa in general. Despite these moderate successes, the formal sector remains generally weak, with a few exceptions such as telecommunications. The preponderance of GDP and an overwhelming proportion of employment are in the informal sector. Formal sector jobs in government and the private sector number in the few hundreds of thousands compared to a total labor force in the millions. Agriculture and other primary activities are nearly exclusively informal. For industry and services, the extent of informal sector dominance varies by subsector. Wholesale retail trade, construction, and transport are among the sectors where informal firms are particularly important.

In contrast to its large role in GDP and employment, the informal sector provides less than 3 percent of fiscal revenue in all of the three countries. We estimate that fiscal revenues would rise by between 25 and 75 percent if the informal sector carried its full share of the tax burden, disregarding the costs of implementing the requisite measures.

The effects of the informal sector on poverty and living standards are much debated. On the one hand, informal employment is a safety valve for the unemployed, particularly in difficult economic times. On the other hand, the standards of living of households engaged in informal work are far below those of households engaged in the formal sector. Overall, the informal sector is a source of income for persons with limited options, but it is not a sustainable source of long-term growth and income generation.

Notes

1. AFRISTAT defines informality using the criteria of firm size and registration.
2. Data provided by the Beninese and Burkinabe authorities are patchy and not reported here.

References

Adams, Arvil V. 2008. "Skills Development in the Informal Sector of Sub-Saharan Africa." World Bank, Washington, DC.

ANSD (Agence Nationale de la Statistique et de la Démographie). 2006. Comptes nationaux du Sénégal. ANSD, Dakar.

———. 2009. Comptes nationaux du Sénégal. ANSD, Dakar.

Calvès, Anne-Emmanuele, and Bruno Schoumaker. 2004. "Deteriorating Economic Context and Changing Patterns of Youth Employment in Urban Burkina Faso: 1980–2000." World Development 32 (8): 1341–54.

Canagarajah, Suddharshan, and DipakMazumdar. 1999. "Employment, Labor Market, and Poverty in Ghana: A Study of Changes during Economic Decline and Recovery." Policy Research Working Paper 1845, World Bank, Washington, DC.

Charmes, Jacques. 1993. "Estimation and Survey Methods for the Informal Sector." University of Versailles-St Quentin en Yvelines, Centre of Economics and Ethics for Environment and Development. Paper prepared for an ILO international seminar.

Chen, Martha Alter. 2001. "Women in the Informal Sector: A Global Picture, the Global Movement." *SAIS Review* 21 (1, Winter-Spring): 71–82.

CSO (Central Statistics Office). 2008. "2007 Informal Sector Survey Preliminary Results." CSO, Gaborone.

DGID (Direction Générale des Impôts et Domaines). 2008. "Statistiques des recettes fiscales et non-fiscales." DGID, Dakar.

DPS (Direction de la Prévision et de la Statistique). 2002. "Enquête sénégalaise auprès des ménages, 2002." Ministère de l'Economie, des Finances, et du Plan, Dakar.

———. 2003. Comptes nationaux du Sénégal. DPS, Dakar.

———. 2004. "Le secteur informel dans l'agglomération de Dakar: Performances, insertion, et perspectives; Résultats de la phase II de l'enquête 1-2-3 de 2003." DPS, Dakar, June.

Gelb, Alan, Taye Mengistae, Vijaya Ramachandran, and Manju Kedia Shah. 2009. "To Formalize or Not to Formalize? Comparisons of Microenterprise Data from Southern and East Africa." Working Paper 175, Center for Global Development, Washington, DC.

Golub, Stephen S., and Ahmadou A. Mbaye. 2002. "Obstacles and Opportunities for Senegal's International Competitiveness: Case Studies of the Groundnut, Fishing, and Textile/Clothing Sectors." Africa Region Working Paper 36, World Bank, Washington, DC.

Haan, Hans Christian. 2006. *Training for Work in the Informal Micro-Enterprise Sector: Fresh Evidence from Sub-Sahara Africa.* Technical and Vocational Education and Training Series: Issues, Concerns, and Prospects, vol. 3. Dordrecht: Springer for Unesco-Unevoc.

ILO (International Labour Organization). 1995. *Gender, Poverty, and Employment: Turning Capabilities into Entitlements.* Geneva: ILO.

———. 2002. *Decent Work and the Informal Economy: Sixth Item on the Agenda.* Report VI, ninetieth session of the International Labour Conference. Geneva: ILO.

INSAE (Institut National de la Statistique et de l'Analyse Economique). 2005. "Questionnaire unifié du bienêtre de base (QUIBB) 2005." INSAE, Cotonou.

———. 2006. Comptes nationaux. INSAE, Cotonou.

———. 2009. Comptes nationaux. INSAE, Cotonou.

INSD (Institut National de la Statistique et de la Démographie). 2003. "Questionnaire unifié du bienêtre de base (QUIBB)." INSD, Ouagadougou.

———. 2006. *Comptes nationaux.* INSD, Ouagadougou.

———. 2009. *Comptes nationaux.* INSD, Ouagadougou.

Levenson, Alec R., and William F. Maloney. 1998. "The Informal Sector, Firm Dynamics, and Institutional Participation, Volume 1." Policy Research Working Paper 1988, World Bank, Washington, DC.

Lindauer, David L., and Ann Velenchik. 2002. "Growth, Poverty, and the Labor Market: An Analytical Review of Senegal's 2002 PRSP." World Bank, Washington, DC, August.

Lund, Francie, and Caroline Skinner. 2004. "Integrating the Informal Economy in Urban Planning and Governance: A Case Study of the Process of Policy Development in Durban, South Africa." *International Development Planning Review* 26(4): 431–56.

Maloney, William. 2004. "Informality Revisited." *World Development* 32 (7): 1159–78.

Mbaye, AhmadouAly. 2005. "Sanitary and Phytosanitary Requirements and Developing-Country Agro-Food Exports: An Assessment of the Senegalese Groundnut Subsector." Agriculture and Rural Development Discussion Paper. World Bank, Washington, DC.

Mbaye, Ahmadou Aly, Sogué Diarisso, and Ibrahima Thione Diop. 2011. *Quel système bancaire pour le financement des économies de l'UEMOA?* Paris: Harmattan France.

Otsuka, Keijiro, and Takashi Yamano. 2006. "The Role of Non-farm Income in Poverty Reduction: Evidence from Asia and East Africa." *Agricultural Economics* 35 (supplement 3): 393–97.

Poapongsakorn, Nipon. 1991. "The Informal Sector in Thailand." In *The Silent Revolution*, ed. A. Lawrence Chickering and Mohamed Salahdine. San Francisco: International Center for Economic Growth.

Ravallion, Martin.1994. "Measuring Social Welfare with and without Poverty Lines." *American Economic Review* 84 (2, May): 359–64.

Schneider, Friedrich. 2000. "The Increase of the Size of the Shadow Economy of 18 OECD Countries: Some Preliminary Explanation." CESifo Working Paper Series 306, CESifo Group, Munich.

Schneider, Friedrich, and Dominik Enste. 2002. "Shadow Economies: Size, Causes, and Consequences." *Journal of Economic Literature* 38 (1): 77–114.

Sen, Amartya.1985. "A Sociological Approach to the Measurement of Poverty: A Reply [Poor, Relatively Speaking]." Oxford Economic Paper, Oxford University, Oxford.

Steel, William F., and Don Snodgrass. 2008."World Bank Region Analysis on the Informal Economy." In *Raising Productivity and Reducing Risk of Household Enterprises*. Annex 1, "Diagnostic Methodology Framework." Washington, DC: World Bank.

Verick, Sher D. 2006. "The Impact of Globalization on the Informal Sector in Africa." Economic and Social Policy Division, United Nations Economic Commission for Africa and Institute for the Study of Labor, Berlin.

Xaba, Jantjie, Pat Horn, and Shirin Motala. 2002. "The Informal Sector in Sub-Saharan Africa." ILO Working Paper on the Informal Economy 2002/10, ILO, Geneva.

World Bank. 2009. World Development Indicators. Washington, DC.

Chapter 4

Large Informal Firms in West Africa

One of the most important features of the informal sector in Africa that emerges from our study is the distinction between large and small informal operators. In West Africa, large informal firms and trading networks coexist with small operators, but little is known about who is involved, the sectors in which they operate, and the nature of their businesses. The existence of large-scale informal operators is well known and acknowledged even by government officials, even if it is undocumented and difficult to prove with the available data.

We approached the issue of the "large informal" sector from several angles. First, we designed our sample in such a way that large informal firms are well represented. Second, we interviewed both government officials and managers or owners of formal and informal firms in our three countries. Third, we matched reported sales and import data for firms, which suggests that some firms are grossly underreporting sales. Fourth, we reviewed press accounts of conflicts and scandals regarding some of the largest informal operators.

In this chapter, we discuss the characteristics of the large informal sector, the main industries in which they operate, and the interactions between the large informal sector, the small informal sector, and the formal sector. We report on case studies of some of the largest informal firms and some of the sectors in which they operate, much of which revolve around importing, wholesale or retail trade, and other services. The findings are derived mainly from our interviews with stakeholders, as described in chapter 2, as well as confidential government customs and fiscal data that were made available to us.

The Large Informal Sector in West Africa

A Few Defining Characteristics
Our interviews reveal some similarities, but many important differences, between the large and small informal sectors.

Large informal firms are like a giant with a clay foot. On the one hand, they have a large volume of sales, rivaling firms in the formal sector. On the other hand, they are much more fragile and less structured than formal firms.

Entrepreneurs, although very talented and hardworking, often have little formal education and lack managerial capacities. A simple disagreement with a customs official can result in bankruptcy. The existence of these firms is usually strongly linked to one individual owner; most firms collapse after the death or incapacitation of the proprietor. The assets and liabilities of the firm and the owner are not clearly separated. Often, those who inherit the firm cannot come to an agreement, and the firm is liquidated. At other times, a dramatic scandal leads to the imprisonment of the owner. This was the case with many actors in the large informal sector in Senegal, such as Cheikh Tall Dioum, Adel Korban, Khadim Bousso, and Moustapha Tall, described later in this chapter. In other cases, disputes with customs or with suppliers undermine the firm.

Although proof is difficult to come by, it is common knowledge that most of these firms engage in informal activities. It is also clear that they benefit from the acquiescence or even collusion of high government officials. Despite their size and political connections, large informal firms are precarious because they are visible to the government and public opinion. As soon as firms lose their political or marabout support, are entangled in incriminating public scandals, or cannot stifle a disagreement with the customs agency, imprisonment of the owner or disappearance of the firm usually follows. Customs laws are particularly restrictive; when a disagreement with the customs agency arises, the entrepreneur usually has no choice but to compromise or go to jail.

Large informal firms do not see themselves as informal; they are even offended at the suggestion that they might be lumped into that category. In truth, they would not be classified as informal if the usual criteria were applied mechanically. They appear, superficially, to meet most of the criteria defining formality: they pay taxes; they are often taxed under the regular business tax regime; their tax filings are sometimes handled by the DGE (Division des Grandes Entreprises, Division of Large Companies), which handles filings for large formal firms (discussed in chapter 3); they have a high level of sales; and they have access to bank credit; among other characteristics. But a closer examination reveals that their practices are, in fact, informal. Even though these firms are large, as measured by sales, their administrative structures and managerial styles resemble those of small informal firms. Formal firms of the same size have distinct departments and a coherent organizational structure; informal firms do not. Apart from the owner and a few permanent employees (rarely more than five), the rest of the personnel are temporary. A single individual manages the firm with little assistance from others. None of the usual departments in formal firms (sales, input sourcing, finance, and human resources, among others) exists in large informal firms, despite their high level of sales. Even the accounting function is outsourced to an independent firm, while all medium-size formal firms have in-house accounting departments. In addition, the accounting for these large informal firms is typically highly inaccurate, massively underreporting sales and profits. The absence of honest accounting is one of the distinctive features of the informal sector, particularly the large informal sector.

The Transition from the Small to the Large Informal Sector

Analysis of results from our interviews and data from studies reveals a huge diversity of informal activities along several dimensions: the sociodemographic characteristics of employees, the interactions of informal firms with the formal sector and with the administration, the level of formality of firms, and the sectors in which they operate.

The characteristics of actors in the large and small firms in the informal sector differ considerably. Although illiteracy is more common in the informal sector than in the formal sector, many participants in the large informal sector are educated. In fact, according to many criteria, the large informal sector is in-between the small informal sector and the formal sector. Actors in the large informal sector are often older than those in the formal sector, having started off in the small informal sector and succeeded in diversifying and developing their activities.

Three categories of small informal firms succeed in transitioning to either the formal sector or the large informal sector as they grow: those whose owners are not educated at all and must remain informal, those that move to a higher level of formality without becoming completely formal, and those that become part of the formal sector.

In the first category, owners have a low level of education, and their firms remain individually operated enterprises despite handling billions of CFA francs. They are found mainly in retail, transportation, or importing and exporting. They conceal their activities completely or reveal only a small fraction of revenues subject to a presumptive tax. These firms are very difficult to apprehend and frequently declare bankruptcy, only to reappear under a different name. They use premises that disguise their activities, pay low rents, and are completely informal. They employ few permanent employees (mainly family members) and sometimes have several fiscal identification numbers under different names, each used for fraudulent import activities.

In the second category, firms declare themselves as formal but maintain many informal practices. They tend to be in construction and in certain service sectors. They often rely on government procurement and realize that they would not be able to obtain contracts without meeting some of the criteria for formality. They are sometimes subject to a presumptive tax, but are often assessed regular business taxes. To meet the requirements of regular business taxes, they employ a minimal number of permanent workers and many temporary workers. Permanent employees are normally confined to an accountant, a chauffeur, and perhaps a messenger. Usually, bookkeeping is outsourced to external accountants, who are paid by the task for end-of-year reporting. As a result, accountants with minimal education do the books for a number of firms simultaneously. Outsourcing accounting has become so widespread that the business associations of accountants in the subregion have asked fiscal authorities to accept only financial documents signed by an authorized accounting expert. This request has hardly stopped the outsourcing of accounting. Instead, there is now just a higher level of complicity between "informal" accountants and their formal counterparts. "Informal" accountants do the work, and authorized accountants provide their seal of approval.

Firms in the final category are essentially part of the formal sector. These are quite rare, and actors in this category often have experience within the administration or in other private companies. They quit their previous occupations to start their own businesses, but, lacking capital, they began with small-scale activities. As they grew, they progressively changed their status and became formal.

In truth, it is hard to find a completely formal firm in the West African subregion. Many entrepreneurs that we met from the formal sector admitted to selling products to firms in the informal sector without declaring or reimbursing the value added tax. Other times, they fail to record transactions in their accounts. Most of these firms claim that they can only compete with informal firms by engaging in these actions. Other firms have both formal and informal activities. They decide which entity to use—formal or informal—depending on the situation of the market in which they are operating. In fact, firms in the formal sector and large firms in the informal sector differ mainly in the share of activities they declare rather than their size: formal firms declare almost all activities (but do not hesitate to renege on this obligation if the opportunity presents itself); meanwhile, large informal firms conceal almost all of their activities. However, when they want access to formal markets or government contracts, they declare just enough to pass as a "formal" entity.

Evidence from Fiscal and Customs Statistics and from Our Studies

To provide some evidence on the magnitude of underreporting of sales by the large informal sector, we carried out a comparison for Senegal of firm-level imports, as reported by customs, and sales, as reported to the tax authorities and recorded by the government statistical agency for those same firms. We selected a number of firms that paid the lump-sum presumptive tax (in principle, reserved for small informal firms). We considered only importing firms with an identification number that allows their declared sales to be traced to the fiscal agency. Given that most importing firms do not have an identification number (which is not a requirement for importing), we were able to match only 132 firms in the fiscal and customs statistics, a small proportion of the firms that pay the presumptive tax. Moreover, it was not possible to identify the largest informal operators from these data. Large informal firms often have many identification numbers and fragment their imports, making it difficult to determine their total imports. Indeed, it would not be surprising if a large number of the 132 identification numbers whose imports and sales we were able to cross-check belonged to one individual.

Notwithstanding these limitations, our analysis starkly reveals the extent of underreporting of sales, demonstrating that many firms that are subject to the presumptive tax because of their underreporting of sales should actually be subject to regular business taxes. These false declarations are facilitated by the lack of cooperation and exchange of data between customs and the fiscal agency. Figure 4.1 shows enormous gaps between imports and sales figures for some firms, with imports sometimes 10 times greater than sales. While some imports are for capital goods, the discrepancies are much too large to be explained this way, particularly given the largely commercial nature of the activities concerned. Among firms in our sample, more than 41 percent report sales below imports. In certain sectors, like jewelry, retail sale, and car mechanics, this proportion is greater than 50 percent. As shown in figures 4.1 and 4.2, in the retail sector, 56 percent of firms in our sample have a greater value of imports than of sales! In fact, the discrepancies between imports and reported sales may be even larger than figures 4.1 and 4.2 suggest, given that imports can also be understated as a result of smuggling and underinvoicing.

Figure 4.1 Proportion of Firms in Senegal for Which Imports Are Larger or Smaller Than Sales, by Industry

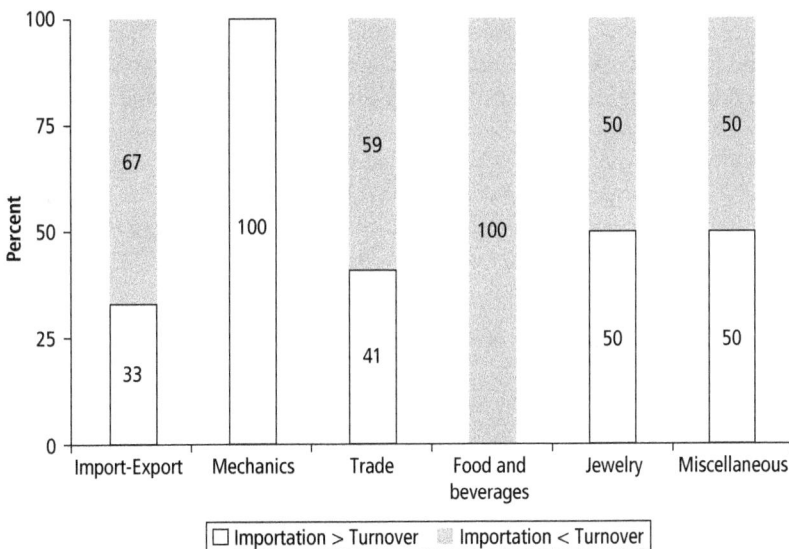

Source: Authors' calculations using customs and fiscal databases.

Figure 4.2 Proportion of Firms in Senegal for Which Imports Exceed Sales, by Industry

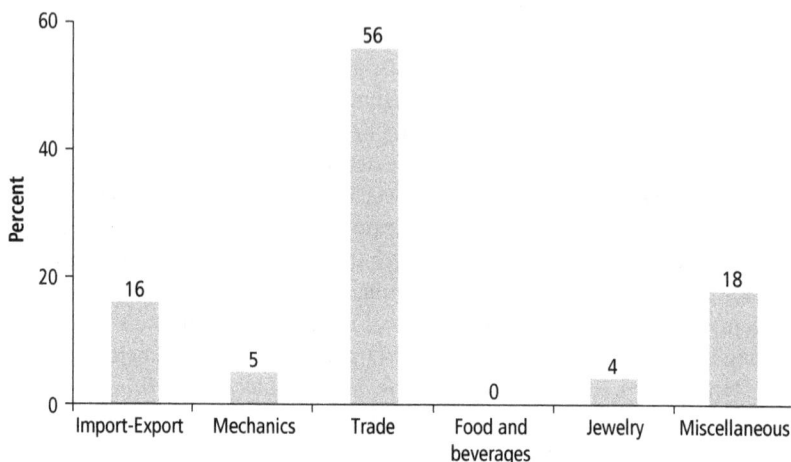

Source: Authors' calculations using customs and fiscal databases.

The government officials we interviewed are well aware of this situation and acknowledged that fraud is common. Joint squads of customs and tax agents identify a significant number of fraudulent tax filings. When they identify tax evasion, they subject the firms to penalties and regular business taxes. Often, however, these firms then declare bankruptcy or simply disappear, only to resume their practices under a different name.

The second phase of our survey, conducted in 2009, focused on formal and large informal firms. Many of the large informal firms identified in the first phase of the survey in 2007 had disappeared by 2009. For example, in Ouagadougou, only 54 percent of large informal firms had survived, compared with 76 percent of formal businesses (table 4.1). The low survival rate of firms in the large informal sector is somewhat misleading, however, as firms often closed and reappeared in a different form.

Table 4.1 Survival Rates of Firms in Ouagadougou
% of firms

Firms	Surviving	Disappeared
Formal	76	24
Informal	54	46
Total	64	36

Source: Based on authors' firm survey data.

Interrelations between the Formal Sector and the Informal Sector

In West Africa, the coexistence of the formal and informal sectors takes complex forms. At times, the two sectors are in competition; at others, they collaborate.

Competition and Cooperation between Formal and Informal Sectors

As noted, it is hard to find a completely formal firm in the region's economies. The only firms that meet all of the necessary criteria are branches of multinational corporations, banks and financial institutions, state-owned enterprises or parastals, certain professions (law firms, notaries' offices), and a few large enterprises. All other firms participate at least minimally in the informal sector. Their informal activities are quite varied, covering undeclared sales or services, value added tax (VAT) collected and not remitted, and so forth. In carrying out these actions, informal firms generally act as subcontractors for formal firms.

The customs clearance process for merchandise at ports and at airports provides a good illustration of this type of interaction. Normally, customs services are performed only by customs clearance agents; these agents are part of the formal sector, which implies a maximum level of transparency in their operations. In reality, many unauthorized agents work in this sector, collaborating with the legally authorized agents. These informal actors offer to help clients to clear merchandise from the port at much lower costs than if they were to deal with authorized customs agents. Because they are not recognized by the customs agency, these fraudulent agents must use the seal of an authorized agent. In return for use of the authorized agent's seal, the informal agent passes on a portion of the fees he collects for clearing clients' merchandise. This practice is common in ports throughout the region and is well known even to customs officials, as they made clear in our discussions with them. The authorized customs agents that we met justified their collaboration with informal firms on the grounds that the latter have the most contact with clients and thus control a good part of the demand in this sector.

Collaboration between the formal and informal sectors is also prevalent in the construction sector. Large contracts for public works can only be acquired by formal enterprises. To win a contract, a firm must produce documents proving that it is in compliance with regular income taxes and that it has the means to finance large investments, pending payment by the government. Formal firms often subcontract with informal firms to do most of the construction, including hiring workers, in exchange for a lump-sum payment from which they pay laborers and retain the surplus as profit. The acquisition and provision of construction materials and other necessary inputs are the responsibility of the lead enterprise with the contract.

Similar types of collaboration between formal and informal firms are common in many other sectors. Many large manufacturing firms use informal distribution channels to sell their products. Cement factories collaborate with merchants with cement depots, which sell their products to retail outlets and, finally, to consumers. Most participants in the value chain are informal. Similar practices occur with breweries, storage depots, and the production of household items.

Despite these examples of collaboration, it would be naive to believe that firms in the formal and informal sectors always cooperate. Fierce competition between the two sectors can escalate into open conflict. The pharmaceutical sector is a case in point: the formal component is under the control of well-educated pharmacists who have formed a pharmacists association. They often sell imported medications, following a strict distribution circuit that involves only formal firms. Low-income customers, however, often cannot afford the high prices at pharmacies and instead purchase medications from informal vendors at much lower prices. Drugs available from informal venders are not, of course, as reliable and can sometimes even be hazardous to the consumer. Informal vendors sell counterfeit and expired medications and almost never store them in proper conditions. Nevertheless, their low prices make them attractive to desperate patients. Formal pharmacies are often burglarized, and professional pharmacists frequently accuse informal vendors of handling their stolen goods.

The Keur Serigne Bi (KSB) case in Senegal provides a good illustration of these dilemmas. This neighborhood, in the heart of Dakar, is home to the largest and best-known informal market for medicines (apart from a hub situated in Touba, the capital of the Mourides, discussed in chapter 8). The Mouride brotherhood owns KSB and gives free reign to its disciples to use the market to sell medications informally. The medications include locally produced counterfeit products and imports from India, China, and Arab countries, which often arrive in dubious condition. In mid-2009, an open conflict broke out between formal pharmacies and KSB. Recurrent thefts of medicines had been occurring at the formal pharmacies, often followed by violence and, in some cases, deaths. The pharmacies accused KSB of instigating the thefts and possessing stolen goods. In an attempt to pressure the government to close KSB, the pharmacies went on strike several times; they were eventually successful, and the government closed KSB in both Dakar and Touba. There was little chance, however, that this order could be implemented, given that the caliph of Touba publicly disavowed the decision and stated his opposition to the closing of KSB. This example illustrates how formal and informal sectors are often in opposition rather than in collusion.

Contrary to the common belief of formal sector actors, informal firms may face more competition than formal firms in many instances.[1] Sectors with a high concentration of informal firms (transportation, retail, certain services like automobile repairs, the clothing industry, carpentry) are usually highly competitive, with low-quality, homogeneous products, flexible prices, and many sellers. Meanwhile, in the modern sector, firms are often protected by special agreements with the government or through membership in professional organizations, which defend their interests.

A More Detailed Analysis of Selected Sectors

In this section, we discuss some sectors in which large informal firms operate, based on our interviews and other research. The sectors we examine here include transport, retail, port transit, and construction. Most of the examples in this and the following sections are related to commerce, as this is by far the most important sector in which the informal sector operates. The 123 survey finds that, for all three countries, around 50 percent of informal enterprises are involved in wholesale-retail trade and a large part of this involves importing.[2] Particularly in Benin but also in the other countries, smuggling is a major arena for large formal firms. The issues involved with customs and smuggling are discussed in chapters 6 and 9.

The characteristics of the large informal sector described earlier emerge clearly in our interviews. In many cases, large informal firms have a large volume of sales but are taxed under the presumptive lump-sum regime. They have few permanent employees, rely heavily on family sources of financing, and have weak organizational structure; many of their activities rely on official corruption and falsified documents.

The Used Vehicle Market in Benin   As also discussed in chapter 9, the used car market plays a crucial role in Benin's economy, accounting for perhaps 10 percent of gross domestic product (GDP). The used vehicle market in Benin is mostly oriented toward informal reexports to Nigeria and landlocked countries to the north (Chad, Niger, Mali, and Burkina Faso). The value chain includes a large number of participants, including shippers, customs clearance agents, used vehicles salesmen, car parks, and drivers, among others.

In Benin's capital, large open-air parking lots have been developed to serve the used vehicle market, for both cars and trucks. These parks are privately owned but lack a strict administrative structure, as is typical of the informal sector. All parks have a director and a general manager responsible for issuing certificates of exit from the park. Apart from these two individuals, temporary workers handle a variety of tasks. The parks claim to serve clients from both the formal and the informal sectors. Each car park houses a large number of importers, with a designated area for displaying their cars. Rents are

CFAF 250,000–CFAF 300,000 (US$500–US$600) a month per hectare. The firm operating the free zone in Cotonou allocates the lots to the various car dealers.

The firms operating in the parking lots import an average of 100 to 150 vehicles per year. The vehicles are an average of 15 years old and generally too dilapidated and too old to be in demand in developed countries, but they are prized by low-income Africans who do not have the means to purchase newer vehicles. Vehicles are transported from their country of origin to Cotonou in 20- and 40-foot containers, with each container costing between CFAF 1.75 million and CFAF 3.5 million, respectively. A 20-foot container can hold three vehicles, and a 40-foot container can hold six. Importing firms, like the parks, have minimal organizational structure. Those that we visited employ only a director and no more than four temporary workers charged with unloading vehicles at the port and transporting them to the car park. These workers said that they take care of customs declarations, bypassing authorized customs agents. In many cases, the majority of buyers are from other countries of the region, usually Nigeria.

To an even greater degree than in the rest of the informal sector, most workers in the parking lots are male. Among workers, levels of education vary: some are illiterate, while others have a high school education or higher. Most of the workers we met had previous professional experience, both in the formal or informal sectors and sometimes in formal firms in other countries. For example, one of the workers we interviewed, who had completed his first year of high school, worked in a formal enterprise in Nigeria for 15 years before coming to the car park. Familial relations are common among employees; one manager even admitted to having his wife as his secretary. Some may not have close relatives but may work with cousins, in-laws, or close friends. "I work morning to night," one interviewee declared, adding, "I created this corporation with my brother and an associate. A brother-in-law who worked as an agent got us started. Relatives (fathers, aunts, etc.) lent us CFAF 10 million to get it off the ground. It started this way for most of us. Sometimes, we get bank loans, but the most we've ever gotten was CFAF 12 million. We got loans from European banks. My brother, who is also an associate, is based in Europe; he works out the loans there and sends the money to us through Western Union. We avoid local banks because they are complicated. We transfer funds in multiple transactions." Another interviewee who transports merchandise stated, "One of my uncles helped me to establish my business. I used to be a taxi driver, but then I transferred to the car park. The initial investment required to transfer was CFAF 12 million, CFAF 5 million of which was supplied by my uncles. We never had any bank credit."

Every manager we interviewed claimed that their businesses were registered. They all stated that they have a fiscal identifier, which is required for an importer card. They all added, however, that it is almost impossible to conduct business in their country without participating in fraudulent activities. For example, some admitted to submitting financial statements to fiscal authorities that misrepresent their sales and profits. In addition, some acknowledged importing on behalf of a third party and billing them afterward. They stated that they often bribe government agents to expedite the paperwork, which otherwise would be bogged down by indefinite delays.

While all of the firms we interviewed are under the lump-sum presumptive tax regime, their annual sales figures are at least CFAF 200 million—four times the limit required to be taxed a lump sum. The offices they rent in town are often small, with monthly rents never above CFAF 20,000 (US$40). They lack internal accounting services and hire external accountants to handle their accounts. On this subject, one of the shippers we met stated, "I am just starting out; I am taxed a lump sum. My head offices are in Boykon, 136 kilometers from Cotonou. It is one of our parents' houses; I rent two rooms that cost me CFAF 7,000 per year. I have a branch office in town, which costs me CFAF 20,000 per year."

Car park managers' perception of the working environment is very negative, consistent with the findings in the previous chapter: they complain about the cost of electricity, telephone, and water. Even more disturbing to them, however, are their relations with the government. They declared that the government is corrupt and predatory and decried the multiple fees they must pay. They must pay the government a CFAF 50,000 fee per imported vehicle, in addition to the port's fees. In theory, vehicles in the transit regime are exempt from customs duties, but other fees add up. Also, if the vehicles are not sold within six months, retailers are fined CFAF 400,000 for each vehicle.

Trucking in Benin   Firm characteristics and perception of the working environment in the trucking sector are similar to those in the used vehicle market. The people we spoke with own some trucks and rent others. One of our interviewees told us, "We buy old trucks that we tinker with. I had to save up to buy all of my trucks; I bought them on credit from local suppliers. I would like to quit this sector because it's too difficult to make money. The last three vehicles that I purchased have been idle for a very long time. I bought them and repaired them, and they cost me CFAF 3 million each." Another stated, "In the past, I would get CFAF 2 million in revenues from a truck. However, for the past while, traffic has slowed and business has decreased. Nowadays, the Lomé port competes fiercely with the Cotonou port, especially over imports destined for reexport to Nigeria. Togolese customs fails to apply the WAEMU [West African Economic and Monetary Union] common external tariff, undercutting Benin's competitiveness; moreover, port delays are not as long in Lomé. One should not stay in this profession for his whole career. I have a master's degree in law. I have two declared permanent employees (an accountant and a chauffeur) and many temporary workers." He added, "Relations with the drivers are very strained because they do not take care of the trucks. The drivers are not serious—they quit and abandon their trucks. My employees who are declared have social security, but the others do not."

On average, truck drivers work two trips a week, at a rate of CFAF 150,000 per trip. The upkeep of the vehicles accounts for 50 to 60 percent of total costs. In this sector, firms pay approximately CFAF 210,000 a year to a tax called *taxe unique sur le transport routier* (TUTR), a form of the lump-sum tax. Enterprises with sales of more than CFAF 10 million per year pay the regular business income tax, with TUTR payments counting as a credit. Our three interviewees at the fiscal administration largely confirmed this information.

Imports and Retail Distribution in the Three Cities   The findings from our interviews in the retail sector are very similar to those from interviews in other sectors. Our most striking interview was with a Beninese civil servant who is involved with smuggling across the Nigerian border. He imports frozen goods, which were prohibited in Nigeria until recently. He sometimes reexports these products to Nigeria and then returns to Benin with goods smuggled from Nigeria. He noted that it is very difficult for authorities to patrol the more than 1,000 kilometers of border that the countries share.

Like others, he claimed that Togo flouts WAEMU agreements on taxes and customs duties, thereby undercutting Beninese competitors. Goods from Lomé enter Benin duty free, fraudulently labeled as goods in transit, with the connivance of Togolese customs agents. Products in transit are supposed to be escorted to the border, but collusion or negligence on the part of customs agents allows large amounts of products to "go missing." According to our interviewee, the informal sector is also encouraged because it is so costly to register formally. He estimated that an importing permit costs about CFAF 750,000, of which the most important costs are the following:

- Public notary costs: CFAF 300,000
- One-stop shop for enterprises: CFAF 40,000
- Licenses: CFAF 120,000
- Contribution to the Chamber of Commerce and Industry: CFAF 50,000
- Tax for the Division of International Trade at the Ministry of Commerce: CFAF 30,000
- Commerce registry: CFAF 50,000
- Land Use Division at the Ministry of Finance: CFAF 160,000

What's more, the retailer's professional identification card costs at least CFAF 140,000. Our interviewee stated that these costs are much too high for many entrepreneurs, who have no choice but to remain in the informal sector.

Another importer with whom we spoke is of the same opinion. He stated that he is part of the formal sector and is subject to regular business taxes. He imports used vehicles and foodstuffs destined for both the Beninese market and the region. His biggest difficulties are related to customs. In his opinion, lack of cooperation on the part of customs agents makes transit difficult because merchandise is searched and containers are opened. Those who do not bribe officials see their business delayed. This is due not only to customs but also to civil servants in the Ministry of Finance. As did others, he noted that electricity, telephone, and water services are expensive and of dubious quality. He said that his electricity generator costs approximately CFAF 1 million a year to maintain.

A customs clearance agent who works for both formal and informal importers said that tax rates in Benin are much too high, because "we stupidly copied French laws. The French also experience many problems in this area." In his daily work, as well as in his relations with employees, he said that he tries to stay clear of the judicial system, which he views as corrupt. Also, the workers are strongly "advised" not to unionize. He acknowledged, however, that despite the difficulties he incurs because of formal status, he is privy to many benefits, such as access to public markets and the possibility of deducting the VAT. He recognizes that informal clearing agents are more dynamic and efficient because they do not pay taxes and can make "deals" with customs. As a result, informal agents can charge as little as a third of what formal firms charge. They cannot, however, handle large shipments that require advance financing.

Construction in Burkina Faso   Among the construction firms that we visited in Burkina Faso, one in particular is revealing. The manager owns two enterprises, with three permanent employees at the first enterprise and five at the second. He also employs numerous contractual employees. The two firms share headquarters, and the combined turnover for the two firms is CFAF 1 billion. He has a tax identification number and separate certified annual statements of accounts for each firm. He is subject to regular business taxes for the two firms and hires an accounting firm to prepare the accounting statements each year. Both firms were created in 1994. He told us that he used to manage a small formal commercial enterprise and has a master's degree in law. All of his employees have a university level of education. He told us, "Our enterprise started with a turnover of CFAF 50 million and has remained a sole proprietorship. We voluntarily participate in the formal sector and pay regular business taxes, with a sales figure of just above the required amount. As an informal firm, we would not be able deduct the VAT. When we created the firm, we started with a few employees, and that has not changed." He also stated that many firms, even corporations, produce two sets of accounting documents. This is facilitated by the lack of collaboration between customs and tax agencies. He said that the regular business tax regime is appropriate for his country because firms that are subject only to presumptive taxes are excluded from the government procurement markets.

This manager admitted that he sometimes creates fake invoices, does not always invoice the value added tax, and omits some activities from his official accounts. He justified these actions on the grounds that the government misuses public funds, while admitting that it is more responsible than many other governments in the region. According to our interviewee, corruption and bribes are rampant in public markets. Customs agencies suffer from the highest level of corruption, and custom clearance agents sometimes sell their identification number to informal agents. Firms attempting to smuggle goods through customs deal with informal customs clearance agents because they undervalue merchandise.

An Example of a Successful Transition from the Informal Sector to the Formal Sector in Burkina Faso   An interesting example of a successful transition from the informal to the formal sector is of SOPAM, an electric power generation corporation with CFAF 200 million in capital. The founder also owns GEOGORFD, a firm with a turnover of CFAF 200 billion and 600 employees. Both of these companies operate in drilling and delivery of water, in addition to energy. SOPAM was created first; before creating these firms, the owner headed the supplier division of a transit company. SOPAM began in the informal sector, with only 10 employees. The owner holds a master's degree in finance and accounting. In his opinion, education was the key to his successful transition from the informal to the formal sector: "I understand foreign languages and have access to a computer, which makes me more efficient." According to him, uneducated economic entrepreneurs usually stay in individual enterprises in the informal sector, even when their firms grow. Nonetheless, he does not think that his success is unique: "There exist many people who, like me, started off with nothing. One expects work and a conscientious attitude. We worked with the government, with SONABEL, the Office National de la Formation Professionnelle, and other governmental and parastatal institutions. I had CFAF 15,000 in start-up capital, and my first loan was for CFAF 200,000, which I obtained from the bank after 14 days of negotiations. The loan was to buy an air conditioner for the university. I still work with the same banker. We obtain loans with short maturities, less than 90 days."

The Stories of Some Large Informal Operators in Senegal

This section focuses on the stories of four large informal operators in Senegal, illustrating the scope of their enterprises, the importance of their political and religious connections, and their fragility. These firms are generally controlled by a single individual and are vulnerable to collapse if the government musters the political will to take them on, for good or bad reasons. These profiles are based mainly on press reports, the most important of which are referenced below.

Moustapha Tall

Moustapha Tall is one of the most important economic actors in Senegal.[3] He controls an estimated 25–36 percent of Senegal's rice market and is involved in other markets, such as sugar. His career's trajectory exemplifies the rags to riches dynamic of a transition from the small to the large informal sector as well as the vulnerability of these firms.

Tall's entry into business is typical of the beginnings of large informal entrepreneurs. Starting with nothing, a select few succeed in building very successful enterprises through tremendous effort and acumen. He described his background in an interview. "I come from Kaolack and completed my primary school studies there, at the Kasaville school. I am my father's first son and my father's brother's namesake. This same uncle put me in school in 1962 and took me out of school 10 years later. My uncle owned a store and was having trouble managing it. The previous manager had left without warning my uncle; the next day, my uncle told me to get the keys to the store and to open it for the day. It was with that order from my uncle that I entered retailing. I think that, in a way, it was retail that chose me. After 10 years, I quit working at my uncle's store and came to Dakar. My uncle had given me nothing, and I came here without a cent."

Tall's experience also illustrates the relations between the formal and informal sectors. He started out in the sugar industry, working as a distributor for Companie Sucrière Sénégalaise, owned by Jean-Claude Mimran, a French national. In Senegal, sugar production has long been monopolized by the Mimran family, which has long-standing ties to the Senegalese government. Sugar is one of the few sectors in Senegal that remains heavily protected, with a variable levy, resisting the trend toward liberalization. Consequently, sugar is much more expensive in Senegal than in neighboring countries, thereby inviting smuggling from The Gambia and Mauritania, as described in chapter 9. Importers who have ventured into this area have wound up in great difficulties, sometimes even in jail. Tall quickly proved to be a very successful trader, claiming to earn CFAF 200,000 to CFAF 300,000 per week. In 1983, within three years of arriving in Dakar, he opened his own store. He said, "By the grace of God, I am where I am today. The liberalization in 1989 allowed me to begin importing rice. In 1995, the liberalization was completed, and as I already had good relations with my bank, I jumped at the opportunity to begin importing greater quantities."

Like many of the other large informal entrepreneurs, he encountered setbacks that almost destroyed his business. He went to prison on charges of smuggling sugar imports estimated at CFAF 1 billion (US$4 million), which he was forced to pay to customs along with a fine of about CFAF 350 million. In regard to his arrest, he stated, "At the time, I paid customs CFAF 1 billion to recover my freedom. In the end, I gave in because I was worried that these people were going to harm me. I had to leave and recoup my activities as soon as possible. My business was badly looted while I was in prison. Both employees and clients escaped with my money. The damage to which I was subjected is immense—I lost about CFAF 3 billion because of my unjust imprisonment. Yet today, thanks to the grace of God, I still survive. I started with zero francs, and even if I have zero francs today, I will still thank God's grace. Regardless of how this conflict affected me financially, I am not complaining. I am beginning to rebuild my business, and I will continue fighting until I reach my previous level."

His relations with government, particularly customs, are typically complex. Large informal traders invariably engage in various forms of smuggling and tax evasion. Their success is contingent on tacit or even explicit complicity. Sometimes, however, for various reasons, an entrepreneur falls out of favor with the authorities, or the government is under pressure to crack down and increase revenues. On paper, customs laws impose draconian sanctions on tax evasion and smuggling. In cases brought to court by customs, the judge reportedly always rules in favor of the government, regardless of the truth of the accusations. The defendant must either settle with customs or go to jail. As Tall put it, "I'm telling you, two customs agents can simply make an accusation against a businessman, fine him, and send him to a tribunal. If the judge is either in collusion with them, is misinformed, or has no courage, he will send the businessman to jail."

Cheikh Tall Dioum

Cheikh Tall Dioum is another successful businessman in Senegal who was imprisoned following a conflict with customs related to allegations of evasion of the laws protecting sugar.[4]

After independence, almost all of the jewelry stores in Senegal were owned by Europeans. Companies like Vendome, Pierrres Precieuses, Taj Mahal, and Comptoir Franco-Suisse were well established in downtown areas. Local so-called "traditional" jewelers were confined to suburbs where they made jewelry and sold it to these big stores, which would then resell the products at a substantial markup.

Dioum, a traditional jeweler, opened a modern jewelry store downtown after accumulating some savings. After establishing the first shop, he opened other jewelry stores everywhere there was a high concentration of Europeans—Hyper Sahm, Score Sarraut, Meridien Hotel in Ngor, the Club Mediterranee des Almadies, the chicest locations in Dakar—by buying out European owners.

He quickly diversified into other sectors, including ice cream. Previously, Miko and Gervais, two French companies, had a monopoly in the ice cream market in Senegal. Dioum's ice cream business was so successful that the French companies exited the market. He also bought a news agency and bought a nightclub in collaboration with the renowned Senegalese singer Youssou Ndour. His biggest investment and near downfall was creating the Nouvelles Brasseries Africaines, a soft drink producer. He repeatedly came into conflict with SOBOA, a Senegalese franchise of Coca-Cola, from which he emerged victorious. He met his match in customs and the Mimran sugar monopoly, however. Customs accused him of abusing his license to import duty-free sugar to manufacture beverages by illegally reselling sugar on the domestic market. Like Tall, he wound up in prison and was only freed after paying a huge fine and losing almost all of his businesses.

Bocar Samba Dieye

Bocar Samba Dieye illustrates another dimension of fragility of large informal entrepreneurs.[5] Dieye is a major Senegalese importer of rice, wheat, and animal feed. Even more than Tall, he is a self-made man. He can neither read nor write French, yet he controls a vast trading network spanning Asia, Europe, and Africa.

Like Tall, his near downfall came from a legal conflict, in this case involving a foreign partner rather than the government. In 2008, he was accused of failing to make payment on a debt of CFAF 17 billion to the Swiss partner, Ascot, a major global rice trading company. The conflict between Dieye and Ascot occurred during a run-up in global food prices, particularly rice, which is the most important food staple in Senegal and is overwhelmingly imported. According to Dieye, the government was worried about social unrest resulting from the soaring price of rice. He imported 160,000 tons of rice, worth CFAF 46 billion from Ascot, with whom he had been working for 15 years. Dieye paid Ascot CFAF 29 billion, with a remaining CFAF 17 billion debt. Dieye claimed that he was selling at a loss due to a sharp unexpected decline in the price of rice. He also complained that Ascot was requesting earlier payment than specified in the contract and that the agreed legal venue for adjudicating the dispute was the Tribunal of Paris rather than that of Dakar. The judge in the case, however, ruled in favor of Ascot and ordered seizure of Dieye's goods, particularly his storage depots of rice.

Marabout Serigne Khadim Bousso

In March 2003, Senegalese society was shaken by the "Khadim Bousso" affair,[6] which revealed the complex linkages between informal sector commercial interests, politics, and religious groups, notably the Mouride Islamic brotherhood. Khadim Bousso was an influential Mouride marabout: a member of the Bousso family (and a descendant of Cheikh Amadou Bamba's mother), founder of the Mouride brotherhood. He also managed two formal firms and was in possession of all the necessary documents. The two firms, NOSOCOM (Nouvelle Societé de Commerce) and IDECOM (Internationale pour le Développement du Commerce Senegalo-Maghrebin), were both commercial enterprises. Bousso also directed the ROES (Rassemblement des Opérateurs Economiques du Sénégal), which was an employers' syndicate. A majority of members of ROES were well-known businesses in Senegal, especially in the informal sector.

In 1999, BICIS Bank—a subsidiary of the French Banque Nationale de Paris (BNP)—took the marabout to court. The case involved a CFAF 2 billion loan (approximately US$5 million) that the bank extended to Bousso, who then proceeded to declare himself insolvent, feigning bankruptcy. When the bank attempted to seize his companies' assets, it quickly realized that there were very few assets to seize. The bank brought the case to court, sparking a political furor that brought into the open the complicity between political and marabout powers. The judge ordered Bousso personally to reimburse the total amount due to the bank and condemned him to the maximum sentence of civil imprisonment. He was incarcerated, and the press put the spotlight on the influence of businessmen based in Touba (the capital of the Mourides).[7]

Touba is a unique city where the state's authority requires the explicit consent of the marabouts, as discussed extensively in chapter 8. A tacit understanding is that the police or customs officers cannot enter the city without authorization of the marabouts. Government officials can be transferred outside of the city on request of the marabout. The caliph-general of the Mourides has also closed public schools, because he decided that the content of the instruction did not conform to Islamic principles. What in other areas of the country would be considered an offense and be severely punished is considered completely normal in Touba. Because of this unusual situation, as long as Khadim Bousso stayed in Touba he would only be at risk if the marabout gave permission to the police to arrest him. The BNP realized this and, with the help of the French government, applied a lot of pressure on Senegalese authorities. Squeezed between the opposing forces of the marabouts and the French powers in Africa, Senegalese authorities attempted to convince the Mourides' caliph to release him. In the end, Bousso was released by the caliph and incarcerated on March 5, 2003. However, he was transferred five days later to the wing for sick detainees at the Artistide le Dantec Hospital in Dakar. Some interpreted the transfer as a condition placed by the caliph on Bousso's arrest.

Several days later, Bousso escaped from prison with the help of his prison guard, who turned out to be his disciple. He then took refuge in Touba and declared on national radio that the conditions in prison were detestable and that he did not intend to return. Under great pressure from the BNP, the authorities again demanded that the caliph authorize Bousso's arrest and succeeded in recapturing him. During his second arrest, Bousso was shot and killed. The reason for the murder and its perpetrator remain unknown. According to the

police, it was a suicide; according to the marabout's family, it was a police blun-
der. Regardless of the cause, this tragedy marked the end of the affair, and the
bank still has not been repaid.

Conclusion

The existence of large informal firms is one of the most important aspects of the
informal sector in West Africa, yet has been almost completely ignored in the
literature until now. There are no publicly available data on these firms, given
that they massively understate their sales and income, yet they are well known
in the countries themselves. We used several methods to obtain information.

We found that large informal firms are fundamentally different from both
formal and small informal firms, while at the same time resembling each of
them in some respects. The main sectors in which they operate include import-
export trade, domestic wholesale-retail, transportation, and construction. These
large informal entrepreneurs often began as small operators with minimal education but became very wealthy and influential due to superior entrepreneurial ability and effort, along with assistance from ethnic and religious trading
groups. In terms of volume of sales and other measures of activity, these firms
do not differ from their formal counterparts. In terms of family-based organization and management, they are very much like small informal firms. Typically, a single person controls all major functions (human resources, accounts,
finance, marketing) in contrast to formal firms, where separate departments
control each activity. In addition, they are fragile insofar as they often are run
by a single individual who may dissolve the business because of a conflict with
tax or customs officials or reappear under another name.

Notes
1. Chapter 5 presents findings on perceptions of competition in formal and informal
   sectors, from our survey data.
2. The 123 study developed by DIAL (Développement, Institutions et Ajustement à
   Long Terme) covers small informal firms. Our interviews and the second wave of
   our surveys focusing on large informal firms showed that a similarly high proportion of large informal firms are involved in trading activities.
3. See "Moustapha Tall, l'importateur de riz," Sud Quotidien, May 17, 2008; http://www
   .nettali.net/Moustapha-Tall-importateur-l-Etat.htm; http://www.rewmi.com/
   Moustapha-Tall-importateur-de-produits-alimentaires-Le-prix-du-riz-ne-baissera-
   pas_a9702.html.
4. See http://www.houblon.net/spip.php?article559; "La chute d'un empereur, Cheikh
   Tall Dioum," Afric.com, December 2, 2001; http://www.xibar.net/ENTRETIEN-
   EXCLUSIF-AVEC-CHEIKH-TALL-DIOUM-Le-golden-boy-ouvre-une-fenetre-

sur-lui_a6801.html;"Entretien exclusif avec Cheikh Tall Dioum: Le golden boy ouvre une fenêtre sur lui," Lissa Magazine, January 22, 2008, http://www.xibar.net.

5. See http://www.nettali.net/Bocar-Samba-Dieye-fait-bloquer-une.html; "Bocar Samba Dieye," Walfadjri, May 26, 2009, http://fr.allafrica.com; Walfadjri, May 26 2009; http://fr.allafrica.com/stories/200807250746.html.

6. See Marsaud (2003); Gueye (n.d.); http://www.socialisme-republiquesn.org/.../oci-khadim-bousso-les... – February 22, 2008; "Senegal: Khadim Bousso; la lettre du continent n°423," AfricaIntelligence.com, May 15, 2003, http://www.africaintelligence.fr/LC-/who-s-who/2003/05/15/khadim-bousso,7360581-ART.

7. See Marsaud (2003).

References

Gueye, El Modou. n.d. "Affaire Khadim Bousso: La famille du marabout dément Me wade." *Walfadjri*. http://www.walf.sn/politique/suite.php?rub=2&id_art=28133.

Marsaud, Olivia. 2003. "La mort du marabout." afrik.com, May 25. http://www.afrik.com/article6126.html.

Chapter 5

Characteristics of the Informal Sector: Findings from Our Surveys

The preceding chapters emphasize the heterogeneity of the informal sector in West Africa, noting in particular the key distinction between large and small informal firms. In this chapter, we examine in detail the characteristics of these two types of firms as well as formal firms, using the findings from our surveys in the three cities.

As discussed in chapter 1, informality is best viewed as a continuum rather than a dichotomy between purely formal and informal firms, with most firms satisfying some, but not all, of the six criteria of informality identified. Likewise, the two categories of large versus small informal firms contain a range of enterprises with various degrees of formality. For the purposes of this chapter, formal firms are those that meet all six criteria and, in particular, pay regular income taxes. Therefore, any firm that fails to meet one of these criteria is informal. We then split the informal firms into two groups: large and small. Small informal firms are those that pay the presumptive tax or no tax at all and have sales below CFAF 50 million. Some of them are registered or have a fixed workplace; very few of them have access to credit, however. Large informal firms are those that underreport sales, often paying the presumptive tax, despite having actual sales above the threshold qualifying for the business income tax regime.[1] They are almost always registered and have a fixed workplace; in some cases, they have access to credit. For this chapter, we ignore the fact that some firms that pay business income taxes are, in fact, largely informal, in the sense that they greatly underreport their sales to the tax authorities, as discussed in detail in chapter 4.

Size and Other Characteristics of Firms in the Sample

Table 5.1 presents descriptive statistics regarding our sample of formal, large informal, and small informal businesses in the three cities. Sales and number of employees are greatest in the formal sector, with the notable exception

Table 5.1 Descriptive Statistics of Firms in the Three West African Cities, by Formal or Informal Status

City and status	Share in total country sample	Average sales (CFAF millions)	Average number of employees (including temporary workers)
Formal			
Dakar	24	833	9.6
Ouagadougou	13	615	21.2
Cotonou	23	725	22.1
Large informal			
Dakar	16	117	4.5
Ouagadougou	11	155	6.1
Cotonou	15	319	22.6
Small informal			
Dakar	60	13	4.2
Ouagadougou	76	11	5.4
Cotonou	62	13	5.8

Source: Based on authors' firm survey data.

of Cotonou, where the average number of employees in large informal firms matches the number of employees in the formal sector, reflecting the role of these firms in Benin's thriving informal cross-border trade, as described in chapter 9. An interesting aspect is the rather weak correlation between firm size as measured by sales and by number of employees, except in the formal sector, where they are both higher than in the others. For example, in Ouagadougou the number of employees in large informal firms is virtually the same as the number in small informal firms, but sales are nearly 20 times greater. Single-person firms (excluding temporary workers) are quite numerous and found at all levels of sales. For example, 75 percent of companies in Senegal with turnover below CFAF 5 million and 67 percent of companies with turnover between CFAF 600 million and CFAF 1 billion are single-employee firms. This again reflects the importance of large informal firms, most of which are sole proprietorships, as discussed in chapter 4.

The size distribution of firms in the sample is rather skewed, with only a few very large firms: in Dakar 11 percent of formal firms and 2 percent of large informal firms in our sample have turnover above CFAF 1 billion, while 34 percent of formal firms and 20 percent of large informal firms have turnover exceeding CFAF 300 million. The distribution is similarly skewed in the other two cities. Also, although the number of employees is higher, on average, in formal than in informal sector firms, there are many small formal firms, contradicting the conventional assumption that small size connotes informality. In Dakar, for example, 50 percent of formal firms have fewer than five employees, compared to 76 percent of the informal sector as a whole. Only 18 percent of firms in the formal sector, 14 percent in the large informal sector, and 6 percent in the small informal sector have more than 10 employees. Table 5.1 shows the average sales and number of employees by category of firms in each of the three cities.

As discussed in chapter 1, the various characteristics of informality are highly correlated. Only 30 percent of small firms (those with less than CFAF 5 million in sales) maintain proper accounts, while all firms with turnover exceeding CFAF 600 million do so. Between 5 and 17 percent of firms with sales exceeding CFAF 50 million, which makes them eligible for formal business income taxes, do not maintain regularly updated accounts. Moreover, 60 percent of companies with turnover below CFAF 300 million do not maintain up-to-date and complete books, compared with 97 percent of companies with turnover exceeding CFAF 300 million. A similar trend is evident in firms' registration decisions. Only 62 percent of firms with turnover below CFAF 5 million are registered, as opposed to 100 percent of firms with turnover at or above CFAF 100 million. The fact that most small firms are registered, however, implies that 88 percent of the firms in our sample are formal, a wholly implausible result. In fact, as mentioned in chapter 1, many informal enterprises are registered with one administrative authority but not with others. As discussed in detail in chapter 1, the most relevant type of registration is lump-sum or regular business taxation. Companies that are taxed at a fixed rate, even if they are well known to the tax authorities, do not generate a formal system of accounting that allows their financial activities to be monitored.

Informality, Market Structure, and Exports

In this section, we examine the domestic and international markets in which the informal sector operates. Previous research on the subject indicates that the informal sector tends to develop in certain industries and is shaped by international trade patterns. Sectors that are the most exposed to international competition are often among those that have the most extensive informal sectors. Several studies of Latin American and African countries show that informalization is most pervasive in retail trade, nonfinancial services, and certain manufacturing sectors. Liedholm (2001) finds that three markets (clothing; food products, including alcoholic drinks; and wood products) constitute 75 percent of the manufacturing activities of small firms in urban areas and 90 percent in rural areas. He also finds that the distribution circuits for these enterprises are very rudimentary: most enterprises sell directly to final consumers.

The data from national income accounts reported in chapter 3 and from our surveys largely confirm the tendency of the informal sector to dominate in certain sectors. In our surveys, 48 percent of small informal firms operate in the industrial sector compared with 38 percent of large informal firms and 18 percent of formal firms; the economy-wide average of firms in the secondary sector is 38 percent. This may seem surprising, but it reflects both the decline of formal manufacturing and the preponderance of informal operators in construction and in artisanal manufacturing of wood products and clothing. In our sample, 17 percent of small informal firms and 15 percent of all firms produce nonmarketable services. The large informal and formal sectors are more involved with wholesale-retail trade, with 59 and 52 percent of their total staff, respectively, engaged in this trade. Financial service and insurance entities, in contrast, are all in the formal sector, as a result of the stringent regulation to which they are subjected by regional organizations such as the Central Bank of West African States (BCEAO). Table 5.2 presents the distribution of the sampled firms by industry.

The formal sector serves a much more diverse clientele than the informal sector. The most important clients of formal enterprises are the public sector and private enterprises—large or small, commercial or noncommercial. For informal firms, the main clients are households and microenterprises. This illustrates the exclusion of informal firms from selling to the public sector. Often, selection committees for the allocation of public sector contracts demand that bidding firms provide proof of good legal standing, particularly vis-à-vis fiscal and social security agencies. These documents are difficult, if not impossible, to procure if the firm is informal. This does not imply, however, that there are no commercial relations between formal and informal enterprises; it only means that most of the business of informal firms comes from households and other informal firms, while formal firms have more diverse buyers.

As in many other countries, exports are usually a small share of firm sales (figure 5.1). Exports as a share of sales are highest in the formal sector, followed by the large informal sector and, finally, by small informal sector firms, but in all cases they are quite low. For firms in Ouagadougou and Dakar, exports do not exceed 10 percent of total sales. In Cotonou, they are slightly higher, at 18 percent of total sales, for firms in the formal sector. In the informal sector, exports are, on average, only 6 to 16 percent of sales.

Table 5.2 Distribution of Sampled Firms in the Three West African Countries, by Sector of Activity

Activity sector	Benin		Burkina Faso		Senegal	
	Number	%	Number	%	Number	%
Industry	67	22.7	61	20.3	120	38.9
Commerce	104	35.3	155	51.7	122	39.6
Service	124	42.0	84	28.0	66	21.5
Total	295	100.0	300	100.0	308	100.0

Source: Based on authors' firm survey data.

Figure 5.1 Share of Exports in Total Sales in the Three West African Cities, by Formal or Informal Status

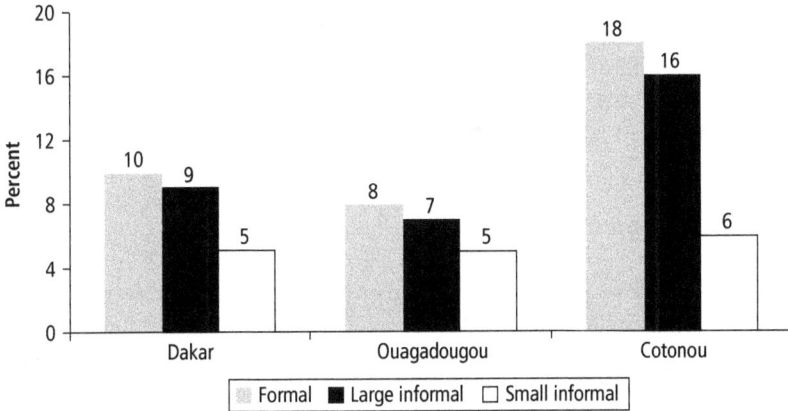

Source: Based on authors' firm survey data.

Patterns of input sourcing in the formal and informal sectors are the opposite of those in output markets: informal firms have a much greater diversity of suppliers than do formal firms. This may be evidence of stricter quality requirements in the formal sector, which would lead formal firms to rely on large commercial enterprises.

Some of the questions in our survey probed the relationship between formal and informal sectors. Given the pejorative connotations of the term "informal," we avoided it in our interview questionnaire. Instead, we used phrases associated with small commercial and noncommercial enterprises, which connote informality to respondents.

Perception of competition among economic actors is acute, particularly among formal firms. Formal firms cited large enterprises as their greatest source of competition, while informal firms cited mainly small enterprises. Competition from imports is also important, particularly for formal firms. Imports account for more than half of the formal domestic market for many products in the three cities. However, for the informal sector, except in Ouagadougou, domestic competitors are viewed as more threatening than foreign competitors.

Formal and informal firms seem to have differing perceptions of the quality of their products. More than 40 percent of formal actors believe that the quality of domestically produced goods is higher than the quality of imported goods. However, less than 20 percent of informal actors share this opinion. This discrepancy suggests that the quality of goods and services provided by the informal sector is low, confirming the hypothesis that a key difference between formal and informal activities is product quality (Gautier 2002).

We attempted to assess the efficiency and dynamism of informal firms relative to their formal counterparts through several indirect questions about product and client turnover. Evidence is mixed. In Cotonou, 30 percent of formal actors reported that product turnover is fast, while only 5 percent of informal actors agreed that products sell quickly, indicating more efficiency in the formal sector. In Dakar and Ouagadougou, informal actors said that products sell quickly, while formal actors complained of slow turnover.

Financing and Investment

Lack of access to credit is generally considered to be a near-universal characteristic of informality and small and medium enterprises, more generally, as noted in chapter 1. Consequently, such firms turn to loans from family, friends, or tontines and usually face high interest rates (Johnson 2004; Akoten, Sawada, and Otsuka 2006).

Our findings largely support the view that informal firms have little access to bank credit, but this is also largely the case for formal firms (table 5.3). Between

Table 5.3 Sources of Financing for Firms in the Three West African Cities, by Method of Financing and Formal or Informal Status

City and status	Internal funding or undistributed benefits	Bank credit	Loan from a family member or friend	Savings, gift, or inheritance
Dakar				
Formal	64	20	4	12
Large informal	62	16	8	14
Small informal	64	8	2	26
Total	64	13	4	20
Ouagadougou				
Formal	67	19	14	0
Large informal	55	14	23	9
Small informal	56	8	20	16
Total	59	10	19	12
Coutonou				
Formal	76	15	7	2
Large informal	64	8	14	14
Small informal	68	15	0	16
Total	70	14	4	12

Source: Based on authors' firm survey data.

4 and 8 percent of small informal firms and between 4 and 12 percent of large informal firms said they had recently been able to borrow from a bank. As noted in chapter 1, in West Africa, formal firms also face substantial credit constraints; the proportion of such firms obtaining a recent bank loan is only 10 percent in Cotonou, 14 percent in Dakar, and 18 percent in Ouagadougou. In addition, a high proportion of firms rely on internal funds (personal savings or undistributed profits) to finance investments. Our results show that most investments in the three countries are financed through personal funds. In Cotonou, for example, more than 70 percent of land purchases in the formal sector and more than 80 percent in the informal sector are financed through personal funds. In Dakar, these proportions are slightly lower, with 65 percent of formal actors and 72 percent of informal actors relying on personal funds to finance land purchases. Almost 100 percent of formal firms and just 40 percent of informal firms in Ouagadougou finance land purchases with personal funds. Remaining investments are financed mostly with grants, loans from family members, or inheritances. Only a minute portion of investments by both informal and formal firms is funded by bank credit.

Interest rates are high across the board, with informal firms facing particularly elevated rates (table 5.4). Formal firms in Dakar and Cotonou typically face rates of about 15 percent, while formal firms in Ouagadougou enjoy the relatively low rate of 12 percent. In Dakar and Cotonou, informal firms must pay rates on the order of 20 percent, while in Ouagadougou rates can rise to 36 percent. The higher rates paid by informal firms can be justified by the

Table 5.4 Interest Rates on Bank Loans in the Three West African Cities, by Formal or Informal Status

City and status	Interest rates on bank loans (%)
Dakar	
Formal	15.3
Large informal	20.7
Small informal	23.2
Ouagadougou	
Formal	12.0
Large informal	35.0
Small informal	36.1
Cotonou	
Formal	15.2
Large informal	22.0
Small informal	24.0

Source: Based on authors' firm survey data.

Table 5.5 Share of Firms Having Difficulty Repaying Loans in the Three West African Cities, by Formal or Informal Status

City and status	% of firms having difficulty repaying loans
Dakar	
Formal	36
Large informal	69
Small informal	70
Total	57
Ouagadougou	
Formal	13
Large informal	58
Small informal	57
Total	45
Cotonou	
Formal	35
Large informal	64
Small informal	92
Total	70

Source: Based on authors' firm survey data.

increased risk involved in lending to them and the high operating costs faced by microfinance institutions.

In Cotonou, 70 percent of all firms interviewed admitted to having great difficulty repaying their loans, whereas in Dakar and Ouagadougou firms reported having relatively less trouble, with 57 and 45 percent, respectively, mentioning the same problems. Formal firms reported fewer difficulties repaying loans than informal firms, especially small informal firms (table 5.5). The share of the small informal sector having difficulty servicing their loans reached 92 percent in Cotonou, 70 percent in Dakar, and 57 percent in Ouagadougou.

Infrastructure

As discussed in chapters 6 and 8, deficiencies in the investment climate are viewed as a primary source of informality, as they raise the costs and lower the benefits of formal sector status.

Our surveys confirm that weaknesses in the business environment are onerous for both formal and informal firms, but more so for firms in the informal sector, as noted in chapter 1. Poor infrastructure is a major dimension of the problem (figure 5.2). Water services in all three cities are surprisingly limited.

Figure 5.2 Proportion of Firms with Access to Public Utility Services in the Three West African Cities, by Formal or Informal Status

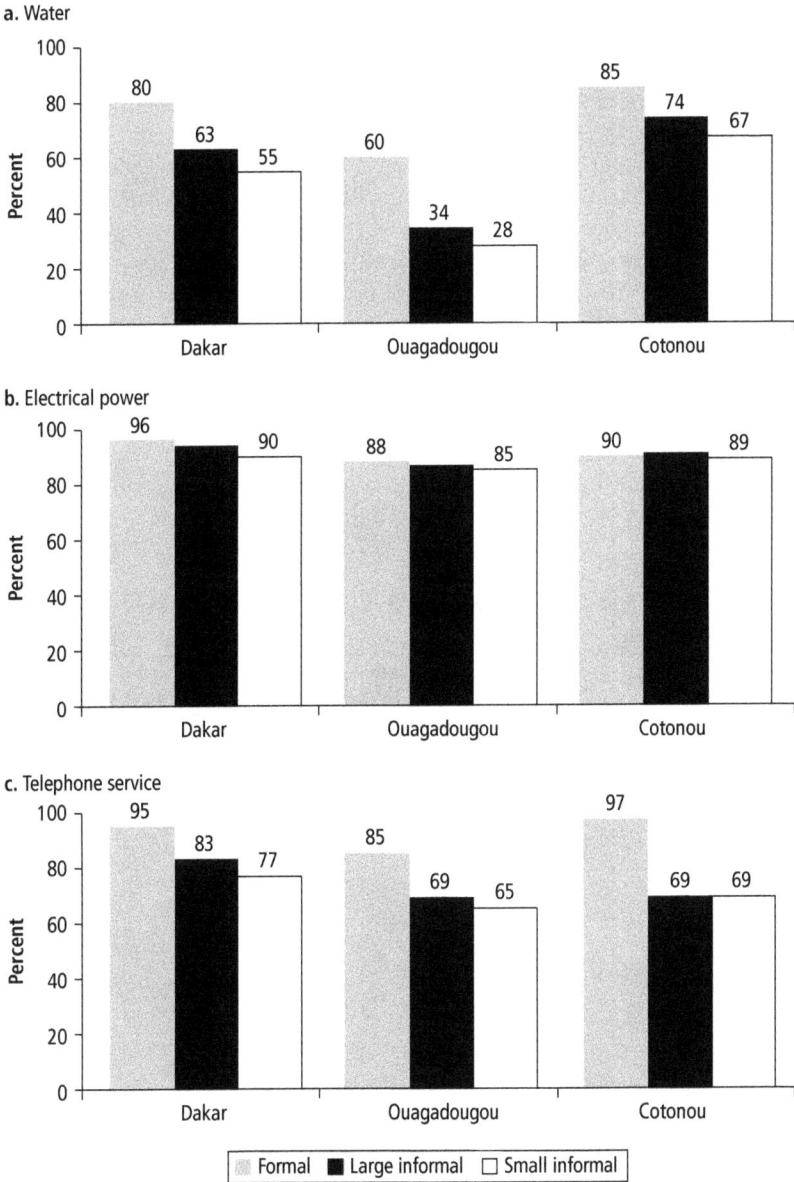

a. Water

b. Electrical power

c. Telephone service

Formal   Large informal   Small informal

Source: Based on authors' firm survey data.

Firms in Cotonou have the best access to water, at 85 percent for formal firms and 67 percent for informal firms. These proportions are 80 and 55 percent, respectively, in Dakar and 60 and 28 percent, respectively, in Ouagadougou. Access to electricity and telephone service is of the same magnitude. In Cotonou, 90 and 89 percent of formal and informal firms, respectively, have access to electricity. In Dakar, 96 percent of formal firms and 90 percent of informal firms have access to electricity, while in Ouagadougou, 88 percent of formal firms and 85 percent of informal firms have access. Access to telephone service is similar, with formal firms enjoying greater access than informal firms, but with inadequacies for both sectors.

Long delays in obtaining connections to utilities are also a problem, with formal firms reporting longer delays than informal firms. For example, in Cotonou, 46 percent of formal firms, 36 percent of large informal firms, and 29 percent of small informal firms reported waiting more than one month for a water connection (table 5.6). Waiting times are lengthier for formal than for informal firms both for electricity (table 5.7) and for telephone services (table 5.8): informal firms are much more likely to obtain a connection within one week. This provides evidence for the claim that access to services is allocated in a corrupt

Table 5.6 Waiting Time for Water Connection in the Three West African Cities, by Formal or Informal Status

City and status	Within a week	Between one week and one month	More than a month
Dakar			
Formal	29	38	33
Large informal	63	13	25
Small informal	50	19	31
Total	46	23	30
Ouagadougou			
Formal	53	40	8
Large informal	73	18	9
Small informal	78	17	5
Total	74	20	6
Cotonou			
Formal	40	15	46
Large informal	32	32	36
Small informal	43	28	29
Total	41	24	35

Source: Based on authors' firm survey data.

Table 5.7 Waiting Time for Electricity Connection in the Three West African Cities, by Formal or Informal Status

City and status	Within a week	Between one week and one month	More than a month
Dakar			
Formal	28	46	26
Large informal	53	24	22
Small informal	32	39	29
Total	35	38	27
Ouagadougou			
Formal	30	63	8
Large informal	48	45	6
Small informal	42	44	14
Total	41	47	12
Cotonou			
Formal	38	17	46
Large informal	30	19	52
Small informal	29	28	42
Total	31	24	45

Source: Based on authors' firm survey data.

Table 5.8 Waiting Time for a Telephone Connection in the Three West African Cities, by Formal or Informal Status

City and status	Within a week	Between one week and one month	More than a month
Dakar			
Formal	55	34	11
Large informal	79	7	14
Small informal	64	30	6
Total	64	27	9
Ouagadougou			
Formal	48	45	8
Large informal	58	36	6
Small informal	60	29	11
Total	58	32	10
Cotonou			
Formal	40	25	35
Large informal	39	26	35
Small informal	48	24	28
Total	44	25	31

Source: Based on authors' firm survey data.

manner and that the informal sector has its own methods for achieving rapid access. Burkina Faso again stands out as a much better performer than Senegal and Benin in the speed of access to telephone services. However, the quality of telephone service is better in Dakar than in Ouagadougou.

Water, telephone, and electricity service outages, one of the signature features of a poor business environment, are pervasive in West Africa (tables 5.9–5.11). Formal and informal actors gave identical responses to questions regarding accumulated interruption times for these services, which is clear evidence of their general unreliability. In Dakar and Cotonou, 90 or more percent of firms reported water and telephone outages lasting up to a week. For electricity, the story is the same in Cotonou and only slightly better in Dakar, with about 60 percent of firms reporting outages of up to a week. Ouagadougou has a lower number of reported service interruptions.

In response to the unreliable supply of electricity, both formal and informal firms have had to purchase expensive generators (figure 5.3): in Dakar and Ouagadougou, 55 percent of formal firms own generators, while about half those percentages of large informal firms own generators. Slightly fewer small informal firms own generators: 31 percent in Cotonou, 20 percent in Dakar, and 20 percent in Ouagadougou.

Table 5.9 Annual Duration of Water Outage in the Three West African Cities, by Formal or Informal Status

City and status	Within a week	Between one week and one month	More than a month
Dakar			
Formal	92	6	2
Large informal	95	3	3
Small informal	92	5	2
Total	93	5	2
Ouagadougou			
Formal	100	0	0
Large informal	100	0	0
Small informal	98	1	1
Total	100	0	0
Cotonou			
Formal	77	13	11
Large informal	71	13	17
Small informal	60	27	13
Total	66	21	13

Source: Based on authors' firm survey data.

Table 5.10 Annual Duration of Electricity Outage in the Three West African Cities, by Formal or Informal Status

City and status	Within a week	Between one week and one month	More than a month
Dakar			
Formal	59	2	39
Large informal	60	5	35
Small informal	64	7	29
Total	62	5	33
Ouagadougou			
Formal	97	3	0
Large informal	96	4	0
Small informal	89	6	4
Total	91	6	3
Cotonou			
Formal	60	8	32
Large informal	45	3	52
Small informal	34	22	44
Total	42	16	42

Source: Based on authors' firm survey data.

Table 5.11 Annual Duration of Telephone Outage in the Three West African Cities, by Formal or Informal Status

City and status	Within a week	Between one week and one month	More than a month
Dakar			
Formal	94	2	4
Large informal	95	2	2
Small informal	96	2	2
Total	96	2	2
Ouagadougou			
Formal	100	0	0
Large informal	92	4	4
Small informal	98	1	2
Total	97	1	2
Cotonou			
Formal	87	4	9
Large informal	85	8	8
Small informal	75	11	14
Total	80	9	11

Source: Based on authors' firm survey data.

Figure 5.3 Share of Firms Owning a Generator in the Three West African Cities, by Formal or Informal Status

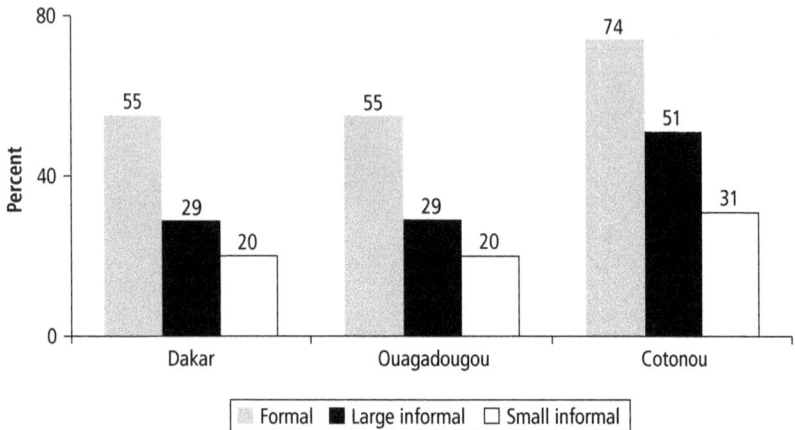

Source: Based on authors' firm survey data.

Taxation

The findings presented in this section derive from the second phase of interviews, focusing primarily on large informal and formal firms. The questions focused on taxation.

Recent literature emphasizes the role of "tax morale" as a crucial determinant of the extent of tax evasion and informalization more generally (Perry et al. 2007). Tax morale refers to the perception of fairness and honesty of the tax system and the government's appropriate use of these revenues. In Latin America, countries in which taxpayers are confident that their money has been put to good use have higher voluntary compliance with tax obligations. This conclusion is strongly corroborated by our findings in West Africa. In Senegal, the proportion of firm managers who expressed dissatisfaction with government use of tax revenues varies between 65 and 100 percent, depending on firm size; the range is 63 to 94 percent in Burkina Faso and 88 to 100 percent in Benin (figure 5.4).

We also examined the effectiveness of the tax authorities in tax collection. One aspect of this issue is fiscal harassment, that is, the extent to which the fiscal authorities disproportionately target formal firms. In Benin, between 17 and 60 percent of managers complained that, once the fiscal authorities identify them as significant taxpayers, they are subject to repeated audits and upward adjustments in payments. In Senegal, 41–55 percent of firms said they feel the same way, compared with 17–50 percent of firms in Burkina Faso (figure 5.5).

Figure 5.4 Share of Firms Expressing Dissatisfaction with the Government's Use of Tax Revenues, by Tax Revenues

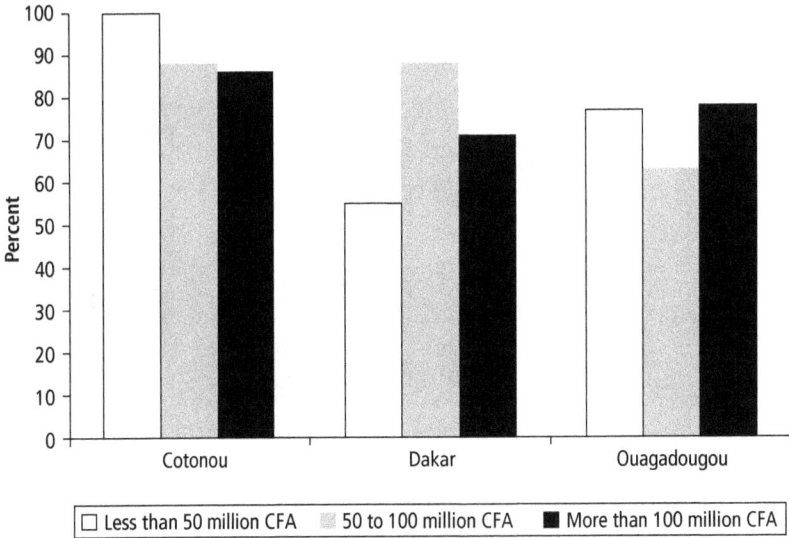

Source: Based on authors' firm survey data.

Figure 5.5 Share of Firms Agreeing That Tax Compliance Entails Subsequent Harassment in the Three West African Cities, by Tax Revenues

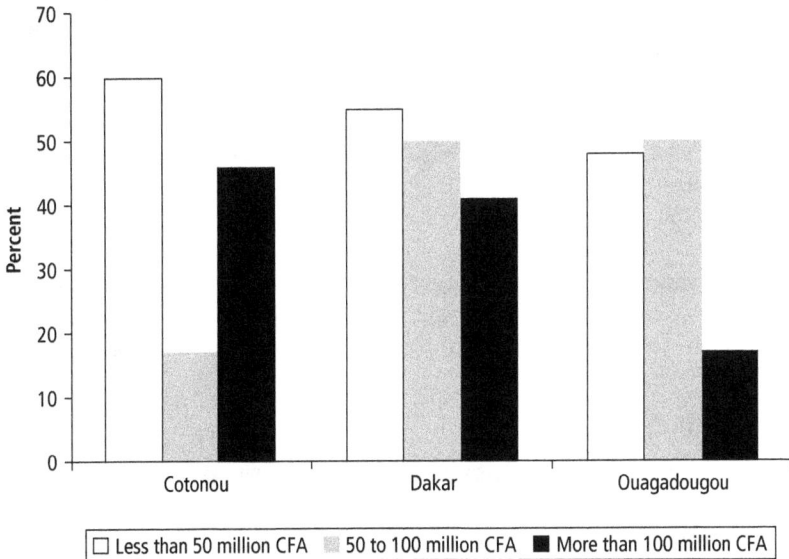

Source: Based on authors' firm survey data.

Figure 5.6 Perception of Time Waiting in Line to Pay Tax Bill in the Three West African Cities, by Formal or Informal Status

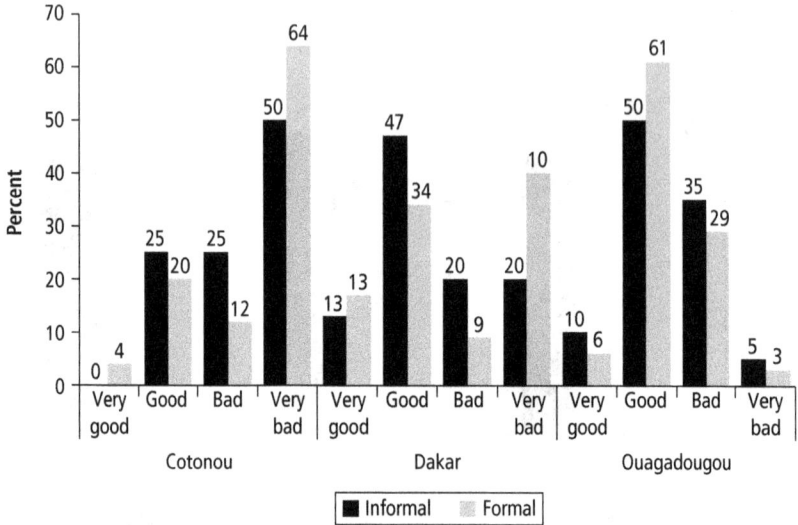

Source: Based on authors' firm survey data.

Tax officials themselves acknowledge targeting formal firms, as discussed in chapter 6. In an environment rampant with corruption, informal firms seem to possess greater flexibility in their relations with the government.

Tax payments must often be made in person, entailing long waits in line. In all three countries, managers view this as a significant hassle for both formal and informal firms. In Benin, for example, 75 and 76 percent of formal and informal firms, respectively, said that this situation is bad or very bad (figure 5.6).

Tax compliance is also weakened by the perceived lack of enforcement by the government. Managers were asked about enforcement in several areas, including social insurance payments, honest accounts, and declarations of income on tax returns. For example, in Senegal, 65 to 100 percent of managers, depending on firm size, said that underreporting of income is pervasive and not sanctioned by the government (figure 5.7).

Other Aspects of the Institutional Environment

In this section, we examine other aspects of the institutional environment beyond those discussed in the previous sections (finance, infrastructure).

Figure 5.7 Share of Firms Saying That Government Adequately Enforces These Obligations in the Three West African Cities, by Tax Remitted

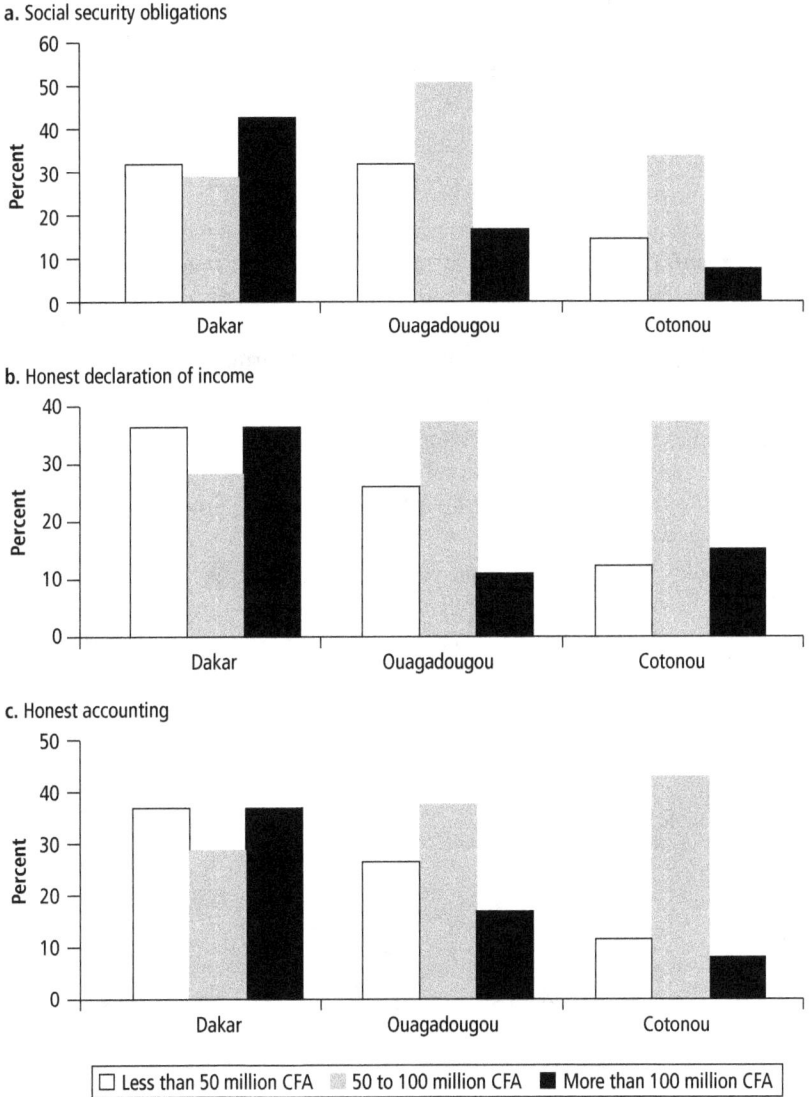

a. Social security obligations

b. Honest declaration of income

c. Honest accounting

☐ Less than 50 million CFA   ▨ 50 to 100 million CFA   ■ More than 100 million CFA

Source: Based on authors' firm survey data.

Information and Communication Technology

A minority of firms use information and communication technology (ICT), such as e-mail and the Internet, for business purposes, particularly in the small informal sector (figure 5.8). Among formal firms, 43 percent in Cotonou, 46 percent in Dakar, and 35 percent in Ouagadougou use ICT; among small informal firms, 14, 20, and 19 percent, respectively, use ICT. For large informal firms, ICT use is between that of formal and informal firms.

Professional Associations

Formal firms are more likely than informal firms to be a member of a professional organization: 35 percent of formal firms and 13 percent of informal firms in Cotonou; 30 and 19 percent, respectively, in Dakar; and 18 and 7 percent, respectively, in Ouagadougou (figure 5.9). The advantages of membership are varied and apply differently to formal and informal firms:

- *Conflict resolution.* Informal firms benefit from conflict resolution services more than formal firms: in Cotonou, 40 percent of informal firms stated that they participate in conflict resolution compared to 12 percent of formal firms; the respective figures are 20 and 10 percent in Ouagadougou and 60 and 40 percent in Dakar.

- *Availability of information on product or input markets.* Again, informal firms benefit from information services more than formal firms in Dakar and Ouagadougou, but formal firms make more use of these services in Cotonou.

Figure 5.8 Proportion of Firms Using ICT in the Three West African Cities, by Formal or Informal Status

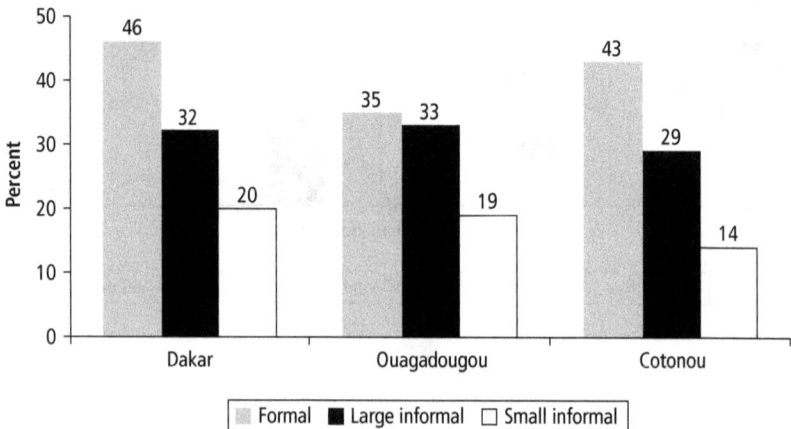

Source: Based on authors' firm survey data.

Figure 5.9 Share of Firms Belonging to a Business Association in the Three West African Cities, by Formal or Informal Status

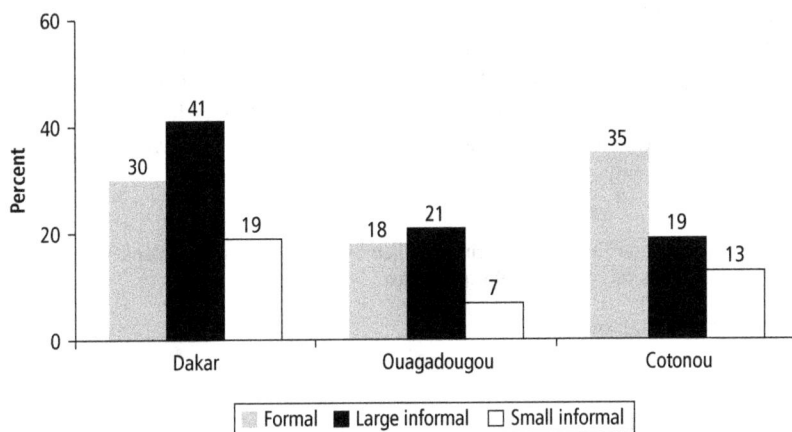

Source: Based on authors' firm survey data.

- *Accreditation to quality standards and reputation.* The informal sector benefits more than formal firms from accreditation in Dakar, while the formal sector reaps more benefits from this recognition in Ouagadougou.

- *Information on current regulations.* In both Dakar and Ouagadougou, informal firms again make more use of information on regulations than formal firms.

- *Perspectives on future prospects.* Both informal and formal firms said they believe that their future prospects are high. In Cotonou, 92 percent of informal actors said they are optimistic about their firm's future. The lowest level of optimism is evident among informal actors in Dakar, where only 82 percent said they are confident of their firm's future. Similarly, a majority of both informal and formal actors responded that they would like their children to pursue their career. Among formal actors in Cotonou, 82 percent responded affirmatively to the prospects of having their children follow in their career footsteps, as did 72 percent of informal actors. In Dakar, 62 percent of formal actors and 60 percent of informal actors responded favorably. Finally, in Ouagadougou, 65 and 72 percent, respectively, responded favorably. This feeling of optimism is also evidenced by the small proportion (30 percent) of workers who said they wish to change professions.

- *Business strategies.* Strategies developed by firms to promote growth in the near term are centered on diversification. We proposed several growth strategies, including (a) canvassing for new clients, (b) changing suppliers in an attempt to cut costs, (c) moving to a less expensive office, (d) limiting pay increases, and (e) none of these strategies. Most interviewees preferred to canvass for clients or did not have a short-term strategy.

- *Relations with government.* More formal than informal firms reported having recent conflicts with government officials. In Cotonou, 34 percent of formal firms reported such conflicts, compared with 21 percent of large informal firms and 20 percent of informal firms (figure 5.10). Very few firms reported conflicts with unions, especially in Ouagadougou, where virtually no conflicts were reported.

Figure 5.10 Share of Firms Experiencing Conflicts with Government or Unions in the Three West African Cities, by Formal or Informal Status

a. Conflicts with government

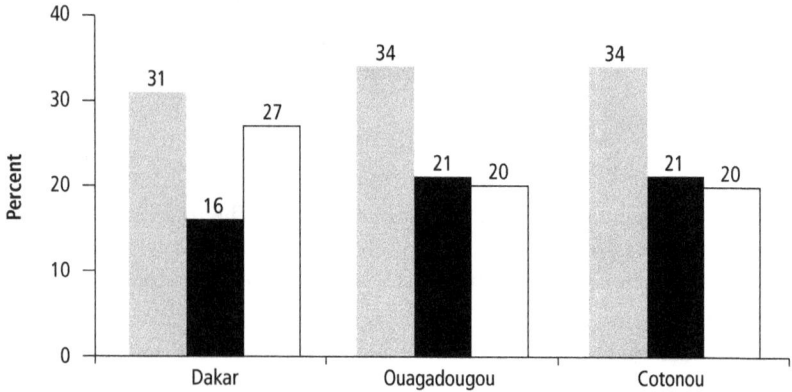

b. Conflicts with unions

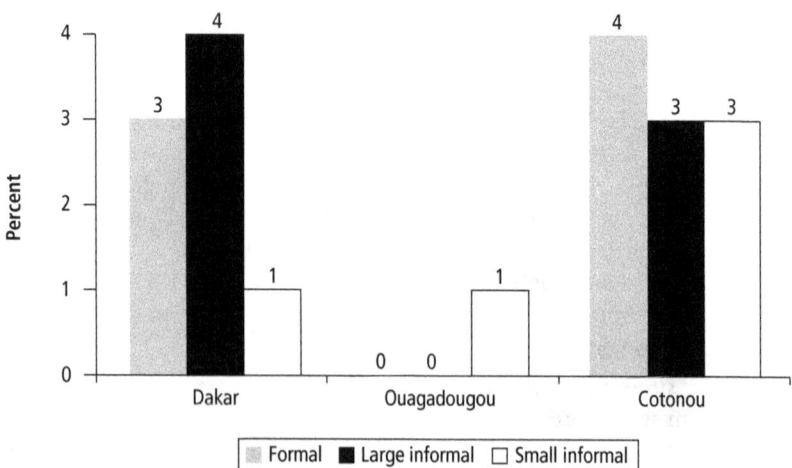

Formal   ■ Large informal   □ Small informal

Source: Based on authors' firm survey data.

The Informal Sector Workforce

Most studies on the informal sector conclude that its workforce differs substantially from that of the formal sector. Self-employment characterizes the informal sector and represents 62 percent of employment in the informal sector in North Africa as well as 70 percent in Sub-Saharan Africa. This proportion rises to 81 percent if South Africa is excluded (Becker 2004). Also, domestic workers and street hawkers represent 10 to 25 percent of nonagricultural employment in developing countries (ILO 2002). A study in Botswana, Kenya, Malawi, and Zimbabwe shows that about two-thirds of informal firms in these countries consists only of the owner (Haan 2006). A study by the Botswana Central Statistics Office finds that most (84.2 percent) informal enterprises are individually operated and that 12.7 percent of enterprises are family owned (CSO 2008). In Latin America, informal self-employment accounts for 40 percent of the workforce (Maloney 2004). Another important characteristic of the informal sector is its high proportion of women: 60 percent of women in the active labor force in the developing world are in the informal sector. In Sub-Saharan Africa, 84 percent of employed women are in the informal sector. According to Steel and Snodgrass (2008), the majority of informal workers (59–83 percent) are women. This confirms the findings of CSO (2008) that 67.6 percent of informal enterprises in Botswana were owned by women in 2007.

Low levels of education among managers also characterize the informal sector. La Porta and Shleifer (2008), using data from African and Asian countries, find that 6.1 percent of managers of informal firms have a university education, compared with 15.9 percent of managers of formal enterprises. In a study of five African countries, Haan (2006) finds that half of informal sector employees have no education at all or have reached only the elementary school level and only 5 percent of employees have reached secondary school. In his study of South Africa, Braude (2005) finds a huge discrepancy between informal sector and formal sector levels of education: 37 percent of informal sector employees have not finished secondary school, compared with only 16 percent of formal sector employees. Similarly, Gelb et al. (2009), based on data from Southern and Eastern Africa, find that, in almost every country, informal entrepreneurs have less education than formal entrepreneurs, except in Tanzania and Uganda, where the proportions are the same.

There are also important discrepancies in earnings between the two categories of workers. El Mahdi and Amer (2005) find that, in the Arab Republic of Egypt, informal sector employees earn only 84 percent as much as formal sector employees. Work in the formal sector is also viewed as preferable because informal sector employees have little job security, work very long hours, and rarely receive social security benefits or are members of a union.

Our surveys confirm these general findings, but with several nuanced differences. Formal sector actors are much better educated than informal sector actors,

Figure 5.11 Distribution of Educational Attainment of Workers in the Three West African Cities, by Formal or Informal Status, as a Share of All Workers in Respective Subgroups

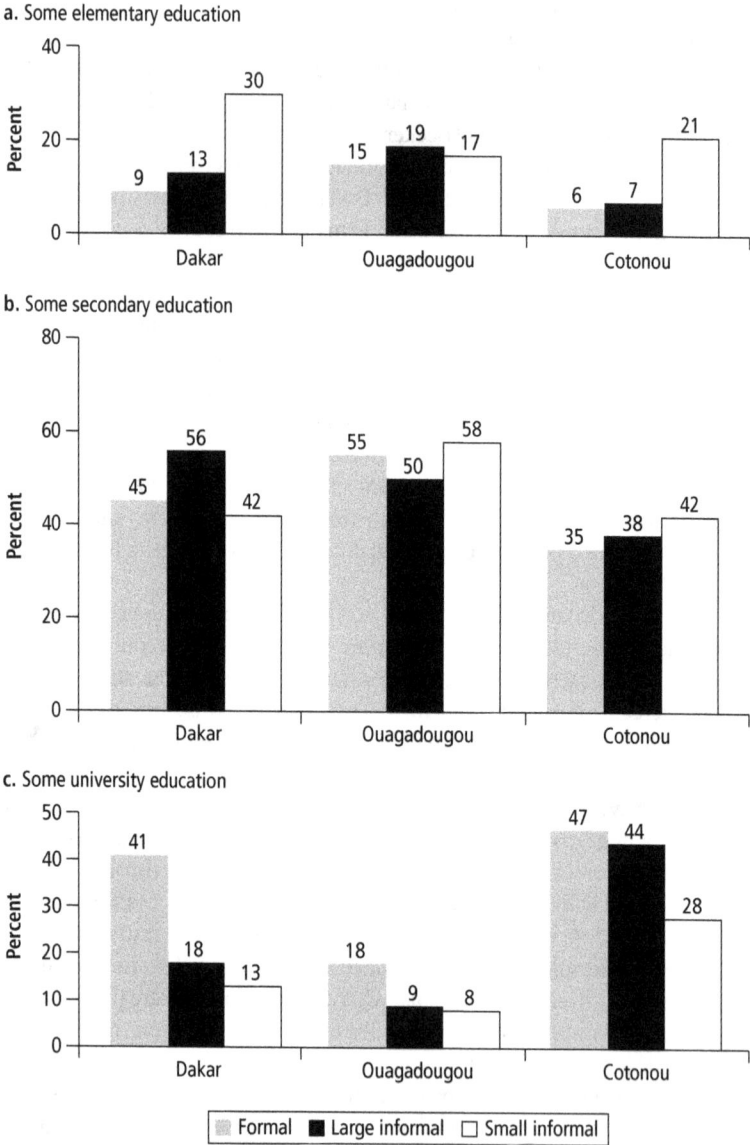

a. Some elementary education

b. Some secondary education

c. Some university education

Formal   ■ Large informal   □ Small informal

Source: Based on authors' firm survey data.

but education among informal sector workers is not as low as one might expect (figure 5.11). In Ouagadougou, 17 percent of small informal workers have stopped their education at the primary level; this is also the case in Cotonou (21 percent) and Dakar (30 percent). Among small informal sector employees, 58 percent in Ouagadougou have reached secondary school, compared with 42 percent in both Dakar and Cotonou. The share of employees in large informal firms with a secondary level of education in the three cities is 50 percent in Ouagadougou, 38 percent in Cotonou, and 56 percent in Dakar. Among formal sector workers, 55, 35, and 45 percent in the three cities, respectively, have some secondary education. In Ouagadougou, 8 percent of small informal sector workers have a university-level education. The figure is 28 percent in Cotonou and 13 percent in Dakar. These relatively high levels of primary and secondary education in the informal sector are surprising. The even higher levels in the large informal sector are especially revealing. Clearly, a substantial proportion of well-educated people are attracted to the informal sector. This is consistent with the finding of Gelb et al. (2009) that productive actors gravitate toward the informal sector in countries with weak business climates and poor enforcement capabilities.

We also find high levels of self-employment in the informal sectors of the three cities, with the highest proportions occurring in Cotonou. In Cotonou, 51 percent of small informal actors work in self-owned enterprises, compared with 39 percent of large informal actors and 25 percent of formal actors. In Dakar, the gap between self-employment in the formal and informal sectors is smaller: only 28 percent of small informal workers, 27 percent of large informal workers, and 20 percent of formal sector workers are self-employed (table 5.12).

Women in the informal sector workforce are less prevalent in West Africa than in other economies. In the three countries examined here, proportions of

Table 5.12 Self-Employment in Two of the Three West African Cities, by Owner of the Enterprise and Formal or Informal Status

City and status	Another individual	Corporation	Myself
Dakar			
Formal	55	25	20
Large informal	54	19	27
Small informal	65	6	28
Total	61	13	26
Cotonou			
Formal	44	30	25
Large informal	43	18	39
Small informal	44	5	51
Total	44	13	43

Source: Based on authors' firm survey data.
Note: No information was available for Ouagadougou.

female workers do not substantially vary between formal and informal sectors, averaging about 11 percent of employment in all sectors combined (table 5.13). At times, women even occupy a greater portion of formal sector jobs than informal sector jobs. Overall, women represent a very small portion of employed workers in both formal and informal sectors in our survey, in contrast to some of the literature reviewed above. Men represent 80–90 percent of managers in all cases, except in Cotonou, where 38 percent of managers in the small informal sector are women (table 5.14).

As expected, a greater portion of formal enterprises have social security contracts than informal entities, although some informal firms have such contracts: 87 percent of formal firms in Cotonou, 81 percent in Dakar, and 79 percent in Ouagadougou have social security benefits. Meanwhile, 24 percent of small informal firms in Cotonou and 14 percent in Dakar and Ouagadougou have signed social security contracts. Firms that do not offer social security benefits justified their decision by citing complex formalities relating to the enrollment of workers and compliance. Most interviewees were in favor of a method of contributions to cover small enterprises. However, informal firms were only willing to contribute up to CFAF 2,000 per month, while formal firms were prepared to contribute greater amounts (figure 5.12).

Table 5.13 Proportion of Female Employees in the Three West African Cities, by Formal or Informal Status
% of firms

City and status	Less than 25% female	25–50% female	50–75% female	75% or more female
Dakar				
Formal	58	20	17	6
Large informal	74	16	6	4
Small informal	80	12	3	5
Total	74	15	7	5
Ouagadougou				
Formal	46	30	17	6
Large informal	59	19	19	3
Small informal	31	16	17	36
Total	39	20	17	24
Cotonou				
Formal	60	18	8	15
Large informal	58	9	3	30
Small informal	64	13	8	15
Total	63	13	8	16

Source: Based on authors' firm survey data.

Table 5.14 Gender of Firm Managers in the Three West African Cities, by Formal or Informal Status

% of firms

City and status	Number of men	Number of women
Dakar		
Formal	82	18
Large informal	94	6
Small informal	91	9
Total	89	11
Ouagadougou		
Formal	81	19
Large informal	87	13
Small informal	62	38
Total	70	30
Cotonou		
Formal	88	12
Large informal	91	9
Small informal	84	16
Total	85	15

Source: Based on authors' firm survey data.

Figure 5.12 Share of Firms Complying with Social Security Obligations in the Three West African Cities, by Formal or Informal Status

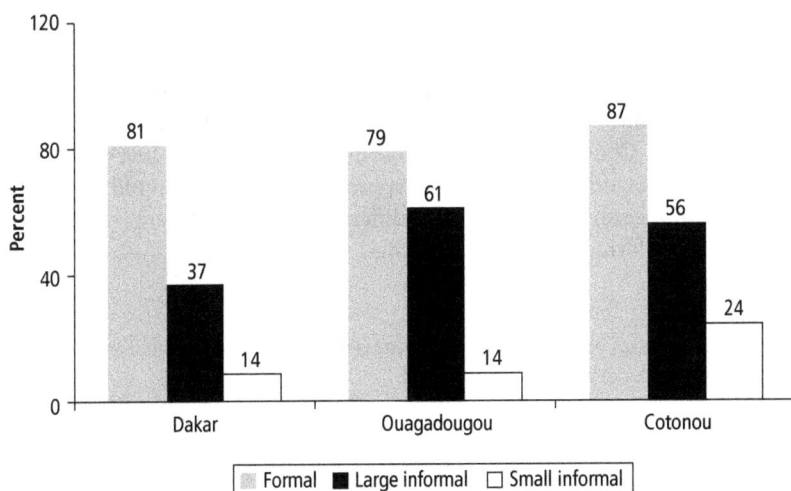

Source: Based on authors' firm survey data.

Conclusions

This chapter compared the characteristics of formal, large informal, and small informal firms. For small informal firms, our survey results largely confirmed the standard findings in previous literature. Small informal firms are concentrated in many of the same sectors as the larger informal firms: commerce, handicrafts, transport, and new and used clothes. Small informal firms sell low-quality products to other microenterprises and low-income households in a highly competitive market. Firm size in this group is tiny, and self-employment is especially prevalent. The level of education of actors is generally low, with a relatively high participation of women in the workforce. Access to bank credit is almost nonexistent due to insufficient documentation, and small informal firms resort to unofficial credit markets with onerous interest rates. Use of ICT is limited. These firms rarely export. Additionally, small informal firms operate in a completely unregulated and competitive labor market, and employees have no social security protection.

Formal firms differ from informal firms in all the characteristics mentioned above. The characteristics of large informal firms tend to fall somewhere in the middle, between formal and small informal firms. The large informal firms' organizational structure differs little from that of smaller informal firms. Volume-of-sales data suggest that large formal firms are generally as big as formal firms, but they have far fewer permanent employees, except in Cotonou. However, formal firms suffer even more than informal firms from deficient infrastructure. In some cases, formal firms have longer wait times for connections to utilities than small informal firms. Moreover, formal and informal firms share the same highly negative view of the business environment.

Overall, all private firms, regardless of formal or informal status and size, face some common problems, notably access to finance, the business climate, lack of competitiveness, and gender imbalance, although to varying degrees. In other respects, however, there are important differences in firm characteristics and challenges. Consequently, policy recommendations from Investment Climate Assessment studies are certainly appropriate, but they should be supplemented with measures targeted to the different segments of the private sector: formal, large informal, and small informal.

Note
1. Some large firms paying the regular business income tax are classified as informal in view of their underreporting of income.

References

Akoten, John E., Yasuyuki Sawada, and Keijiro Otsuka. 2006. "The Determinants of Credit Access and Its Impacts on Micro and Small Enterprises: The Case of Garment Producers in Kenya." *Economic Development and Cultural Change* 54 (4): 927–44.

Becker, Kristina F. 2004. *The Informal Economy*. Stockholm: SIDA Publications.

Braude, Wolfe. 2005. "South Africa: Bringing Informal Workers into the Regulated Sphere; Overcoming Apartheid's Legacy." In *Good Jobs, Bad Jobs, and No Jobs: Labour Markets and Informal Work in Egypt, El Salvador, India, Russia, and South Africa*, ed. Tony Avirgan, L. Josh Bivens, and Sarah Gammage. Washington, DC: Global Policy Network, Economic Policy Institute.

CSO (Central Statistics Office). 2008. "2007 Informal Sector Survey Preliminary Results." CSO, Gaborone.

El Mahdi, Alia, and Mona Amer. 2005. "Egypt: Growing Informality, 1990–2003." In *Good Jobs, Bad Jobs, and No Jobs: Labour Markets and Informal Work in Egypt, El Salvador, India, Russia and South Africa*, ed. Tony Avirgan, L. Josh Bivens, and Sarah Gammage. Washington, DC: Global Policy Network, Economic Policy Institute.

Gautier, Jean-Francois. 2002. "Taxation optimale de la consommation et biens informels." *Revue Economique* 53 (3, May): 599–610.

Gelb, Alan, Taye Mengistae, Vijaya Ramachandran, and Manju Kedia Shah. 2009. "To Formalize or Not to Formalize? Comparisons of Microenterprise Data from Southern and East Africa." Working Paper 175, Center for Global Development, Washington, DC.

Haan, Hans Christiaan. 2006. *Training for Work in the Informal Micro-enterprise Sector: Fresh Evidence from Sub-Sahara Africa*. Technical and Vocational Education and Training. Dordrecht: Springer.

ILO (International Labour Organization). 2002. "Decent Work and the Informal Economy: Sixth Item on the Agenda." Report VI, ninetieth session of the International Labour Conference, Geneva, June 20.

Johnson, Susan. 2004. "Gender Norms in Financial Markets: Evidence from Kenya." *World Development* 32 (8): 1355–74.

La Porta, Rafael, and Andrei Shleifer. 2008. "The Unofficial Economy and Economic Development." *Brookings Papers on Economic Activity* 2: 275–364.

Liedholm, Carl. 2001. "Small Firm Dynamics: Evidence from Africa and Latin America." *Small Business Economics* 18 (Winter): 227–42.

Maloney, William. 2004. "Informality Revisited." *World Development* 32 (7): 1159–78.

Perry, Guillermo E., William F. Maloney, Omar S. Arias, Pablo Fajnzylber, Andrew Mason, and Jaime Saavedra-Chanduvi. 2007. *Informality: Exit and Exclusion*. Washington, DC: World Bank.

Steel, William F., and Don Snodgrass. 2008. "World Bank Region Analysis on the Informal Economy." In *Raising Productivity and Reducing Risk of Household Enterprises*. Annex 1, "Diagnostic Methodology Framework." Washington, DC: World Bank.

Chapter 6

The Institutional Environment
of the Informal Sector in West Africa

With Ibrahima Thione Diop and Birahim Bouna Niang

In this chapter, we examine the institutional environment facing the informal sector in the three countries that are the focus of this book. We begin with a review of the literature. We then provide a detailed description of the institutions and rules governing the informal sector. We conclude with an assessment of the institutional environment, emphasizing that cumbersome regulations, bad governance, and weak enforcement contribute to the spread of the informal sector, as does the influence of powerful political and religious actors.

State Failures and the Informal Sector:
Hypotheses and Literature Review

State failures are often identified as a central factor contributing to the spread of the informal sector in developing countries. Recent literature views informality as a rational choice in response to the costs and benefits of formal versus informal status (for example, Perry et al. 2007; Kanbur 2009; Djankov et al. 2002; Loayza, Oviedo, and Serven 2005; Ishengoma and Kappel 2006; Aterido, Hallward-Driemier, and Pages 2007; Marcouiller and Young 1995; Johnson et al. 2000). The institutional environment heavily conditions this choice. Formalization means greater access to public services but also requires compliance with regulations and payment of taxes. The extent to which the government enforces rules and sanctions noncompliance is also critical. Many studies have corroborated the importance of these considerations. Three factors affect firms' choice of formal or informal status:

- The benefits of formalization, including the quality of public services and differential access to these services for formal and informal firms

- The costs of formalization in the form of higher taxes and regulatory compliance costs

- The extent to which informal firms are sanctioned for failing to comply with tax and regulatory obligations.

In this section, we review the literature on those aspects of the institutional environment affecting the informal sector.

Access to Public Services

Steel and Snodgrass (2008) and Verick (2006) argue that lack of access to services is a major determinant of informality. Relevant services span infrastructure, capital, education, health, and social security. According to Liedholm (2001), many government programs discriminate against small enterprises and small informal enterprises in particular. He states that most tax exemptions for imports apply only to large enterprises, and most small enterprises do not qualify. By simply eliminating such distortions, governments could stimulate the growth of small enterprises. These authors argue that we should be concentrating less on formalizing the informal sector and more on improving the provision of public services.

Education and training have been identified as important factors in assisting informal firms to grow and transition toward formality. According to many authors (Atchoarena and Delluc 2001; Brewer 2004; Haan 2006; NISER 2007), even more so in the informal than in the formal sector, education has largely failed to promote the kinds of skills and knowledge that are helpful for private sector development. Formal education in Africa retains an antiquated orientation toward preparation for a career as a government official and fails to develop practical skills (such as management and entrepreneurship) that are needed by private firms. According to Adams (2008), most schools that offer training to informal actors in Africa are themselves unregistered and informal. These organizations offer training of dubious quality (Johnson and Adams 2004). Churches and nongovernmental organizations have attempted to close this training gap but have had difficulty meeting the needs of informal actors (Haan 2006). Similarly, although large enterprises devote considerable resources to employee training, small enterprises—especially informal enterprises—do not. According to Nielson, Rosholm, and Dabalen (2007), only 4.6 percent of firms with fewer than 10 employees in Kenya, Zimbabwe, and Zambia offer training programs for their staff. Of firms with 151 employees or more, 81 percent offer training programs. This lack of training confines informal actors to low-productivity and low-profitability endeavors. The most common form of training in informal sectors in Africa is the traditional apprenticeship, which is of dubious quality. Others stress that informal firms and workers have less access than formal firms and workers to some training programs, lines of credit, and insurance. In Peru in 1985, the interest rate for firms in the informal sector was 22 percent, while it was only 4.9 percent for firms in the formal sector (De Soto 1989). This could reflect both cause and effect of the fact that informal businesses tend to be smaller, more inefficient, and more inexperienced and to have a higher mortality rate.

The Regulatory and Tax Environment

Loayza (1997) views excessive taxes and regulations as the main factors determining informality. His empirical model for Latin America finds that tax burdens and labor market restrictions greatly influence the size of the informal sector: a one standard deviation change in these variables raises informality by 0.33 and 0.49 standard deviation, respectively. De Soto (1989) also stresses the role of excessive regulation in informality. Similarly, Loayza, Oviedo, and Serven (2005) conclude that excessive regulation reduces growth and favors the development of the informal sector. Branstetter et al. (2010) and Bruhn (2011) find that relaxation of entry regulations leads to an increase in registration of enterprises, although the effects are concentrated on wage earners who are opening a business or "marginal" firms that are small and have low survival rates.

In the same vein, Arias et al. (2005) find that excessive labor market restrictions reduce productivity and inhibit the adoption of new technology, adversely affecting economic growth. Dabla-Norris, Gradstein, and Inchauste (2008) find that the regulatory framework is the greatest determining factor in the development of an informal sector, followed by access to certain services—financial services in particular—for small enterprises. Gelb et al. (2009) confirm, but refine, this view: they argue that the quality of the regulatory framework, along with the state's capacity to enforce regulations, is vital in determining a firm's decision to join the informal sector. According to these authors, it is important to distinguish between two scenarios: (a) educated individuals manage productive informal firms that have a high potential for growth, in which case improving the regulatory framework and access to services might lead them to formalize, and (b) an adequate regulatory framework is already in place, and the only firms in the informal sector are those that are practicing survival strategies. In this scenario, helping firms to access social services would, at best, enable them to survive. Ingram, Ramachandran, and Desai (2007) test a probit model where perceptions of constraints in the business climate are a determinant of locating in the formal or informal sector. The results show a robust correlation between formality and certain attributes of the business climate—access to electricity, finance, land—but the authors acknowledge that, without panel data, these attributes cannot be established as "causing" formality.

Using data from 69 countries, Friedman et al. (2000) find that the high costs of corruption and bureaucracy push firms toward the informal sector. Similarly, Azuma and Grossman (2002) blame development of the informal sector on predatory governments that siphon off tax revenue for the benefit of the elites. Tax evasion by these elites places excessive tax burdens on formal firms, pushing them to seek refuge in the informal sector.

La Porta and Shleifer (2008) distinguish between the cost of becoming formal, the cost of remaining formal, and the benefit of becoming formal. To determine the cost associated with becoming formal, they take the log of the number of procedures required to start an enterprise legally. To measure the cost associated with remaining formal, they define three categories of proxy variables: the cost of having to pay taxes, the cost of abiding by work legislation, and the cost associated with bureaucratic red tape. The authors define the benefits of remaining or becoming formal as having easier access to public goods and services and being able to defend one's legal rights in a court of law. Analyzing data from several countries, they determine that these three categories of variables are strongly correlated with the size of the informal sector. Apart from these variables, gross domestic product (GDP) per capita has a strong negative correlation with the size of the informal sector, as found in other studies.

Beyond tax and regulatory issues, governmental behavior and enforcement capabilities have a strong impact on private sector behavior. Perry et al. (2007) argue that actors' decisions are strongly influenced by their perception of and relationship with the government. Willingness to abide by laws and pay taxes is strongly influenced by one's perception of the level of honesty and efficiency of the government.

Informal sector firms are also particularly vulnerable to arbitrary state action such as extortion and confiscation of assets by police, customs officials, and others. De Soto (1989) argues that in order to protect themselves against abuse of power by the government, firms in the informal sector pay between 10 and 15 percent of their income in bribes, compared with only 1 percent for firms in the formal sector. Moreover, informal businesses are obliged to remain small so as not to attract attention, inhibiting their development and the consequent gains to the overall economy.

Enforcement of Regulations

Kanbur (2009) argues that a key determinant of informality is lack of enforcement of regulations. Gelb et al. (2009) also find that firms opt for formality when access to public utilities and credit are favorable and where tax and registration rules are enforced. Comparing several countries in Eastern and Southern Africa, they test a probit model, also following Lucas (1978), where the market sorts the more talented managers and productive firms into the formal sector. They find that the model is far more applicable in countries with stronger business climates and better enforcement of regulations. In some countries with weaker business climates, they find that formal and informal firms are similar to each other in all other aspects besides formal registration. They explain:

> To the extent that enforcement and provision of public services are characterized by a high degree of arbitrariness and variability, the concealment func-

tion will be less sharply convex. Therefore, it would pay for an entrepreneur in one country to remain informal while a similar entrepreneur in another country would be better off by operating formally. The benefits of formal registration might not be realized because of poor delivery of financial or other services, or because the concern of business—such as reliable power—is similar for formal and informal firms.

Building on the general equilibrium model of Lucas (1978), which focuses on government enforcement capability, Dabla-Norris, Gradstein, and Inchauste (2008) analyze informal sales by formal firms using data from 40 middle- and high-income countries, none of which is in Africa. They find that the informal sector's growth is more sensitive to the government's capacity to enforce laws (measured by the rule-of-law index developed by Kaufmann, Kraay, and Zoido-Lobatón 1999) than to the quality of public services. According to Dabla-Norris, Gradstein, and Inchauste (2008), firms choose to enter the informal sector to avoid costs associated with formal sector regulations; the firm does, however, run the risk of being apprehended and having to pay a fine. In many developing countries, however, the weakness of the legal system considerably lowers the probability of being apprehended and sanctioned. Consequently, the informal sector grows to a much greater extent. In a related vein, Gatti and Honorati (2008) use data from 40 countries, including several from Africa, to show a strong relation between tax compliance and access to credit. They find that, as noncompliance with tax codes weakens the informational content of balance sheets, access to credit declines. They conclude, "From a policy perspective this underscores the fact that policies directed at improving the functioning of capital markets are unlikely to be fully successful unless they are complemented by policies—such as increased enforcement and simplification of tax codes—aimed at decreasing the level of informality and improving transparency."

Lack of adherence to regulations may not necessarily be due to failures of enforcement but rather to lack of knowledge and capacity. Hence the appropriate response is not necessarily to crack down but rather to educate. Results from the 123 study in Senegal show, for example, that lack of firm registration of small firms cannot be completely explained by deficient government services or excessive regulations. At least 60 percent of these actors claim to be unaware of any particular regulation; either they do not know that registration is obligatory, or they do not know with which institution they must register (Brilleau et al. 2005). UNACOIS, the trade association that represents informal firms in Senegal (Ndiaye 2004), claims that lack of training of informal actors, most of whom are illiterate, is the reason for noncompliance, rather than deliberate violation of rules. Of course, this view should be taken with a grain of salt, but it has some validity, given the lack of training and education of most informal entrepreneurs.

The Institutional Framework in West Africa

In the following section, we describe and analyze the governmental, and in some cases, semi-official institutions that regulate and assist the informal sector in West Africa.

Regional Institutions

WAEMU Commission   In West African Economic and Monetary Union (WAEMU) countries, monetary, fiscal, and trade policies are administered by the WAEMU Commission, which establishes the rules that are applicable to all member countries. In recent years, the commission's purview has been extended to policies in sectors such as agriculture, industry, and education.

WAEMU Customs Union   Benin, Burkina Faso, and Senegal are all members of WAEMU, which features a single currency—the CFA franc—and a customs union. Domestic taxation has also been substantially harmonized.

In principle, the common external tariff and other liberalization and harmonization measures should reduce smuggling. Moreover, customs systems are almost wholly computerized, which should reduce the scope for fraud. But smuggling remains pervasive, as discussed below.

OHADA   The Organization for Harmonization of Business Law in Africa (OHADA) is a system of business laws adopted by the francophone countries of Central and West Africa with the ambitious goal of providing a unified legal framework for business. The goal is to promote investment and growth through harmonization. It prescribes various levels of reporting and tax obligations for enterprises of differing sizes, including microenterprises. While countries have followed some general OHADA principles in their fiscal and regulatory systems, in reality most countries establish practices largely at the national level. In particular, as mentioned in chapter 1, OHADA stipulates differential tax treatment depending on firm size. Countries follow this general principle, but the application differs considerably. The presumptive tax regime, which prevails under many fiscal agencies in the subregion, goes well beyond what OHADA prescribes with regard to establishing a relaxed regime for informal firms (Ndjanyou 2008).

Taxation and Customs

Domestic Taxes   Informal firms avoid the proliferation of taxes faced by formal firms. Formal enterprises are subject to numerous taxes, including the following: corporate income tax, corporate lump-sum tax, wage tax, property tax on buildings that the corporation owns, property tax on real estate, surcharge on undeveloped or partially developed land, registration fees, stamp tax, taxes on consumption of certain products, tax on motor vehicles, special tax on corporate cars, fees for licenses, and more.

Most of these taxes are cumulative and can amount to a significant portion of income. Informal firms are, however, denied exemptions and deductions that reduce the tax burden on formal firms. Value added taxes (VAT) on inputs, for example, are deductible only for formal firms.

The tax systems of WAEMU member countries are similar, but not identical. Revenue collection is split among several agencies, of which the following are the main three:

- The Division of Large Companies (Division des Grandes Entreprises, DGE) collects taxes from the largest companies in the country
- Secondary collection centers, which collect taxes from companies that are subject to formal income taxes but do not qualify for the DGE
- The centers responsible for the taxation of informal enterprises, which specialize in businesses eligible for lump-sum tax collection as well as local taxes, usually collected on behalf of local communities.

The fiscal systems in francophone West Africa in practice do distinguish between firms by size, but not exactly in the way prescribed by OHADA. Here we distinguish between two main fiscal regimes in WAEMU: the regular business tax regime and the lump-sum tax regime.

The Regular Business Tax Regime   Taxable income for firms subject to this regime is obtained from declared sales figures. This assumes that the enterprises maintain regular accounts. The thresholds for eligibility are set, but limits vary significantly among countries and activities. Within this regime, firms are further divided into large and small. Larger firms with sales in excess of a predetermined threshold report to the DGE. The threshold is currently CFAF 500 million (US$1 million) or above in the three countries. In all three countries in our study, the DGE collects around 90 percent of tax revenue. Enterprises assigned to the DGE are subject to a more restrictive declaration procedure: in addition to the accounting documents required of other firms under the regular tax regime, these firms must also submit a detailed table of receipts, expenditures, and sources and uses of funds.

In addition to the DGE, Burkina Faso and Benin further distinguish between the normal regular business tax regime and the simplified regular business tax regime. Firms subject to the normal regular business tax regime have sales of more than CFAF 80 million in Benin and more than CFAF 50 million in Burkina Faso. Firms subject to the simplified regular business tax regime have sales between CFAF 40 million and CFAF 80 million in Benin and between CFAF 30 million and CFAF 50 million in Burkina Faso. Senegal does not distinguish between normal and simplified and has only one unified regular business tax regime.

The Lump-Sum Tax Regime   Firms under the lump-sum tax regime must have sales below CFAF 40 million in Benin, CFAF 30 million in Burkina Faso, and CFAF 50 million in Senegal. This is intended to apply to informal enterprises with limited capacities to maintain records. Enterprises subject to this regime have minimal reporting obligations. In view of the lack of documentation of sales and profits, fiscal agencies mostly estimate tax liabilities and usually apply a single tax for each firm. This single rate is in lieu of taxes on profit, licensing fees, and several other types of taxes that firms subject to regular business taxes must pay. In Senegal, the single tax applied to informal firms is called the uni-fied levy (*contribution globale unique*); in Benin, it is the unified professional tax, and in Burkina Faso, it is the informal sector contribution (*contribution du secteur informel*).

However, certain enterprises cannot become informal, regardless of the level of their sales. These include certain professions such as lawyers and customs agents, corporations, and foreign subsidiaries.

The thresholds and ranges on sales vary considerably within countries, depending on the firm's product lines, and over time. For example, although Benin previously had similar limits to Burkina Faso, it has recently made sig-nificant changes, and further modifications are to be expected.

In addition to these special regimes for informal operators, governments have instituted a variety of programs to reduce tax evasion by informal firms, such as various withholding requirements at the level of customs. In Benin, customs withholds 1 percent on all taxable imports, inclusive of the value of duties paid (with the exception of the VAT) on firms that are registered, includ-ing firms subject to presumptive taxation. For informal importers that are not registered with fiscal authorities, the withholding rate rises to 5 percent. If the importer is subject to the regular business tax regime, this withholding is a pro-visional deposit to be deducted from tax liability at the end of the tax year. If the importer is subject to the lump-sum tax or is unknown to fiscal authorities, the withholding is not recovered. The same system is applied to the road transport tax (TUTR) in Benin, which is a presumptive tax paid annually by businesses in the road transport sector. At the end of the year, the road transport tax becomes definitive for any firm with sales below CFAF 10 million; for others, it is a pro-visional payment that is deducted from year-end taxes.

Despite these efforts, tax evasion remains pervasive. Fiscal officials cite the incoherence of the registration system, with different agencies each providing their own identifiers and failing to exchange information, as the key reason for their inability to ascertain and tax informal sector incomes.

These difficulties are illustrated by one of the largest bastions of informality in Benin, the sprawling Dantokpa market in Cotonou, which houses 23,000 known economic operators with fixed workplaces. This understates the number of operators, as many do not have a fixed locale. Benin's fiscal administration has created a division assigned exclusively to Dantopka (the Dantopka Tax Agency), along with other agencies, including the national management committee for fiscal verification and registration, the rapid intervention brigade, the agency for taxation at the port and other borders, in addition to the customs withholding procedures, noted earlier. Despite all of these efforts, many wealthy operators who handle billions of CFA francs avoid paying for business licenses. Our interviewees noted that many politicians have interests in the Dantopka market and send their brothers and spouses to work there. Many large informal transportation companies operate out of Dantopka. Furthermore, many formal firms engage in informal activities in that market.

Taxpayers are recorded with a unified tax identification number (TIN). But this does not prevent large-scale evasion, for several reasons. First, agents often import more than they declare, and many import on behalf of others. Furthermore, according to our interviews, customs enforcement is handicapped by the lack of links between government computer networks, forcing officials to cross-check records manually. Since 2009, Beninese enterprises under the DGE system are no longer subject to tax withholding. Firms routinely provide false statements and refuse to pay on time, without being sanctioned. According to fiscal authorities, the financial documents presented to them are not reliable. Many firms subject to regular business taxes do not make their payments on time. The informal sector contributes mainly to local government revenues. According to our interviewees, fraudulent accounting is rampant, and the underlying documentation for verifying statements does not exist. Beninese authorities now require account certification to reduce fraudulent bookkeeping.

To identify informal activities more accurately, fiscal administrations have resorted to some similar measures in all three countries. Within each, collection has been decentralized by region and by sectors, such as the Dantokpa branch in Benin mentioned earlier. Officials also attempt to cross-check reported sales figures with other information. In Burkina Faso, officials look at the mobility of workplace, the capital stock, and other factors. Consequently, the actual tax burden varies according to the locale of the activity, the profession, the means of displacement, and the firm's activities and capital equipment.

Overall, despite these efforts, the informal sector largely continues to escape taxation. In Burkina Faso in 2008, the informal sector accounted for a paltry CFAF 2 billion out of a total of CFAF 226 billion in revenues, or less than 1 percent—completely out of proportion to its predominant role in economic activity.

Why are so few taxes collected from informal firms, when they account for such a large share of the economy? Tax collection officers explain that it is very difficult to determine the level of taxable income of informal firms. Suspicions of underreporting of sales are almost impossible to prove. The human and financial resources devoted to investigating and pursuing informal sector tax cheats are, in most cases, larger than the amounts recouped. Consequently, it is more cost-effective for officers to direct efforts toward collecting taxes from formal firms, which are in government databases and pay their taxes. However, many formal actors perceive this approach to be the most significant reason for the expansion of the informal sector. Entrepreneurs in the formal sector complain of unrestrained tax harassment, dissuading informal actors from shifting to formal status.

Informal firms, even large ones, find it quite easy to avoid paying taxes. Informal actors generally have several accountants and can easily find accountants who will authenticate fraudulent documents underreporting income. According to our interviewees, fraudulent accounting is rampant and the underlying documentation for verifying statements does not exist. Beninese authorities now require the certification of accounts to reduce multiple books, but there is little evidence of improvement.

Some informal actors also slip through customs without paying duties by presenting themselves as casual importers, exempting them from providing proper identification. According to our interviewees, even more blatant fraud occurs in the real estate market: buildings with five or more floors in Cotonou do not have identified owners. Tax authorities are unable to monitor the bulk of land and real estate transactions. Estimates of real estate values approved by notaries are drastically understated. Normally, notaries are agents sworn under oath, and their documents are used as evidence in a court of law—at least until they are challenged or proved invalid. Notaries have the exclusive power to grant land and real estate titles and record values. Because of the high cost of fees and taxes for real estate transactions (21 percent of the total value of the transaction for the buyer and 5 percent for the seller in Senegal), buyers and sellers have an incentive to undervalue buildings. Often, clerks (assistants to the notary) will offer to record undervalued prices in exchange for a suitable side payment.

Customs   There is no specific customs regime for informal firms. Much of the merchandise that crosses borders is known to be informal. Indeed, importation of merchandise does not require a business license. No inspection is necessary for imports valued between CFAF 500,000 and CFAF 2 million. Many firms whose imports exceed this limit will divide their merchandise into smaller lots and import them fraudulently under separate orders. In addition, formal firms will often contract with informal operators to smuggle in merchandise and then purchase the goods. Individuals importing no more than CFAF 500,000 worth of goods are allowed to import duty-free after a simple declaration, and there are often gross abuses of this allowance. Most people caught fraudulently importing are only front men.

Smuggling is common through ports because customs supervision is imperfect. Customs verifies only 10 percent of goods presented for inspection; the rest undergoes a risk analysis. Many fraudulent imports pass through borders under false declarations. Fraud occurs most often among imports of the most highly taxed products. These products include petroleum products, tobacco (which is subject to import permits), sugar (also subject to prior authorization), as well as cooking oils. Motorcycle trade between Benin, Burkina Faso, and Togo is an often-cited example: informal operators drive imported motorcycles from Togo to Burkina Faso, taking the opportunity to smuggle goods that they transport on the back of motorbikes or smuggle the motorbikes themselves.

According to customs officials, all economic actors participate at least somewhat in the informal sector, particularly in commerce, from wholesalers to retail distributors. They all import, sometimes legally and sometimes illegally. In the transit sector, formal customs clearance agents often take part in informal business transactions. They sell their seals to informal actors and no longer play a role in customs clearance. These formal sector agents seek out informal agents who have more clients. Certain customs clearance agents are importers as well. Many formal enterprises import merchandise through informal importers in order to lower costs. Customs officials are rather fatalistic about the high level of smuggling, attributing it to long-standing social relationships among ethnic groups such as the Mourides and the Yoruba, as discussed in detail in chapters 8 and 9.

Customs officials reported that, among informal actors, various family members often have separate identification numbers. People change names frequently to evade customs. Customs agents observe this practice when they stop someone for an infraction and charge them a fine. When the perpetrator reports to the authorities, it is often clear that he is an agent for someone else and cannot afford to pay the fine. Often, the individual will claim to be a relative who is not linked to the fraud in question but is stepping in to help. He will then offer to remit a token amount well below the proposed fine. Seeing through these hoaxes, our interviewees noted that the supposed "good Samaritan" is often an employee of the importer. However, in the absence of conclusive evidence, customs agents are forced to accept the token amount or risk not recovering any part of the fine. Customs agents argue that this strategy is more beneficial than reporting the offender to the police. Offenders convicted of such frauds are released after only a short period of time, and, in the interest of recovering anything, it makes more sense for customs agents to deal with offenders directly. Both tax officials and customs agents reported cases of agents selling their identification number to importers. They also reported cases of firms that had declared bankruptcy but were later discovered to be continuing to import.

According to customs authorities, large informal actors are responsible for the bulk of fraudulent activities and it is more advantageous for customs officials to deal with large informal firms than with smaller ones. Large informal firms are more solvent, are better known to customs officials, and have more assets to protect than do small informal firms. Consequently, it is easier to enforce fines on large informal firms than on small informal ones.

Coordination between Tax and Customs Administrations   The customs and domestic taxation agencies share responsibility for raising revenue. Domestic tax authorities themselves are quite fragmented. Tax and customs agencies levy and collect direct taxes, while the treasury collects income taxes and administers spending. However, in certain countries, such as Benin, tax agencies collect their own revenues before turning them over to the treasury. This does not apply to the VAT levied at the border, which is collected by customs. Similarly, many agencies collect taxes on behalf of the treasury. For example, airport taxes are collected by airline companies, and rental charges for cell phones are collected by the national regulatory authority.

The authorities claim that there is a good relationship between the fiscal agency and other finance agencies—customs and the treasury in particular—but acknowledge that these relationships could be improved. To improve the coordination of customs and tax agency interventions, a common identifier (TIN) was created in Benin and Burkina Faso. A similar step is planned in Senegal.

In order to improve communication between customs and tax authorities, an investigative unit was created to bring together officers from both agencies. This unit undertakes after-the-fact investigations, selecting cases based on a few factors:

- Information obtained from informants
- A random sample of certain products
- Whether or not the product is politically sensitive

Once the sample has been selected, investigators compile the taxpayers' fiscal and customs information. In Burkina Faso in 2008, 3,409 violations were recorded, amounting to CFAF 3.6 billion. This process is impeded, however, by the lack of connectivity between networks.

In reality, collaboration between tax and customs remains minimal. Information exchange is limited because both sides are unwilling to collaborate. WAEMU commission officials go even further, arguing that lack of communication exists even within departments. Within tax agencies, for example, departments in charge of the VAT and departments in charge of property taxes do not share files. We confirmed this lack of communication during our visits to national fiscal agencies. We consolidated the lists of enterprises used in different divisions, compared them to the list of enterprises used in the department that oversees all of the divisions, and found many discrepancies between the two. On top of this, competition between customs in different countries to attract greater activity can trump cooperation. For example, Benin and Togo compete for serving as the gateway to the landlocked countries such as Burkina Faso, Mali, and Niger and for smuggling into Nigeria, as discussed in Chapter 9.

Business Support Agencies

The governments of the subregion support small and medium enterprises (SMEs)—informal sector ones in particular—through support centers for financial and administrative regulation. This support is provided mainly through the *centres de gestion agréés* and takes many forms:

- Assistance in credit applications as well as provision of information relating to available financial sources
- Training in accounting, finance, and management and information about fiscal, social, and legal legislation relating to private enterprises
- Preparation of accounting statements
- Assistance relating to fiscal and social security declarations
- Assistance in fulfilling registration procedures
- Assistance in registering with social security institutions
- Organizational assistance—help in creating an organizational chart for personnel management and preparing administrative and accounting procedure manuals
- Assistance in increasing sales

In order to entice SMEs to obey regulations, governments offer them limited tax allowances. In Senegal, for example, eligibility is limited to firms with no more than CFAF 30 million in sales for commercial enterprises, CFAF 20 million for artisan enterprises, and CFAF 10 million for other enterprises. Beneficiaries of the tax allowances are required to produce sincere accounting documents. An external, centralized accounting system was meant to help to ensure the honesty of accounts, but the system rarely conducts evaluations. The official report on this program found that it has had little effect, with fewer than 200 out of 200,000 informal enterprises participating.

In most countries, support funds for the informal sector are available from the ministry responsible for SMEs, the treasury, or other agencies. Government funding for the informal sector in Burkina Faso provides a good illustration of this system. Several organizations have been established to improve access to credit. Loan repayment for these facilities has been dismal. Theoretically, individuals who default on their loans can be pursued through legal means. In reality, however, they always end up being released by the police or by the courts without making good on their obligations.

The ultimate objective of this assistance is to promote transition to formal status, in particular as measured by the number of firms that switch from lump-sum tax status to regular business taxes. By this measure, little has been accomplished, in part due to the poor functioning of the support agencies.

Business support agencies for the informal sector tend to be very bureaucratic, with much red tape inhibiting the effective provision of services. Programs suffer from a grievous lack of coherence: numerous overlapping organizations support informal firms without coordination and with much duplication in their missions and services. This leads to strong competition for the same public resources and turf battles among agencies. In Senegal, for example, several organizations provide support to SMEs: the Agency for the Development of SMEs, the Directorate for SMEs at the Ministry of SMEs, the Directorate of Industry, the National Agency for the Promotion of Youth Employment, the National Fund to Promote Youth, and more. Most of these institutions are managed by different ministries, are autonomous, or are affiliated with the presidency of the republic. Their missions often overlap, and they rarely consult each other.

Registration Procedures

Numerous institutions are involved with registering firms, imposing substantial costs and time for managers. The Ministry of Commerce distributes commercial licenses, commercial registrations, import licenses, and other documents necessary for obtaining a fiscal identification number. The national statistical agency also plays a role in the registration of enterprises and in the compilation of data on enterprises. All registered enterprises must submit some of their accounting and financial statements to the fiscal and national statistical agencies. Of course, they are also supposed to register with the tax authorities at the national and local levels. Firms must also pay fees to register with the Chamber of Industry and Commerce and must certify that they have paid social security contributions and other fees.

There are long delays in obtaining import and commercial licenses. Firms are given temporary certificates and have two years to obtain a permanent commercial permit. The cost of a business license varies depending on the activity and the issuing country. The various officials we interviewed acknowledged the delays and costs, but all blamed other agencies rather than their own. Private sector actors found fault with all of the agencies.

State Failures and the Informal Sector in West Africa

Government policies and institutions, and their failures, shape the informal sector in West African countries. These issues are similar to those highlighted in the literature review presented earlier. All of the following contribute to informal sector growth: the length and complexity of registration procedures, the failings of the judicial system, the inadequacy of organizations charged with recovering loans and providing support to small enterprises (informal enterprises in particular), and the ability of large and influential actors—often with the government's help—to bypass regulations. In this section, we analyze a few of these obstacles to formality.

In West Africa, informal activity is pervasive. Given governments' limited monitoring and enforcement capabilities and widespread corruption, informal enterprises can easily conceal their activities and evade taxes. Firms simply do not list certain activities in their accounting, present falsified financial statements, import goods under multiple fiscal identification numbers, or smuggle goods outright. These practices are, however, not without some risks for the actors involved. Fiscal and customs legislation mandates severe penalties for these types of fraud. Sometimes, perpetrators are apprehended and suffer very severe sanctions, which can put their enterprises in danger of bankruptcy, as seen in chapter 4.

Large informal firms are much more vulnerable to detection and sanctions than are small informal firms. In fact, a sort of fool's bargain exists between the government and large informal firms: the government is often aware of the actions of large informal firms, but tolerates and even indulges them. At the same time, the government has at times cracked down on large informal actors, as described in chapter 4, with large fines or even imprisonment. The customs code is especially draconian, forcing the accused to choose only between accepting the sanctions and going to jail.

The Business Climate

The quality of services (infrastructure, judiciary, finance) affects the choices of firms insofar as one of the benefits of formal sector status is greater access to these services; if these services are of poor quality, what is the point of being formal? Likewise, if formal firms must comply with onerous regulations and high taxes, informal sector status is more appealing. Most studies on the investment climate confirm that countries in the subregion experience a more adverse business environment than do other developing countries (see rankings from the World Economic Forum's World Competitiveness Report and the World Bank's Doing Business indicators). Countries in West Africa are generally ranked well below other developing countries. Steel and Snodgrass (2008) conclude that, in the African context, getting registered and becoming formal are not advantageous for informal firms.

Our findings largely confirm the results of these surveys, but with certain variations. Few enterprises see registration as an obstacle. Of all the enterprises included in the second phase of our study, which focused on formal and large informal firms, only 12 percent had encountered obstacles in registering. Enterprises did, however, cite many other inadequacies in public services.

Our interviews revealed that perceptions of the institutional environment are consistent with the findings of the surveys reported in chapter 5. Actors from the formal sector and the large and small informal sectors all responded similarly concerning their perception of the business environment in their country. Invariably, they pointed to arbitrariness and delays in the judicial system, the high cost of factor inputs, as well as the poor quality of water, electricity, and telephone services. Corruption and inefficiency in government, especially fiscal, customs, and commercial agencies, were also often mentioned. Opinions regarding time for obtaining access to these services vary: some actors said the delays are abnormally lengthy, reduced only by bribes, while others cited some improvement and did not report that bribes are necessary to gain access. Customs clearance agents, for example, cited some improvements in a generally unwelcoming business environment: "We have seen progress in terms of ease of starting a business. The time for obtaining permits has dropped from 126 days to two days. The administration (the legal system, customs, the fiscal agency) is still too slow, however. Our energy costs are the highest in the region. The informal sector provides unfair competition for the formal sector."

Formal and informal actors in retail distribution hold similar views on the informal sector. A supermarket owner complained that the government mismanages its relations with both the formal and informal sectors. He argued that the informal sector mostly arises from this poor management. He told us that the building that houses his firm may be demolished and that the government plans to compensate the owner of the building for lost business, but not him. He admitted that most of his local suppliers are informal. Although the law requires payment by check for all transactions exceeding a certain amount, local suppliers only accept cash. Taking these firms to court accomplishes nothing. He claimed that the state is inefficient and predatory. Advertisements and parking spots are excessively taxed. Moreover, the administration is slow and corrupt. Power outages are frequent, forcing him to buy a generator that is costly to maintain. Credit is expensive, compounding his difficulties. He finished by stating that if his firm were informal, he would earn much more and have fewer hassles. A high-ranking Beninese government official adopted a similar position, stating that the presence of informal firms is justified by the need to provide products and services for poor consumers, for whom formal market products are too expensive. He also claimed that the informal sector is beneficial because it supplements the meager salaries of civil servants. He himself is a civil servant in the highest salary bracket, yet he earns a salary of only about CFAF 300,000. His informal activities cover his end-of-month bills. He noted that the informal sector acts as a sort of social security system, absorbing unemployed labor and providing cheap products; if it were not for informal firms, there would be food riots.

The lack of credible policies to promote private sector development becomes obvious when heads of enterprises are asked about their taxation. Two-thirds said that the state does not make good use of tax revenue, and this proportion rises to 88 percent among medium-size firms (enterprises with sales of between CFAF 50 million and CFAF 100 million). Furthermore, 69 percent of respondents said that the state uses public funds unethically. This proportion rises to almost 100 percent among medium-size firms. Most firms also claim that the state imposes excessive tax burdens on firms, leading to tax evasion. Many also agree that they are exposed to even greater hassles if they formalize their firms. Among all respondents in Senegal, 52 percent said that paying taxes exposes a firm to greater hassles; 59 percent of large enterprises said they share this view.

A Senegalese tax agent explained the problem to us this way: "Informal actors are expensive in terms of the research that we need to carry out to tax them." Indeed, the fiscal administrations of the three countries seem to be of the opinion that the cost of obtaining information on informal firms outweighs the benefit of the increased revenues that would result. Consequently, they focus their efforts on the firms they can easily identify and from which they can collect the full amount of taxes due—in other words, formal firms, as stated earlier.

Most respondents have a negative view of the level of taxes and the management of tax collections. The majority said that fiscal pressure is very high (60 percent of all firms and 67 percent of large informal firms). In addition, 46 percent of respondents reported long queues that make tax payment more difficult; 20 percent said they find it hard to declare taxes and 42 percent said that the collection service is poorly managed.

The state's failure to enforce obligations is also widely recognized. In Senegal, for example, 68 percent of interviewees said that the state does not adequately enforce regulations concerning workers' social security; the same proportion said there is inadequate verification of honesty in revenue declarations and accounting. The perceived lack of enforcement capabilities on the part of government is one of the most important determinants of informality.

Inadequate Public Services

Discrimination against the informal sector in access to services does not seem to be a major problem in West Africa. Public services are poor for both formal and informal firms. All firms suffer from similar constraints in this respect.

Education   The problem with education is not so much lack of resources but misdirected focus. Governments devote a large share of their resources to education and training services. In Senegal, education and training account for more than 40 percent of the operating budget. These resources, however, are devoted mainly to general education, with very little allocated for practical training for enterprises. Formal enterprises suffer as much as informal enterprises from the lack of practical orientation. Training is mostly on the job and, for most informal firms, in the form of apprenticeships. Young people who drop out of school are often pushed by their parents toward informal firms, where they can be enrolled as apprentices. They are used for small tasks and are paid so little (or not paid at all) that they are basically a source of free labor. The same apprenticeship training occurs in formal enterprises. All formal and informal actors, regardless of whether they work in textiles, fishing, or other manufacturing sectors, decry government's failure to provide much-needed practical training for workers (Golub and Mbaye 2002).

Financial Services   As we have seen, most informal firms, and almost all small firms, have little access to credit. These enterprises must resort to informal forms of credit, such as loans from family, friends, or tontines, which generally charge high rates of interest (Johnson 2004; Akoten, Sawada, and Otsuka 2006), as reported in chapter 5 based on our survey data.

Although firms in the large informal sector have access to bank credit, many of them continue to make use of personal funds or funds from their families or other personal relations. However, this use of personal savings is a matter of choice rather than necessity—these firms have all the necessary documents required to obtain a bank loan. Most of these documents are, of course, fraudulent, but this would not be an impediment to accessing bank credit. These firms generally eschew bank credit because the conditions of this credit are onerous and because the increased transparency of their business income could increase their exposure to the tax authorities. In an interview, one large informal firm complained about the high cost of credit, citing interest between 13 and 17 percent.

Tax Incentives   Discrimination against small informal firms occurs, however, with regard to exemptions and subsidies for which informal firms are ineligible. The VAT, which is collected by the firm and transferred to the government, is an example of this type of tax. Firms are supposed to pay the VAT in advance, when purchasing inputs, and are then supposed to be reimbursed by the fiscal administration for exemptions. Firms must, however, present credible documents for reimbursement, which most informal enterprises cannot do. Informal firms also do not benefit from exemptions on other inputs, like machines and equipment, which formal firms can obtain under several regimes, such as the investment code and the free zones. However, many formal firms frequently fail to receive refunds owed to them, while large informal firms usually have little trouble obtaining exemptions and refunds.

The investment code regime excludes small informal firms because the minimum amount that firms must invest to benefit from the exemption is higher than what most small firms are capable of investing. The free trade zone regime, the free trade point regime, and the free status regime also exclude informal firms because of investment minimums. As with the other exemptions, small informal firms are excluded; large informal firms, however, have the necessary connections and have no trouble providing the required paperwork to benefit from the exemption.

Corruption and the Power of Large, Influential Actors

Corruption and failure to enforce rules and regulations are also major determinants of informality. The corruption that exists at all rungs of society contributes to the flourishing of large informal firms. Often, they are well connected politically, which offers them some impunity. Court decisions are frequently challenged, and the press often reports corruption scandals in the courts. Large informal firms are supported by a chain of collusion that involves customs, the administration, and the courts. A customs authority from one of the countries we visited confided to us, "When we arrest a person for fraud, we quickly offer him a deal and do our best to ensure that the case does not get to the tribunal or to the police; once there, one is never sure what the outcome will be."

In our interviews, truckers confirmed this negative view of the judiciary. One of them explained, "The judicial system is slow and corrupt; we have created arbitration centers, in conformity with OHADA provisions. There are designated arbitrators and mediators, who can be lawyers, heads of enterprises, or others, but arbitration rulings are often challenged."

Some large informal firms also rely on Islamic brotherhoods for support, as discussed in chapter 8, particularly in cross-border trade (chapter 9). Cross-border trade between Senegal and The Gambia offers a good illustration (Golub and Mbaye 2009). This trade has long been dominated by well-identified social and religious groups, such as the *baolbaol* (traders from the Mouride brotherhood), Guineans, and Mauritanians. The Mouride brotherhood plays an important role in this process. Collusion between the Senegalese state and heads of the Mourides has been well documented. In 1986, after the partial deregulation of rice imports, with 25 percent of the market allocated to private enterprises, one of the largest transporters benefiting from the clientelistic allocation of market shares was the personal secretary to the caliph of the Mourides.

Conclusion

This chapter focused on how the institutional and policy environment affects the decision of firms to operate in the informal sector. As in much of the previous literature on developing countries, weaknesses in the business climate are very important determinants of the spread of informality in West Africa. Formal businesses are subject to a proliferation of taxes, resulting in numerous duplicative levies that entail onerous compliance costs. Another major problem is lack of cooperation among government agencies, particularly between customs and tax authorities. Also, there are a large number of underfunded and ineffective government agencies with overlapping and unclear mandates.

State failures also include corruption, bureaucracy, and the establishment of state rent-seeking systems. Corruption at all rungs of society contributes to the flourishing of large informal firms. The weaknesses of the state are also manifest at the level of tax collection. Fiscal authorities disproportionately target formal firms. Many firm managers also believe that underreporting of income is pervasive and not sanctioned by the government.

Due largely to these problems, indicators of the business climate are poor. In this regard, our surveys and interviews for the most part corroborate standard international rankings and indicators of the business environment.

References

Adams, Arvil V. 2008. "Skills Development in the Informal Sector of Sub-Saharan Africa." World Bank, Washington, DC.

Akoten, John E., Yasuyuki Sawada, and Keijiro Otsuka. 2006. "The Determinants of Credit Access and Its Impacts on Micro and Small Enterprises: The Case of Garment Producers in Kenya." *Economic Development and Cultural Change* 54 (4): 927–44.

Arias, Omar, Andreas Blom, Mariano Bosch, Wendy Cunningham, Ariel Fiszbein, Gladys Lopez Acevedo, William Maloney, Jaime Saavedra, Carolina Sanchez-Paramo, Mauricio Santamaria, and Lucas Siga. 2005. "Pending Issues in Protection, Productivity Growth, and Poverty Reduction." Policy Research Working Paper 3799, World Bank, Washington, DC, December.

Atchoarena, David, and A. M. Delluc. 2001. *Revisiting Technical and Vocational Education in Sub-Saharan Africa: An Update on Trends, Innovations, and Challenges.* IIEP/Prg. DA/1, 320. Paris: International Institute for Educational Planning.

Aterido, Reyes, Mary Hallward-Driemeier, and Carmen Pages. 2007. "Investment Climate and Employment Growth: The Impact of Access to Finance, Corruption, and Regulations across Firms." IZA Discussion Paper 3138, Institute for the Study of Labor, Bonn, November.

Azuma, Yoshiaki, and Herschel I. Grossman. 2002. "A Theory of the Informal Sector." NBER Working Paper 8823, National Bureau for Economic Research, Cambridge, MA.

Branstetter, Lee G., Francisco Lima, Lowell J. Taylor, and Ana Venancio. 2010. "Do Entry Regulations Deter Entrepreneurship and Job Creation? Evidence from Recent Reforms in Portugal." NBER Working Paper 16473, National Bureau for Economic Research, Cambridge, MA, October.

Brewer, Laura. 2004. "Youth at Risk: The Role of Skills Development in Facilitating the Transition to Work." Skills Working Paper 19, ILO, Geneva.

Brilleau, Alain, Siriki Coulibaly, Flore Gubert, Ousman Koriko, Mathias Kuepie, and Eloi Ouedraogo. 2005. "Le secteur informel dans l'agglomération de Dakar: Performances, insertion, perspectives; Enquête 123, phase 2." Stateco 99, 65–88. Direction de la Prévision et de la Statistique, Dakar.

Bruhn, Miriam. 2011. "License to Sell: The Effect of Business Registration Reform on Entrepreneurial Activity in Mexico." *Review of Economics and Statistics* 93 (February): 382–86.

Dabla-Norris, Era, Mark Gradstein, and Gabriela Inchauste. 2008. "What Causes Firms to Hide Output? The Determinant of Informality." *Journal of Development Economics* 85 (1-2): 1–27.

De Soto, Hernando. 1989. *The Other Path: The Invisible Revolution in the Third World.* New York: Harper and Row.

Djankov, Simeon, Ira Lieberman, Joyita Mukherjee, and Tatiana Nenova. 2002. "Going Informal: Benefits and Cost." World Bank, Washington, DC, April.

Friedman, Eric, Simon Johnson, Daniel Kaufmann, and Pablo Zoido-Lobatón. 2000. "Dodging the Grabbing Hand: The Determinants of Unofficial Activity in 69 Countries." *Journal of Public Economics* 76 (3): 459–93.

Gatti, Roberta, and Maddalena Honorati. 2008. "Informality among Formal Firms: Firm-Level, Cross-Country Evidence on Tax Compliance and Access to Credit." Policy Research Working Paper 4476, World Bank, Washington, DC.

Gelb, Alan, Taye Mengistae, Vijaya Ramachandran, and Manju Kedia Shah. 2009. "To Formalize or Not to Formalize? Comparisons of Microenterprise Data from Southern and East Africa." Working Paper 175, Center for Global Development, Washington, DC.

Golub, Stephen S., and Ahmadou Aly Mbaye. 2002. "Obstacles and Opportunities for Senegal's International Competitiveness: Case Studies of the Groundnut, Fishing, and Textile/Clothing Sectors." Africa Region Working Paper 36, World Bank, Washington, DC.

———. 2009. "National Policies and Smuggling in Africa: The Case of The Gambia and Senegal." *World Development* 37 (37): 595–606.

Haan, Hans Christian. 2006. *Training for Work in the Informal Micro-Enterprise Sector: Fresh Evidence from Sub-Sahara Africa.* Evidence from Sub-Sahara Africa Series: Technical and Vocational Education and Training: Issues, Concerns, and Prospects, vol. 3. Dordrecht: Springer.

Ingram, Michael, Vijaya Ramachandran, and Vyjayanti Desai. 2007. "Why Do Firms Choose to Be Informal? Evidence from Enterprise Surveys in Africa." World Bank, Washington, DC.

Ishengoma, Esther, and Robert Kappel. 2006. "Economic Growth and Poverty: Does Formalisation of Informal Enterprises Matter?" GIGA Working Paper 20, German Institute of Global and Area Studies, Hamburg.

Johanson, Richard, and Arvil V. Adams. 2004. "Skills Development in Sub-Saharan Africa: Regional and Sectoral Studies." World Bank, Washington, DC.

Johnson, Simon, Daniel Kaufmann, John McMillan, and Christopher Woodruff. 2000. "Why Do Firms Hide? Bribes and Unofficial Activity after Communism." *Journal of Public Economics* 76 (3, June): 495–520.

Johnson, Susan. 2004. "Gender Norms in Financial Markets: Evidence from Kenya." *World Development* 32 (8): 1355–74.

Kanbur, Ravi. 2009. "Conceptualizing Informality: Regulation and Enforcement." Working Paper 09-11, Department of Applied Economics and Management, Cornell University, Ithaca, NY.

Kaufmann, Daniel, Aart Kraay, and Pablo Zoido-Lobatón. 1999. "Aggregating Governance Indicators." World Bank, Washington, DC.

La Porta, Rafael, and Andrei Shleifer. 2008. "The Unofficial Economy and Economic Development." *Brookings Papers on Economic Activity* 2: 275–364.

Liedholm, Carl. 2001. "Small Firm Dynamics: Evidence from Africa and Latin America." *Small Business Economics* 18 (Winter): 227–42.

Loayza, Norman. 1997. "The Economics of the Informal Sector: A Simple Model and Some Empirical Evidence from Latin America." Policy Research Working Paper 1727, World Bank, Washington, DC.

Loayza, Norman V., Ana Maria Oviedo, and Luis Serven. 2005. "The Impact of Regulation, Growth, and Informality: Cross-Country Evidence." Policy Research Working Paper 3623, World Bank, Washington, DC.

Lucas, R. E. 1978. "On the Size Distribution of Business Firms." *Bell Journal of Economics* 9 (2, Autumn): 508–23.

Marcouiller, Douglas, and Leslie Young. 1995. "The Black Hole of Graft: The Predatory State and the Informal Economy." *American Economic Review* 85 (3): 630–46.

Ndiaye, Ousmane. S. 2004. "Contribution de l'UNACOIS á la cérémonie de lancement du projet de promotion des exportations du Sénégal." Dakar.

Ndjanyou, Laurent. 2008. "Portes du système comptable OHADA sur la production et la diffusion de l'information financière des entreprises de petite dimension." *Revue Africaine de l'Intégration* 2 (2, July): 1–26.

Nielson, Helena S., Michael Rosholm, and Andrew Dabalen. 2007. "Evaluation of Training in African Enterprises." *Journal of Development Economics* 84 (1): 310–29.

NISER (Nigerian Institute of Social and Economic Research). 2007. "Report of Baseline Study of Employment Generation in the Informal Sector of the Nigerian Economy." Report prepared for the Africa Capacity Building Foundation and the ILO, Ibadan.

Perry, Guillermo E., William F. Maloney, Omar S. Arias, Pablo Fajnzylber, Andrew Mason, and Jaime Saavedra-Chanduvi. 2007. *Informality: Exit and Exclusion.* Washington, DC: World Bank.

Steel, William F., and Don Snodgrass. 2008. "World Bank Region Analysis on the Informal Economy." In *Raising Productivity and Reducing Risk of Household Enterprises.* Annex 1, "Diagnostic Methodology Framework." Washington, DC: World Bank.

Verick, Sher D. 2006. "The Impact of Globalization on the Informal Sector in Africa." Economic and Social Policy Division, United Nations Economic Commission for Africa and the Institute for the Study of Labor, Bonn.

Chapter 7

Informality and Productivity

With Dominique Haughton

Central to the impact of informality on development is its relation to productivity. Previous research has shown that informality is associated with lower growth and productivity. The productivity gap could be either a consequence or a cause of informality. Our results for West Africa confirm that informal firms have lower productivity than formal firms, with an important twist: the differential between formal and informal firms is much smaller for large informal firms than for smaller informal firms. We also investigate the sources of productivity differences and the direction of causality between productivity and informality.

The Importance of Productivity

In recent years, there has been renewed interest in examining the trends and determinants of productivity, both in the economic literature and among policy makers. Krugman (1994) states concisely, "Productivity isn't everything, but in the long run, it is almost everything. A country's ability to improve its standard of living over time depends almost entirely on its ability to raise its output per worker." Indeed, there is no disputing that productivity is central to a country's growth and standard of living. Furthermore, productivity affects international competitiveness, employment, and overall well-being.

In the empirical literature on growth accounting, total factor productivity (TFP) growth is estimated to account for one-third to half of the observed growth rate of gross domestic product (GDP) per capita (Nehru and Dhareshwar 1994). The Organisation for Economic Co-operation and Development (OECD 2008) estimates that the contribution of TFP to GDP growth averaged somewhere between 1 and 3 percentage points between 1985 and 2006 for G7 countries and up to 6 percentage points for other OECD countries. Some economists, such as Nordhaus (2001) and Krugman (1990), consider productivity to be a good indicator of standard of living. Causa and Cohen (2005) note, "The industrial productivity of a country is one of the key determinants of its prosperity." Schreyer and Pilat

(2001) observe that computed productivity reflects a variety of factors, including technological progress, competition in product markets, scale economies, and state of the business cycle, among others. In recent years, a controversy over the nature of the relationship between productivity and growth has arisen from what is now commonly referred to as the productivity paradox. Several studies have found that investment in information and communication technologies (ICTs) does not, in general, appear to raise productivity (Sharpe 1997). It has become increasingly clear that the difficulty of measuring productivity in the service sector can explain much of this productivity paradox.

Many studies have also focused on the relationship between productivity and international competitiveness. Mbaye and Golub (2003) define competitiveness in terms of relative unit labor costs—the ratio of wages to labor productivity in one country compared to the ratio in others. If productivity grows more rapidly than labor compensation, cost competitiveness tends to improve, boosting exports. Mbaye and Golub confirm that relative unit labor costs affect exports of manufactured products for Senegal. Golub and Edwards (2004) obtain similar results for South Africa using the same methodology. Likewise, Causa and Cohen (2005) find a correlation between low productivity in developing countries and difficulties in exporting. The OECD (2008) also finds that increasing productivity boosts competitiveness by lowering unit labor costs.

Productivity also largely determines the standard of living, since per capita income is clearly associated with output per worker. Poverty tends to decline with increasing output and, therefore, with increasing productivity. For example, in Senegal, the elasticity of poverty is much greater with respect to per capita income than with respect to inequality, as measured by the Gini coefficient (Mbaye 2006).[1]

Productivity and Informality in Developing Countries

A large literature shows a strong negative correlation between informality and productivity of firms in developing countries. In their review of factors explaining firm growth, Steel and Snodgrass (2008) distinguish between factors external to the firm (market demand for goods produced by the firm, a favorable business environment, quality of infrastructure, access to resources, financing, inputs, training and other firm development services, and information on the market) and factors internal to the firm (quality of staff, management, and supervisors). They find that the productivity differential between the two categories of firms is due mainly to unequal access to public services. Using a model of endogenous growth, Loayza (1997) develops a mechanism whereby informal sector expansion is negatively correlated with overall economic growth. The negative effect of informality on growth is due to the fact that the informal sector creates a sort of congestion in the use of certain public goods. Informal actors consume these goods, but do not contribute to their financing through taxes. He finds support for his model with empirical tests on Latin American data. Gelb et al. (2009) compare the productivity of formal firms and informal firms using surveys on the investment climate for several countries in Southern and Eastern Africa. Their results confirm that formal sector firms are, on average, more productive than informal ones, but the gap between formal and informal firms is much less for East African countries than for Southern African countries. They attribute this to the difference in the quality of the business environment and the enforcement of rules. The relative weakness of the state in East Africa undermines the performance of formal firms, thereby lowering the gap between formal and informal firm productivity. That is, the benefits of formalization are low in terms of productivity differentials if business services are of poor quality or if informal operators can evade taxes and regulations.

La Porta and Shleifer (2008) obtain related results using World Bank informal sector surveys covering registered and unregistered firms in 13 countries (6 from Africa) and microenterprise surveys covering 14 countries (India and 13 from Africa). Their most salient result is that the productivity of formal firms is substantially greater than that of informal firms, although most strongly so in India. However, once they control for expenditure on inputs, human capital of the top manager, and firm size, being unregistered has little additional impact on productivity. By contrast, Perry et al. (2007) find a residual negative impact of informality on productivity, even when other characteristics are controlled for. Dabla-Norris, Gradstein, and Inchauste (2008) also find a fairly strong correlation between informality and productivity of firms. None of these studies, however, considers large informal firms.

Perry et al. (2007), using aggregated data, find that the connection between informality and low productivity is nuanced in Latin America. According to them, informal entrepreneurs are well aware of their limitations with regard to access to capital and skilled labor. Therefore, they tend to operate in sectors where it is possible to produce more efficiently on a small scale. This is facilitated by the fact that product demand in sectors where the informal sector thrives tends to be negatively correlated with per capita income, and those sectors predominate in most developing countries. Moreover, even in instances where a productivity differential favors formal businesses, informal businesses compete successfully by evading taxes and other charges levied on formal firms. Perry et al. also cast doubt on the negative effect of informality on growth, finding that the coefficient of informality is not robust in a regression on per capita income. The problem is that most of the variables used to explain growth are also correlated with the informal sector. Thus it is quite difficult to distinguish their direct impact on growth from the impact of informality. When they consider the relationship between informality and productivity using disaggregated data, they find a 29 percent difference, on average, in labor productivity between the formal and informal sectors of seven Latin American and Caribbean countries in their sample. They find that the productivity of firms that started as informal but later formalized was higher than that of firms that started and remained informal, suggesting that formalization may have a positive effect on productivity and growth.

Methodology

To compare productivity levels between the formal and informal sectors for our survey sample, we compute two alternative measures of productivity with our survey data: labor productivity and total factor productivity (Harrigan 1997; Mbaye 2003; Mbaye and Golub 2003). Labor productivity, LP, is measured using the following ratio:

$$LP_i = \frac{Q_i}{L}, \qquad (7.1)$$

where Q is the value added and L is the number of employees for firm i, both permanent and nonpermanent.

In order to measure total factor productivity, we use the Cobb-Douglas production function: $Q_i = AL_i^{\alpha}K_i^{\beta}$, where K is capital stock and α and β are the respective shares of labor and capital in total factor income:

$$TFP_i = \frac{Q_i}{L_i^{\alpha}K_i^{\beta}} = A. \qquad (7.2)$$

Under the usual assumption of constant returns to scale, we have $\alpha + \beta = 1$. TFP can be estimated using a log-linear version of the Cobb-Douglas production function, where ε is a random error:

$$\text{Log}\, Q = A + \alpha \, \text{Log}\, L + \beta \, \text{Log}\, K + \varepsilon. \qquad (7.3)$$

Total factor productivity is usually computed as the constant term in equation 7.3. Equation 7.3 would then be run separately for each of the three subgroups in our sample (formal, large informal, and small informal firms). This would provide measures of average TFP for the various firms in the three categories, assuming that the production functions for the individual firms are of the Cobb-Douglas type with constant returns to scale.

LP and TFP are related as follows:

$$LP = \frac{AL^{\alpha}K^{\beta}}{L} = TFP\left(\frac{K}{L}\right)^{\beta}. \qquad (7.4)$$

$$\ln\left(\frac{LP_t}{LP_{t-1}}\right) = \ln\left(\frac{TFP_t}{TFP_{t-1}}\right) + \beta \ln\left(\frac{K_t/L_t}{K_{t-1}/L_{t-1}}\right). \qquad (7.5)$$

Recall that β represents the capital share of income.

Estimations of TFP using equation 7.3-like regressions have given rise to several criticisms in the literature: (a) TFP is computed under the assumption of constant returns to scale, which might lead one to attribute to technological variation the effect of scale on input efficacy, and (b) factor shares in total costs are assumed to be identical across sectors, which is not necessarily always the case, since technology may vary across firms and industries (Harrigan 1997; Mbaye 2002). Mbaye (2002) tests the first hypothesis using the Wald test as well as an alternative specification of the TFP equation and rules out the scale effect in both cases for Senegal. To allow for different production functions and technologies across firms, we calculated factor shares at the firm level. Results presented below are based on this method using firm-specific parameters.

Equation 7.4 indicates that labor productivity is a function of TFP and capital intensity, while equation 7.5 shows the same relationship in rates of change. A rise in capital intensity will lead to a rise in labor productivity, holding A constant. These equations suggest that productivity differentials between sectors could be due either to differences in efficiency or technology (TFP) or to differences in capital-labor ratios. Differences in capital-labor ratios could, in turn, reflect differential access to financing between formal and informal firms or between large and small firms. Our results indicate that productivity differences between formal and informal firms reflect differences in both efficiency and capital intensity.

Survey Results

Our results confirm a significant productivity gap between the formal and informal sectors of the three cities, but the gap is much smaller for the large informal sector. Labor productivity and TFP are higher, on average, in formal firms than in large informal firms, which, in turn, have higher productivity than small informal firms. This is consistent with the literature on labor productivity cited above. Few other studies, however, have considered TFP. As noted, this is important because differences in labor productivity between firms may reflect capital intensity rather than differential technology. Another improvement over previous literature is the use of alternative indicators or correlates of informality. Our estimates proved to be robust with respect to these various measures.

Figure 7.1 displays boxplots of the distribution of productivity levels for the formal and informal sectors, using the continuous definition of informality described in chapter 1 for the three cities. Informality here is on a 0–5 scale, where 0 is completely formal and 5 is completely informal, based on the number of criteria of formality a given firm meets.[2] Productivity gaps are sizable in all three cities and are particularly pronounced in Ouagadougou. This particularly

Figure 7.1 Productivity of Firms in the Three West African Cities, by Level of Informality

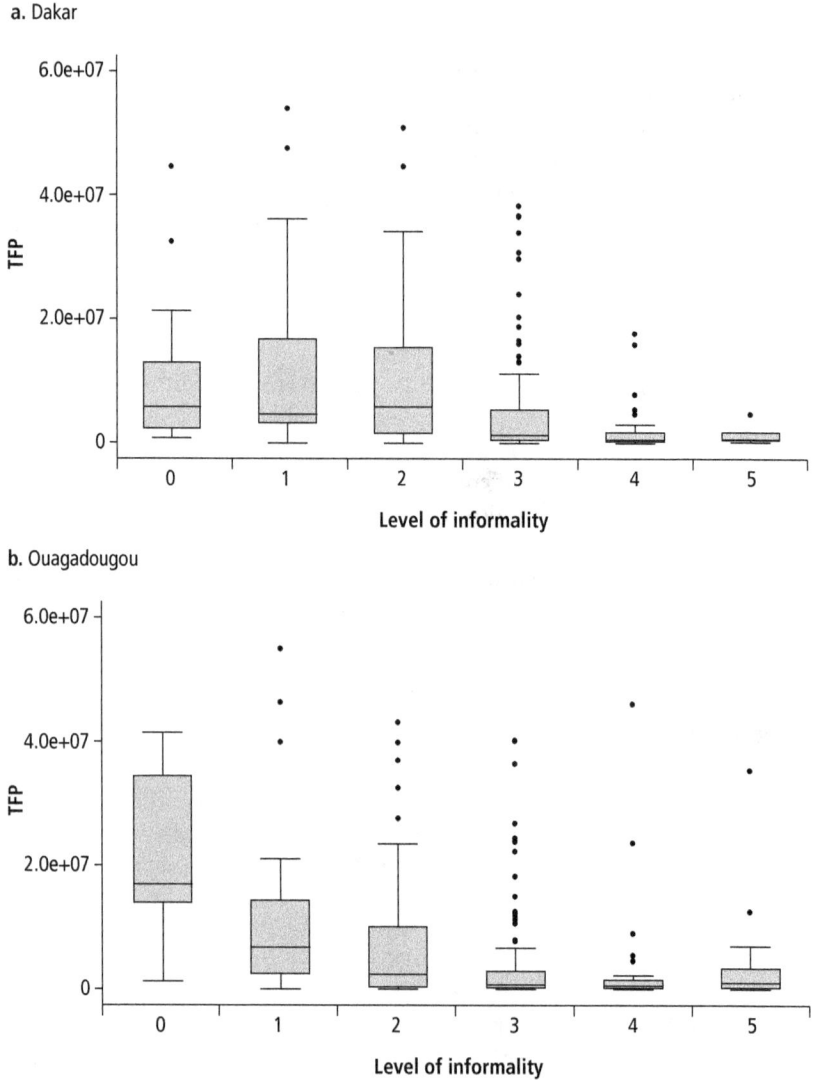

a. Dakar

b. Ouagadougou

large discrepancy in Ouagadougou is likely to be related to firms' perception of the business environment, which is considerably better in Burkina Faso than in the other countries. Whether one considers access to basic social services, the amount of time necessary to obtain access to these services, or average duration of service disruptions, the results of our surveys indicate that the situation is far

Figure 7.1 continued

c. Cotonou

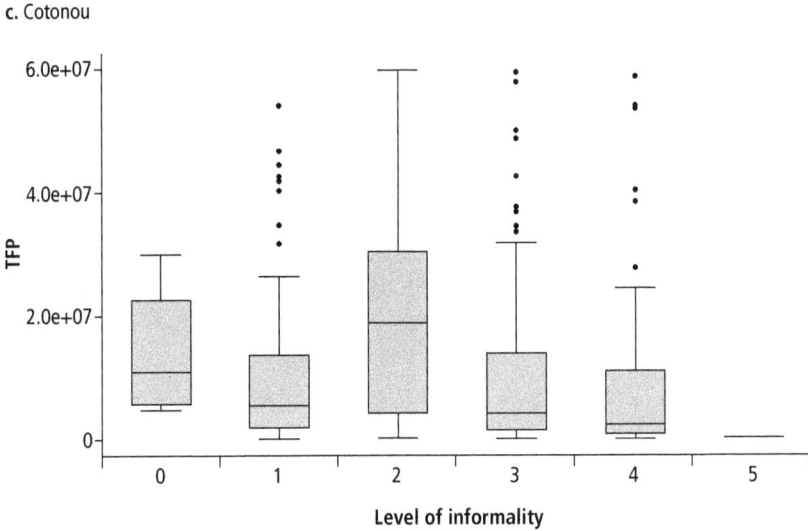

Source: Based on authors' firm survey data.
Note: Informality is on a scale of 0–5, where 0 is completely formal and 5 is completely informal.

more favorable in Ouagadougou than in the other cities. This lends credence to the hypothesis proposed by Gelb et al. (2009) that the two most important determinants of the productivity differential between the formal and informal sectors are the quality of the business environment and the ability of the state to establish and enforce laws and regulations.

Figure 7.2 shows the distribution of productivity for formal, large informal, and small informal firms in the three cities. Formal firms account for the bulk of firms with the highest labor productivity, whereas informal firms constitute a large majority of firms with low productivity. For example, in the case of Dakar, among the companies with a productivity level between CFAF 100 million and CFAF 300 million per worker, 77 percent are in the formal sector, with 23 percent and 0 percent in the large and small informal sectors, respectively. Conversely, among firms with productivity levels below CFAF 5 million, only 13 percent are in the formal sector, 8 percent are in the large informal sector, and the remaining 79 percent are in the small informal sector (see figure 7.3).

We are also interested in the magnitude of absolute productivity gaps between the three types of firms. As it turns out, the productivity differential

Figure 7.2 Labor Productivity of Firms in the Three West African Cities, by Formal or Informal Status (Share of Firms in Each Productivity Range)

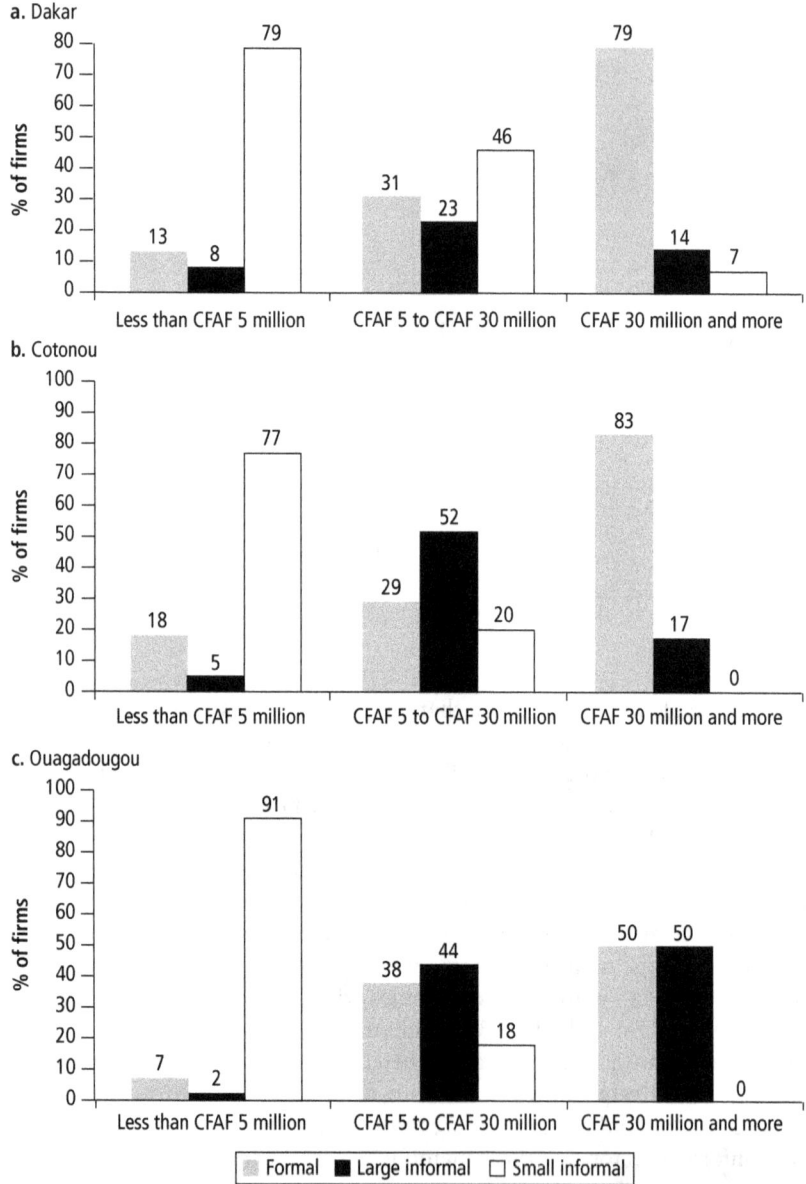

a. Dakar

b. Cotonou

c. Ouagadougou

Formal ■ Large informal □ Small informal

Source: Based on authors' firm survey data.

Figure 7.3 Firm Distribution according to Informality and the Level of Productivity in Dakar, Ouagadougou, and Cotonou

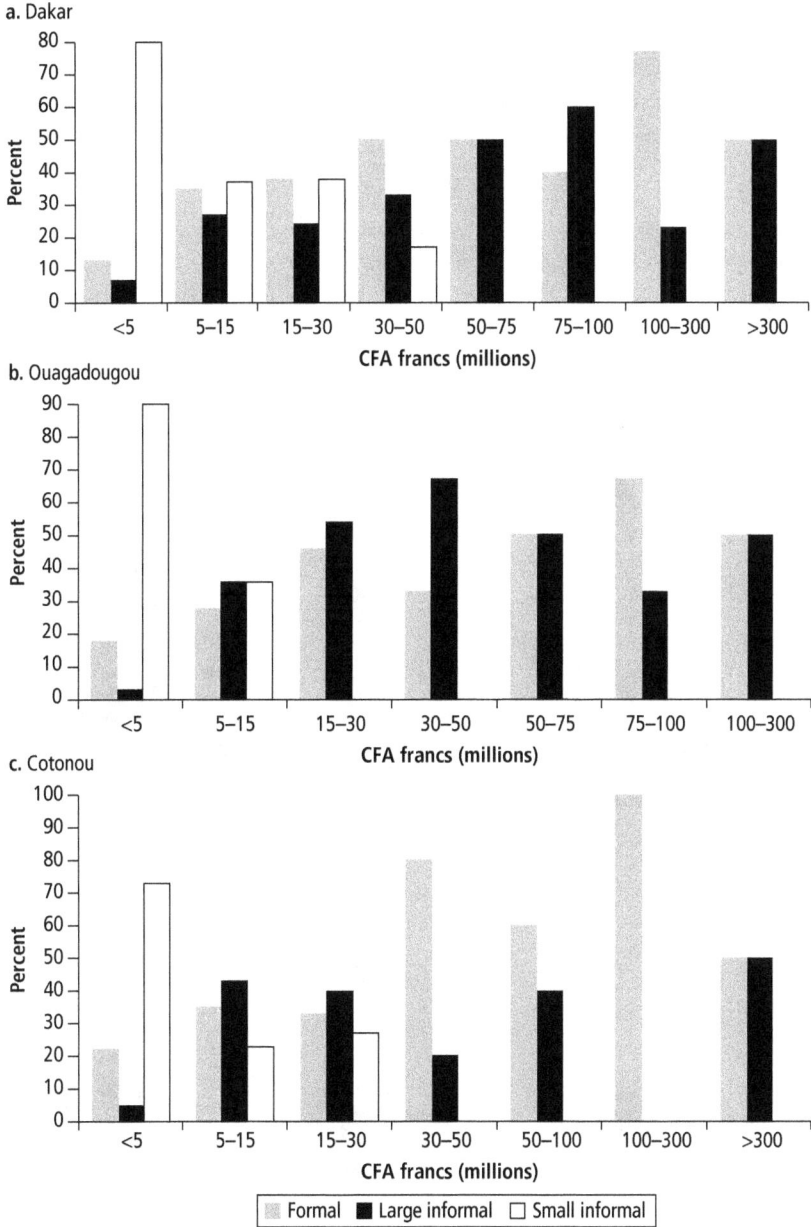

Source: Based on authors' firm survey data.

is relatively small between the formal and large informal sectors, whereas the gap between either of those subgroups and the small informal sector is quite pronounced. For example, in Dakar, 22 percent of the firms in the formal sector and 21 percent of firms in the large informal sector achieve productivity levels higher than CFAF 50 million, but no firms in the small informal sector do so. At higher productivity levels, the differences between the formal and large informal sectors are clearer. For example, in Senegal, 17 percent of formal sector

Figure 7.4 Labor Productivity of Firms in the Three West African Cities, by Formal or Informal Status and Various Correlates of Informality

a. Access to bank credit

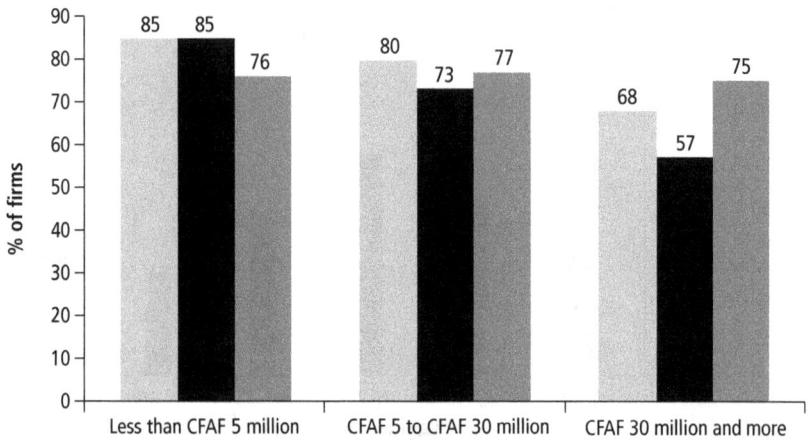

b. Compliance with social security obligations

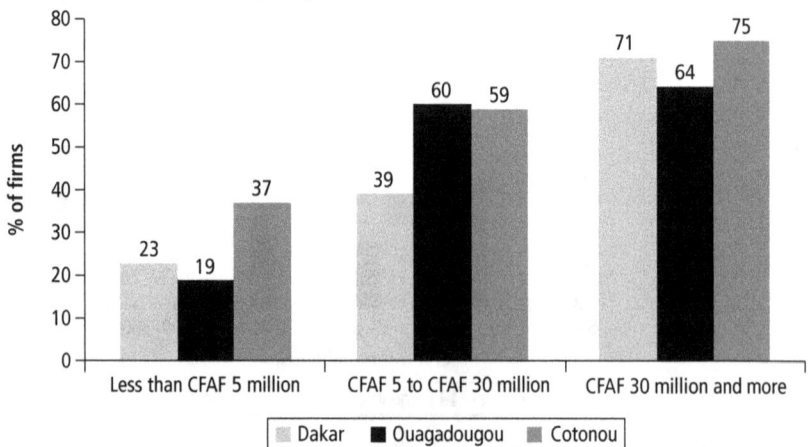

firms have productivity levels that exceed CFAF 100 million, as compared with only 10 percent of firms in the large informal sector.

These productivity differences are robust to alternative indicators or correlates of informality such as social insurance contributions for employees and maintenance of honest accounts (figure 7.4). For example, firms that offer

Figure 7.4 (continued)

c. Honest accounting

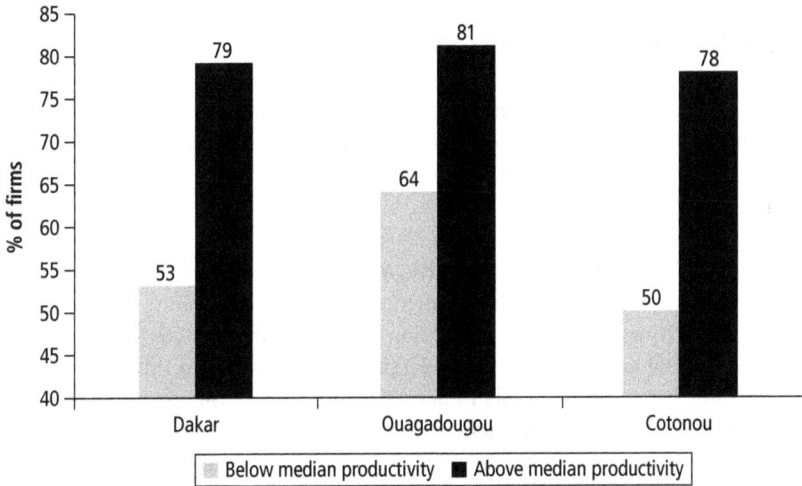

d. Registration with authorities

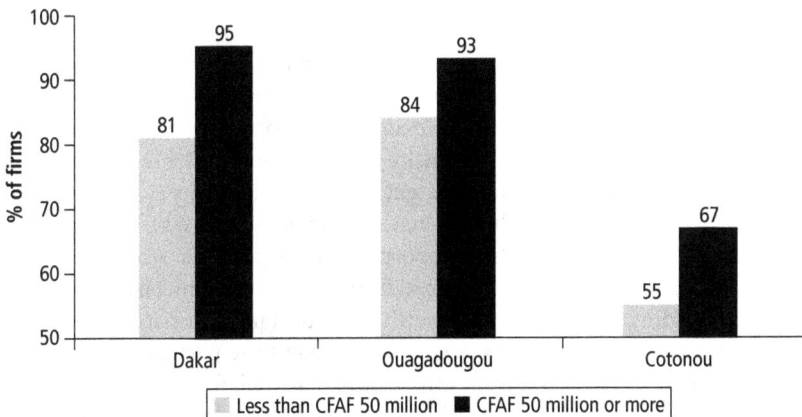

Source: Based on authors' firm survey data.

their employees social security coverage (that is, mainly formal firms) have markedly higher productivity than firms that do not offer such coverage. Thus among firms with productivity levels below CFAF 5 million in Ouagadougou, 81 percent offer no social insurance coverage for employees. Conversely, in the same country, among firms in Ouagadougou that achieve a productivity level superior to CFAF 30 million, 64 percent have social security coverage, while the remainder of firms belonging to the large informal sector do not.[3] Access to bank credit is an exception, because formal firms have only slightly greater recourse to bank loans than informal firms, as shown in chapter 5.

Factors Explaining the Productivity Gap

As mentioned in the previous section, many factors have been identified to explain the productivity differentials between the formal and informal sectors. Here, we discuss a few of them and then proceed to a multivariate econometric analysis.

Access to Credit, Capital Intensity, and Total Factor Productivity

This section discusses the issue of unequal access to credit and its impact on capital intensity as a possible explanation for the labor productivity differential between formal and informal firms. Firms in the formal and informal sectors have somewhat different levels of access to funding. While formal firms can obtain bank financing, informal firms are financed almost exclusively by equity capital as well as by various microfinance institutions or help from friends and family. The question that arises is the extent to which the observed differences in financing explain the productivity gap between the two sectors. Some insight into this question can be obtained from the breakdown of labor productivity into total factor productivity and capital intensity in equations 7.4 and 7.5.

Capital intensity is the ratio of capital stock to the number of employees of the firm. Capital stock is calculated as the sum of net investments in the past five years; employment includes both permanent and seasonal workers. According to equations 7.4 and 7.5, capital intensity accounts for any differences between labor productivity and TFP. To the extent that capital intensity is larger for formal than for informal forms, this difference could be explained by greater access to financing. We provide partial support for this hypothesis. Access to credit does differ between formal and informal firms, but not by as much as one might expect, according to our surveys. Nevertheless, substantial disparities in capital intensity between formal and informal firms may arise partially from differences in access to credit but from other sources as well; for example, informal firms are skittish about large capital investments that could be confiscated and are attracted to endeavors with rapid returns on investment.

The distribution of firm-level total factor productivity by formal or informal status is quite similar to that of labor productivity—that is, formal firms tend to have higher TFP than informal firms. Taking the example of Cotonou, 34 percent of small informal firms have TFP above the median for Cotonou, whereas 63 percent of formal firms have TFP above the median (figure 7.5).

TFP is found to be correlated with the age of the firm, regardless of formality status—older firms tend to be more productive (table 7.1). For example, for firms over 14 years old in Dakar, the probability that TFP will be above the sample average is 50 percent for formal firms, 30 percent for large informal firms, and only 7 percent for small informal firms. Firm size also affects TFP within the formal and informal sectors. The probability that small firms (fewer than five employees) in our Dakar sample will have above-average TFP is 25, 20, and 4 percent for the formal, large informal, and small informal sectors, respectively. However, if we consider firms in Dakar with more than 10 employees, the likelihood of achieving TFP above the sample average is 30, 33, and 0 percent, respectively, for formal, large informal, and small informal firms (table 7.2).

Capital intensity also differs between formal and informal firms. Formal firms have higher labor productivity, efficiency (TFP), and capital intensity than large and small informal firms. This suggests that differences in labor productivity reflect both differences in efficiency (TFP) and differences in capital intensity.

Figure 7.5 Share of Firms in which TFP is above Economy-wide Median TFP Levels, by Formal or Informal Status

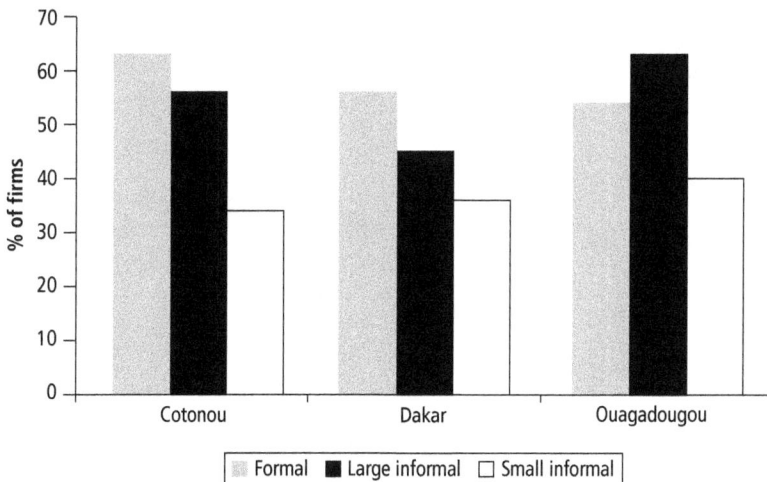

Source: Based on authors' firm survey data.

Table 7.1 Probability of Reaching Average TFP in the Three West African Cities, by Firm Age and Formal or Informal Status

Firm age and status	Dakar	Ouagadougou	Cotonou
Formal			
Below 10 years	0.14	0.14	0.33
10 to 14 years	0.33	0.60	0.18
Over 14 years	0.50	0.22	0.25
Large informal			
Below 10 years	0.17	0.63	0.30
10 to 14 years	0.40	0.40	0.19
Over 14 years	0.30	0.33	0.21
Small informal			
Below 10 years	0.00	0.07	0.00
10 to 14 years	0.00	0.04	0.03
Over 14 years	0.07	0.09	0.06

Source: Based on authors' firm survey data.

Table 7.2 Probability of Reaching Average TFP in the Three West African Cities, by Firm Size and Formal or Informal Status

Firm size and status	Dakar	Ouagadougou	Cotonou
Formal			
Below 5 employees	0.25	0.29	0.21
5 to 10 employees	0.33	0.25	0.22
Over 10 employees	0.30	0.31	0.27
Large informal			
Below 5 employees	0.20	0.45	0.20
5 to 10 employees	0.25	0.25	0.19
Over 10 employees	0.33	0.50	0.21
Small informal			
Below 5 employees	0.04	0.03	0.00
5 to 10 employees	0.00	0.07	0.06
Over 10 employees	0.00	0.09	0.11

Source: Based on authors' firm survey data.

Firm longevity and size are correlated with capital intensity as well as productivity. Among firms that have been in operation for less than 10 years, the probability of reaching the average level of capital intensity is 21 percent for formal, 11 percent for large informal, and 0 percent for small informal firms. For firms in operation for more than 14 years, the probability rises to 33 percent for formal, 25 percent for large informal, and 5 percent for small informal firms (table 7.3). When we consider the criterion of size, the same pattern emerges. For smaller firms in our sample (fewer than five employees), the probability of above-average capital intensity is 37 percent for formal, 18 percent for large informal, and 3 percent for small informal firms. For larger companies (more than 10 employees), the probability is 36 percent for formal, 25 percent for large informal, and 20 percent for small informal firms (table 7.4).

Table 7.3 Probability of Reaching Average Capital Intensity in the Three West African Cities, by Firm Age and Formal or Informal Status

Firm age and status	Dakar	Ouagadougou	Cotonou
Formal			
Below 10 years	0.21	0.33	0.33
10 to 14 years	0.25	0.60	0.32
Over 14 years	0.33	0.39	0.25
Large informal			
Below 10 years	0.11	0.63	0.43
10 to 14 years	0.25	0.50	0.47
Over 14 years	0.25	0.22	0.42
Small informal			
Below 10 years	0.00	0.04	0.19
10 to 14 years	0.00	0.08	0.14
Over 14 years	0.05	0.05	0.14

Source: Based on authors' firm survey data.

Table 7.4 Probability of Reaching Average Capital Intensity in the Three West African Cities, by Firm Size and Formal or Informal Status

Firm size and status	Dakar	Ouagadougou	Cotonou
Formal			
Below 5 employees	0.37	0.62	0.36
5 to 10 employees	0.33	0.50	0.38
Above 10 employees	0.36	0.23	0.27
Large informal			
Below 5 employees	0.18	0.53	0.36
5 to 10 employees	0.25	0.25	0.41
Above 10 employees	0.25	0.20	0.18
Small informal			
Below 5 employees	0.03	0.08	0.21
5 to 10 employees	0.06	0.02	0.16
Above 10 employees	0.20	0.09	0.05

Source: Based on authors' firm survey data.

Gender and Educational Level of the Managers and Employees

The factors that explain the productivity gap seem quite varied and are very similar to factors associated with informality. The gender and education level of top management are other key factors that condition the productivity differential between the formal and informal sectors. If the head of a firm is male, the likelihood of reaching the average productivity threshold in Dakar is 34 percent for formal firms, 33 percent for large informal firms, and 2 percent for small informal firms. However, if the head is female, then the probability drops to 15, 21, and 2 percent, respectively (table 7.5).

The skill level of the firm's staff, which is proxied by average monthly salary, also matters for labor productivity. When the staff averages a monthly salary below the minimum wage, the probability that the firm will reach average productivity levels is 0 percent for the formal sector (probably because the proportion of staff paid minimum wages in the formal sector is negligible), 33 percent for the large informal sector, and 3 percent for the small informal sector, again using Dakar data. However, if the head of the firm has a monthly salary of more than CFAF 200,000, the proportion then becomes 34 percent in the formal sector, 45 percent in the large informal sector, and 8 percent in the small informal sector (table 7.6).

The average education level of a firm's staff is also correlated with productivity: 44 percent of employees in formal firms that perform at an average level of productivity or higher are university educated, while in the large informal sector only 20 percent of employees are university educated (table 7.7). In general, only 18 percent of firms with university-educated staff perform at a productivity level below CFAF 5 million. In the case of firms with turnover rates

Table 7.5 Probability of Achieving Average Productivity in the Three West African Cities, by Gender of the Manager and Formal or Informal Status

Gender of the manager and status	Dakar	Ouagadougou	Cotonou
Formal			
Male	0.34	0.52	0.24
Female	0.15	0.75	0.36
Large informal			
Male	0.33	0.81	0.46
Female	0.21	0.50	0.50
Small informal			
Male	0.02	0.04	0.03
Female	0.02	0.03	0.04

Source: Based on authors' firm survey data.

Table 7.6 Probability of Achieving Average Productivity in the Three West African Cities, by Average Salary of Employees and Formal or Informal Status

Monthly salary and status	Dakar	Cotonou	Ouagadougou
Formal			
Below CFAF 35,000	0.00	0.25	0.13
CFAF 35,000 to CFAF 200,000	0.50	0.56	0.38
Over CFAF 200,000	0.34	0.86	0.55
Large informal			
Below CFAF 35,000	0.33	0.38	0.21
CFAF 35,000 to CFAF 200,000	0.33	0.67	0.33
Above CFAF 200,000	0.45	0.80	0.50
Small informal			
Below CFAF 35,000	0.03	0.00	0.05
CFAF 35,000 to CFAF 200,000	0.03	0.21	0.06
Over CFAF 200,000	0.08	0.20	0.10

Source: Based on authors' firm survey data.

Table 7.7 Share of Firms with Above-Average Productivity in the Three West African Cities, by Education Level of Employees and Formal or Informal Status
% of firms

City and status	None	Primary	Secondary	University	Total
Dakar					
Formal	0	25	31	44	100
Large informal	10	20	50	20	100
Ouagadougou					
Formal	0	33	33	33	100
Large informal	50	0	50	0	100
Coutonou					
Formal	0	0	80	20	100
Large informal	0	0	100	0	100

Source: Based on authors' firm survey data.

between CFAF 100 million and CFAF 300 million, the proportion of firms with university-educated staff is 38 percent.

Use of Information and Communication Technologies

The use of new ICTs is strongly correlated with informal status and productivity levels. Among firms with productivity below CFAF 5 million, 76 percent do not use e-mail to communicate with customers, as opposed to 38 percent among firms with turnover between CFAF 100 million and CFAF 300 million. Likewise, among firms with productivity below CFAF 5 million, 85 percent do not use websites to interact with customers, as opposed to 77 percent of firms with turnover between CFAF 100 million and CFAF 300 million.

Informal Sector and Productivity: Econometric Modeling and Testing Causality

In this section, we analyze the relationship between the informal sector and labor productivity using multivariate regressions. We also analyze causality between the two variables using the DAG (directed acyclic graphs) method.

An Econometric Analysis of the Relationship between Informality and Productivity

To test the impact of informal status on productivity more fully, we use a simple ordinary least squares (OLS) regression. The dependent variable is the log of labor productivity, which is regressed on a variety of explanatory variables such as informality, the characteristics of corporate managers, the sectors in which firms operate, as well as their perceptions of the business environment and the labor market. These sets of candidate variables and their expected effects are presented in table 7.8. Using the stepwise backward procedure, we proceed to eliminate certain variables in order to retain only the most significant.

The results obtained with our baseline regression are presented in table 7.9. Our results indicate that all variables are significant with the expected sign. Informality is here considered as a categorical variable that takes on the values 1, 2, and 3, respectively, for large informal, formal, and small informal firms. The variable for formal firms is considered to be the reference variable and is dropped. The variable for small informal firms has a negative coefficient that is significant at the 1 percent level, while the large informal variable has a positive coefficient that is significant at the 1 percent level. Other factors involved in determining labor productivity are capital intensity (positive and significant at 1 percent) and the firm's industry affiliation.

The three potential problems could bias the results of our regressions:

1. Most variables are not normally distributed, and many have highly skewed distributions.

2. A nonlinear specification might yield superior results.

3. While our descriptive statistics, along with the results obtained from our basic regression, indicate a negative correlation between informality and productivity, this does not indicate the direction of causation; bidirectional causality between these two variables could induce endogeneity bias.

Table 7.8 Explanatory Variables and Their Expected Effects

Variable	Expected sign
Household characteristics of head of enterprise or its ***employees, aggregated at the enterprise level***	
Age	−/+
Sex	−/+
Matrimonial status	−/+
Education level	+
Illiteracy	−
Household position (head of the household, other)	−/+
Sectoral characteristics	
Capital intensity	+
Level of import protection	+/−
Exports as a % of total output	−/+
Agents' views of weak regulatory framework and labor market	
Perception of the high cost of labor and other nontradable factors	−
Perception of the restrictiveness of labor legislation	−
Fiscal harassment	−
Perception of low efficacy of government inspection services (security, quality control)	−
Perception of financing constraints	−
Perception of the credibility of overall economic policy	−

Source: Authors.

Table 7.9 Regression of the Log of Labor Productivity (lprod) on Formal or Informal Status and Other Explanatory Variables

Lprod	Coefficient	Standard error	T	P>|t|	[95% Conf. Interval]	
Capital labor ratio	0.096	0.027	3.550	0.000	0.43	0.149
Services	0.463	0.218	2.130	0.034	0.035	0.891
Trade	0.836	0.220	3.790	0.000	0.402	1.270
Buildings	0.709	0.425	1.670	0.097	−0.128	1.546
Legal structure	0.606	0.340	1.780	0.076	−0.064	1.275
Small informal	−1.401	0.239	−5.860	0.000	−1.872	−0.930
Big informal	0.658	0.295	2.230	0.027	0.077	1.239
Constant	13.054	0.521	25.050	0.000	12.028	14.080

Source: Authors.
Note: Number of observations = 286; F(7, 278) = 22,05; Prob > F = 0; R^2 = 0.36.

To address the first and second problems, we used the CART (classification and regression trees) method, a nonparametric relational analysis method. The results (obtained with IBM-SPSS decision trees) are presented in figure 7.6 (IBM n.d.). This method considers several potential independent variables and examines which one provides the single best split of the dependent variable (log of labor productivity) into the two most homogeneous groups (that is, those having the smallest standard deviation). In the three cities, whether or not a firm is informal provides the best split. The procedure is then repeated iteratively on each of the two groups generated by the previous split. The fact that informal or formal status emerges as the variable that best splits labor productivity observations into two distinct groups indicates the decisive connection

Figure 7.6 Classification and Regression Trees

a. Dakar

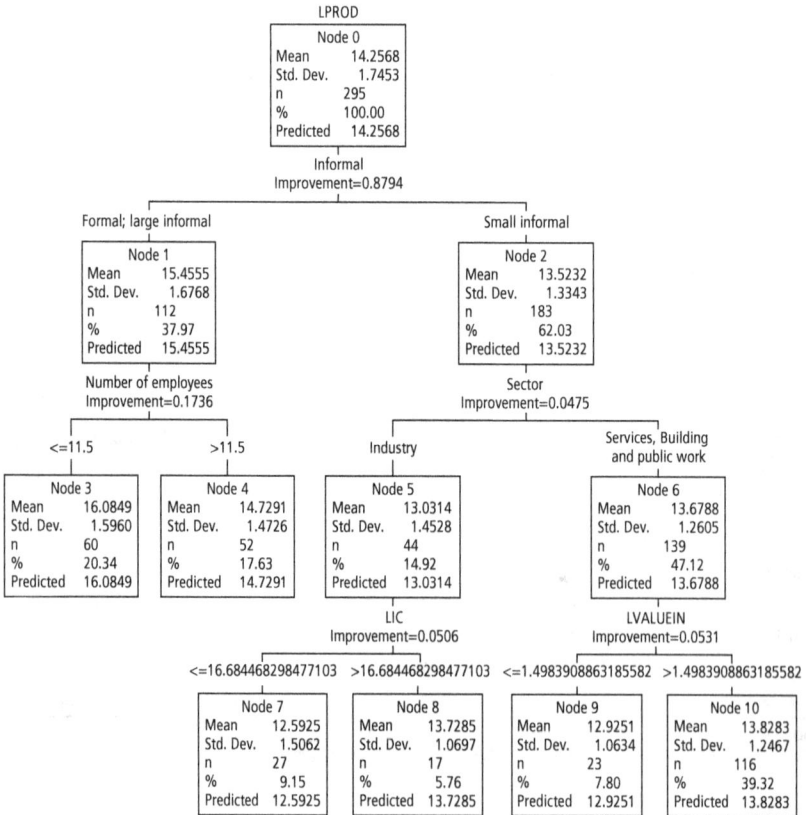

Figure 7.6 (continued)

b. Ouagadougou

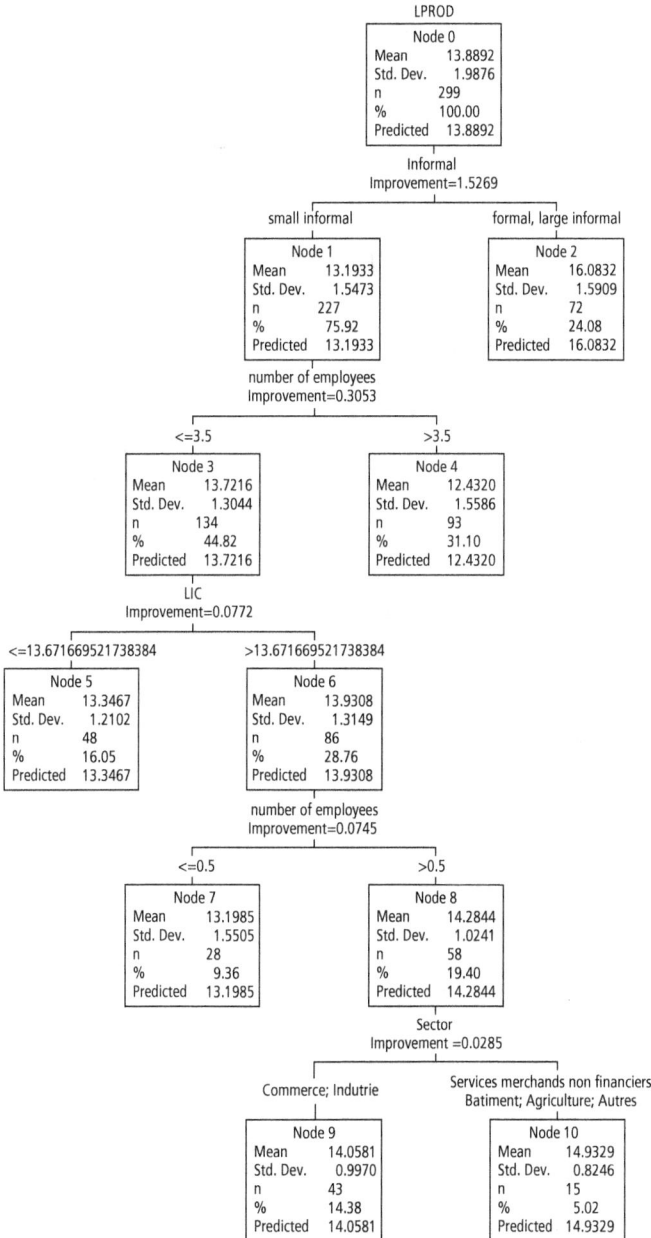

LPROD

Node 0	
Mean	13.8892
Std. Dev.	1.9876
n	299
%	100.00
Predicted	13.8892

Informal
Improvement=1.5269

small informal   formal, large informal

Node 1	
Mean	13.1933
Std. Dev.	1.5473
n	227
%	75.92
Predicted	13.1933

Node 2	
Mean	16.0832
Std. Dev.	1.5909
n	72
%	24.08
Predicted	16.0832

number of employees
Improvement=0.3053

<=3.5   >3.5

Node 3	
Mean	13.7216
Std. Dev.	1.3044
n	134
%	44.82
Predicted	13.7216

Node 4	
Mean	12.4320
Std. Dev.	1.5586
n	93
%	31.10
Predicted	12.4320

LIC
Improvement=0.0772

<=13.671669521738384   >13.671669521738384

Node 5	
Mean	13.3467
Std. Dev.	1.2102
n	48
%	16.05
Predicted	13.3467

Node 6	
Mean	13.9308
Std. Dev.	1.3149
n	86
%	28.76
Predicted	13.9308

number of employees
Improvement=0.0745

<=0.5   >0.5

Node 7	
Mean	13.1985
Std. Dev.	1.5505
n	28
%	9.36
Predicted	13.1985

Node 8	
Mean	14.2844
Std. Dev.	1.0241
n	58
%	19.40
Predicted	14.2844

Sector
Improvement =0.0285

Commerce; Indutrie   Services merchands non financiers
Batiment; Agriculture; Autres

Node 9	
Mean	14.0581
Std. Dev.	0.9970
n	43
%	14.38
Predicted	14.0581

Node 10	
Mean	14.9329
Std. Dev.	0.8246
n	15
%	5.02
Predicted	14.9329

Figure 7.6 (continued)

c. Cotonou

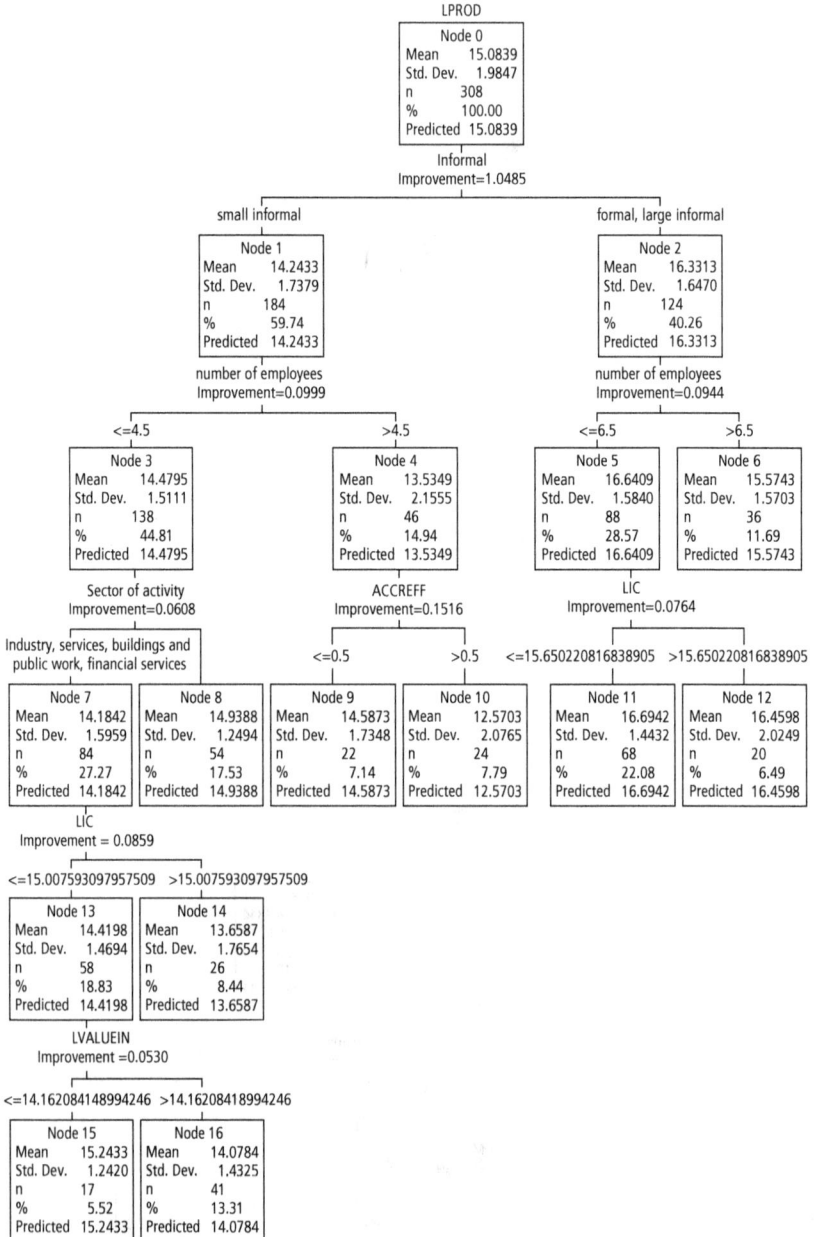

Source: Based on authors' firm survey data.

between informality and firm productivity. Moreover, the CART analysis lumps large informal and formal sectors together into one homogeneous group, while placing the small informal sector into a separate group. The gap in average log productivity between the grouped formal and large informal sectors relative to the small informal sector is 2.09, 1.93, and 2.89 for Dakar, Cotonou, and Ouagadougou, respectively. For further details on the CART methodology and a discussion of its use in the literature on the analysis of living standards, see Haughton and Haughton (2011, ch. 4).

In addition to the informal sector classification, other factors also affect labor productivity according to the CART analysis: namely, the sector in which the firm operates, firm size, and capital intensity. These findings are quite consistent with the findings from our regressions and the descriptive statistics. However, interaction effects seem to be strong between certain explanatory variables, particularly the sector of activity and informality status, implying that the impact of informality status on productivity is likely to depend on the sector of activity, as one might expect. We, therefore, interacted these two variables in a second model, the results of which are presented in table 7.10. This new specification improved the results, while confirming the main findings. Capital intensity is still significant at 1 percent, with the expected positive sign. The coefficient on the variable representing the small informal sector remains significant at 1 percent with negative sign. Industry classification is also significant, most notably affiliation with trade

Table 7.10 Regression of the Log of Labor Productivity (lprod) on Formal or Informal Status with Interaction of Explanatory Variables

Lprod	Coefficient	Standard error	T	P>|t|	[95% Conf. Interval]	
Capital labor ratio	0.100	0.027	3.720	0.000	0.047	0.153
Small informal*financial services	2.362	1.401	1.690	0.093	−0.395	5.119
Buildings	0.706	0.423	1.670	0.096	−0.126	1.538
Big informal*commerce	−1.298	0.594	−2.190	0.030	−2.468	−0.129
Small informal	−1.090	0.278	−3.920	0.000	−1.638	−0.543
Small informal*commerce	−1.056	0.471	−2.240	0.026	−1.984	−0.129
Big informal	1.086	0.364	2.990	0.003	0.371	1.802
Services	0.499	0.216	2.310	0.022	0.073	0.925
Legal structure	0.761	0.342	2.220	0.027	0.087	1.434
Commerce	1.788	0.440	4.070	0.000	0.922	2.654
Constant	12.694	0.530	23.930	0.000	11.650	13.738

Source: Estimation based on authors' firm survey data.
Note: Number of observations = 286; $F(10, 275) = 16,67$; Prob > F = 0; R^2 = 0.38.
* = significant at 10 percent.

and service sectors. The R^2 statistic also improved. In order to address whether or not the existence of a bidirectional relationship could cause residuals to be correlated with explanatory variables, most econometrics textbooks recommend the use of estimation with instrumental variables. However, we refrained from searching for appropriate instruments in view of recent research that casts doubt on the validity of instrumental variable procedures and their alleged superiority over OLS methods (Murray 2006; Larcker and Rusticus 2010).

An Analysis of Causality between Informality and Productivity

DAG is a fairly standard procedure used in the literature on survey data to test for causality. It is a simple graph that uses arrows and vertices (variables). It is defined as an ordered triplet $<V,M,E>$, where V is a nonempty set of vertices, M is a nonempty set of symbols attached to the ends of segments connecting two variables, and E is a set of ordered pairs (Bessler 2003; Zhang, Bessler, and Leatham 2006; Awokuse, Chopra, and Bessler 2009; Bessler and Loper 2001; Awokuse 2006; Canalda, Chatonnay, and Josselin 2004; Haughton, Kamis, and Scholten 2006). For an introduction to DAGs and a discussion of causality issues in the context of the analysis of living standards data, see Haughton and Haughton (2011, ch. 5). The DAGs represent the conditional independence obtained by the following recursive decomposition:

$$Pr(v_1, v_2, v_3, ..., v_n) = \prod_{i=1}^{n} Pr(v_i / pa_i) \tag{7.6}$$

where Pr denotes the probability of events concerning the variables v_1, v_2, v_3, ..., v_n, and pa_i ("parents" of v_i) is a subset of the aforementioned variables, with arrows leading directly to ("causing") v_i.

What determines the direction of causality in a representative DAG is each extremity of the segment connecting the two variables. For example, given three vertices A, B, and C, a representation of A $\leftarrow$ B $\rightarrow$ C would indicate that A and C are simultaneously caused by B. The unconditional correlation between A is C is not zero, because they have a common cause, while the conditional correlation between A and C, given B, is zero.

The inferences made on the existence or absence of causal links between variables are derived from interpreting whether or not different segments connect the vertices and, if so, what is the nature of the extremity of these vertices. In instances where there is a zero correlation between a pair of variables, no segment connects the two variables. The DAG was obtained from our data using the software Tetrad version 4.3.9-0 (Tetrad Project 2012) and the FCI (full conditional independence) algorithm (figure 7.7). The advantage of the FCI algorithm is that it allows for the (likely) possibility of unrecorded common causes of pairs of variables in the dataset. The DAG displays segments connecting variables related to informality with those related to productivity, indicating the existence of a correlation between the two subsets of variables (refer to the right-hand-side group of variables in figure 7.7). However, the lack of arrowheads at the ends of these segments indicates that the direction of causality could not be ascertained, given the algorithm used. As an interesting by-product, the DAG also reveals which groups of variables tend to be correlated with each other: size of the firm (lvalueinvt) and (log of) capital intensity (lic), the group of three variables that express confidence in the future of the firm (avenirt, contenfant, gardad), sector variables (secteur), and status (statut) variables.

Figure 7.7 Analysis of Causality between Informality and Productivity Using Directed Acyclic Graphs for Cotonou

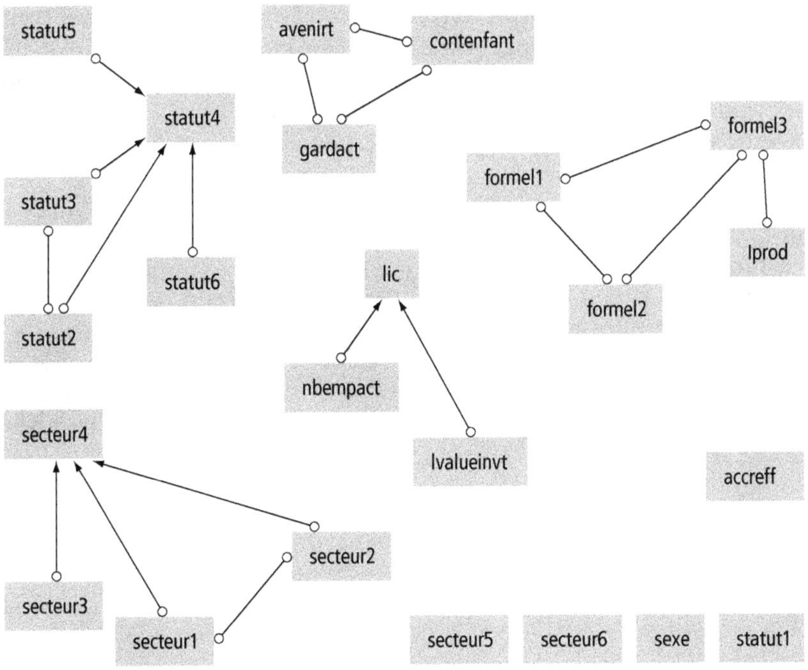

Source: Authors.
Note: An edge with an arrowhead from X to Y indicates that Y is not a cause of X. Two arrowheads connecting X and Y indicate the existence of an unrecorded common cause of X and Y. If an edge extremity is marked with an "o," the algorithm cannot determine whether an arrowhead should be at that extremity or not. Variables Secteur1–6 are dummy variables for the different activity sectors. Variables Formel1–3 are dummy variables for the three formality levels (formal, large informal, small informal). The variable lprod denotes the log of productivity; lic is the log of capital intensity; nbempact and lvalueinvt are measures of the size of the firm; avenirt, gardact, and contenfant are measures of the interviewee's confidence in the future of the firm. Variables Status1–6 represent the status of the firm (public, for example).

Conclusion

Consistent with previous literature, this chapter showed a large productivity gap between formal and informal firms. This finding is robust with respect to alternative indicators and correlates of informality and is confirmed using alternative multivariate regression specifications. The correlation between productivity and informality may reflect two-way causation. Low productivity may lead to informal sector status through self-selection of firms by quality of management. Reverse causation running from firm status to productivity could be due to the reduced access to public services that informality entails.

We investigated productivity differentials between large and small informal firms. Our results indicate that large informal firms also have lower productivity than formal firms, but the differential is minor, whereas the productivity gap between large and small informal firms is much greater. Thus with regard to productivity, large informal firms resemble formal firms much more than their smaller informal counterparts. We also examined total factor productivity in addition to labor productivity. TFP controls for capital intensity, yet we find the same positive correlation between TFP and formality as we do for labor productivity. This shows that capital intensity alone cannot explain differences in labor productivity.

Notes

1. This study finds that the elasticity of poverty headcount is –1.38 with respect to per capita income and 0.89 with respect to the Gini coefficient.
2. In chapter 1, six criteria of formality are spelled out. Here, we use five criteria, conflating tax status and registration, given their close connection since registration usually entails contact with the fiscal authorities.
3. By definition, no small informal firm can achieve a level of turnover and thus a level of productivity above this threshold.

References

Awokuse, Titus O. 2006. "Export-Led Growth and the Japanese Economy: Evidence from VAR and Directed Acyclic Graphs." *Applied Economics* 38 (5, March): 593–602.

Awokuse, Titus O., Aviral Chopra, and David A. Bessler. 2009. "Structural Change and International Stock Market Interdependence." *Economic Modeling* 26 (3): 549–59.

Bessler, David A. 2003. "On World Poverty: Its Causes and Effects." Research Bulletin, Food and Agricultural Organization of the United Nations, Rome.

Bessler, David A., and Nathan Loper. 2001. "Economic Development: Evidence from Directed Acyclic Graphs." *The Manchester School* 69 (4): 457–76.

Canalda Philippe, Pasal Chatonnay, and Didier Josselin. 2004. "Énumeration d'arbres couvrants tentaculaires, une solution au problème de transport à la demande en convergence." In *IEEE International Conference on Sciences of Electronic, Technologies of Information and Telecommunications (SETIT) 2004*, 146–54. Sousse, Tunisia, March.

Causa, Orsetta, and Daniel Cohen. 2005. "Productivité industrielle et competitivité." OECD, Paris, September.

Dabla-Norris, Era, Mark Gradstein, and Gabriela Inchauste. 2008. "What Causes Firms to Hide Output? The Determinant of Informality." *Journal of Development Economics* 85 (1-2): 1–27.

Gelb, Alan, Taye Mengistae, Vijaya Ramachandran, and Manju Kedia Shah. 2009. "To Formalize or Not to Formalize? Comparisons of Microenterprise Data from Southern and East Africa." Working Paper 175, Center for Global Development, Washington, DC.

Golub, Stephen S., and Lawrence Edwards. 2004. "South Africa's International Cost Competitiveness and Exports in Manufacturing." *World Development* 32 (8, August): 1323–39.

Harrigan, James.1997. "Cross-Country Comparison of Industry Total Productivity: Theory and Evidence." Research Paper 9734, Federal Reserve Bank of New York.

Haughton, Dominique, and Jonathan Haughton. 2011. *Living Standards Analytics: Development through the Lens of Household Survey Data*. Berlin: Springer-Verlag.

Haughton, Dominique, Arnold Kamis, and Patrick Scholten. 2006. "A Review of Three Directed Acyclic Graphs Software Packages: MIM, Tetrad, and WinMine." *American Statistician* 60 (3): 272–86.

IBM (International Business Machines). n.d. SPSS Decision Trees. http://www-01.ibm .com/software/analytics/spss/products/statistics/decision-trees/.

Krugman, Paul. 1990. "Increasing Returns and Economic Geography." NBER Working Paper 3275, National Bureau of Economic Research, Cambridge, MA.

———. 1994. "Fluctuations, Instability, and Agglomeration." NBER Working Paper 4616, National Bureau of Economic Research, Cambridge, MA.

La Porta, Rafael, and Andrei Shleifer. 2008. "The Unofficial Economy and Economic Development." *Brookings Papers on Economic Activity* 2: 275–364.

Larcker, David F., and Tjomme O. Rusticus. 2010. "On the Use of Instrumental Variables in Accounting Research." *Journal of Accounting and Economics* 49 (3): 186–205.

Loayza, Norman V. 1997. *The Economics of the Informal Sector: A Simple Model and Some Empirical Evidence from Latin America*. Washington, DC: World Bank.

Mbaye, Ahmadou A. 2002. "Capital humain, compétence et productivité du travail au Sénégal: Une analyse empirique." *Economie et Société*, Serie F, no. 20.

———. 2003. "Competitiveness, Manufacturing, and Exports in Senegal." In *Senegal: Policies and Strategies for Accelerated Growth and Poverty Reduction*. Country Economic Memorandum. Washington, DC: World Bank.

———. 2006. "Mise à jour des indicateurs de pauvreté au Sénégal." Centre de Recherches Economiques Appliquées, Université de Dakar, for the Ministère de l'Economie et des Finances Cellule de Suivi du Programme de Lutte contre la Pauvreté, Dakar.

Mbaye, Ahmadou A., and Stephen Golub. 2003. "Relative Unit Labor Costs, International Competitiveness, and Exports: The Case of Senegal." *Journal of African Economies* 2 (11): 219–48.

Murray, Michael P. 2006. "The Bad, the Weak, and the Ugly: Avoiding the Pitfalls of Instrumental Variables Estimation." Bates College, Lewiston, ME.

Nehru, Vikram, and Ashok M. Dhareshwar. 1994. "New Estimates of Total Factor Productivity Growth for Developing and Industrial Countries." Policy Research Working Paper 1313, International Economics Department, World Bank, Washington, DC.

Nordhaus, William D. 2001. "Productivity Growth and the New Economy." NBER Working Paper 8096, National Bureau of Economic Research, Cambridge, MA.

OECD (Organisation for Economic Co-operation and Development). 2008. *Compendium 2008 sur les indicateurs de productivité*. Paris: OECD.

Perry, Guillermo E., William F. Maloney, Omar S. Arias, Pablo Fajnzylber, Andrew Mason, and Jaime Saavedra-Chanduvi. 2007. *Informality: Exit and Exclusion*. Washington, DC: World Bank.

Schreyer, Paul, and Dirk Pilat. 2001. "Measuring Productivity." *OECD Economic Studies* 33 (2): 127–69.

Sharpe, Andrew. 1997. "Pourquoi les Américains sont-ils plus productifs que les Canadiens?" Centre d'Études des Niveaux de Vie, Observateur International de la Productivité, Montreal.

Steel, William F., and Don Snodgrass. 2008. "World Bank Region Analysis on the Informal Economy." In *Raising Productivity and Reducing Risk of Household Enterprises*. Annex 1, "Diagnostic Methodology Framework." Washington, DC: World Bank.

Tetrad Project. 2012. "The Tetrad Project: Causal Models and Statistical Data." Carnegie Mellon University, Pittsburgh, PA. http://www.phil.cmu.edu/projects/tetrad/.

Zhang, Jin, David A. Bessler, and David Leatham. 2006. "Does Consumer Debt Cause Economic Recession? Evidence Using Directed Acyclic Graphs." *Applied Economics Letters* 13 (7): 401–07.

Chapter 8

Informal Trading Networks in West Africa: The Mourides of Senegal/The Gambia and the Yoruba of Benin/Nigeria

By Stephen Golub and Jamie Hansen-Lewis

A theme of this study is that the informal sector in West Africa stems largely from the institutional environment and the incentives that firms face (chapter 6). In particular, weak and corrupt state administrations fail to provide the foundations of formal markets such as property rights, contract enforcement, and information dissemination. An additional consideration, however, is that informal business operations are perpetuated by informal institutions that substitute for state provision of public goods. Informal institutions are pervasive in all economies, but they are particularly significant in developing countries (Casson, Guista, and Kambhampati 2009). Ethnic and social kinship groups are an especially significant informal institution, providing a set of norms of conduct and enforcement mechanisms that substitute for formal rules and regulations.

Ethnic and social networks are a form of "social capital" (Barron, Field, and Schuller 2000), which can have positive as well as negative effects on economic development. On the plus side, social networks create bonds of trust that enable contract fulfillment, access to financing, and information exchange without documentation or official involvement (Putnam 1995; Fafchamps 2004). Kinship groups play a particularly important part in international trade, helping to overcome transaction costs created by lack of information and differences in business practices across countries (Rauch 2001). Kinship networks have a major role in informal cross-border trading in West Africa, as will be described further and in the following chapter. On the negative side, however, social capital in general and informal networks in particular can be exclusionary, accepting or even promoting antisocial behavior and violation of the rules and norms in the formal economy (for example, Adhikari and Goldey 2009;

Field 2003; Portes 1998). Munshi and Rosenzweig (2006) provide an illustration of the complex interactions in India between a traditional network—the caste system—and the modern global economy. Again, this is clearly manifested in West Africa insofar as kinship networks are heavily involved in illegal activities, particularly smuggling and tax evasion. Overall, ethnic and religious networks are particularly significant in West Africa because of the combination of weak formal institutions and the continuing importance of kinship ties dating from the precolonial era and the resistance to colonialism.

North's (1989) concept of institutions also provides a helpful conceptual framework for understanding the informal sector. North distinguishes between formal institutions ("rules") and informal institutions ("norms") and argues that both are important in shaping the possibilities for economic development. In both modern and traditional societies, formal and informal institutions have evolved to mitigate opportunistic behavior, but modern arm's-length capitalism involves a very different set of institutions than traditional village society. In chapter 6, we focus on formal institutions involving the protection of property rights and the functioning of state institutions. This chapter completes the picture by analyzing some of the informal institutions, particularly kinship ties, that shape informal sector behavior in West Africa.

In this chapter, we analyze these issues by reviewing the history, functioning, and consequences of two informal networks in West Africa—the Mourides and the Yoruba. The Mourides are a Muslim brotherhood that originated in the nineteenth century, while the Yoruba are an ethnic group predating the colonial era. These networks retain important economic functions. The bonds of solidarity among members of the group provide a social foundation for informal markets in West Africa, particularly in cross-border trade, both filling the void left by deficient official institutions as well as contributing to the weakness of these institutions.

The Mourides in Senegal and The Gambia

The Mouride Islamic brotherhood plays a major role in the informal sector in Senegal and The Gambia and has developed an extensive global trading network spanning West Africa, Europe, and the United States.[1] The Mourides' strong group solidarity and unsurpassed work ethic have enabled their remarkable transition from rural groundnut farmers to one of the most dynamic urban trading groups in Africa.

Historical Background
The Mouride movement arose in the aftermath of the defeat of the Wolof nation by the French colonial army in the late nineteenth century (O'Brien 1971).

Wolof society was in a state of political and social disarray. In this context, Islam, which had been implanted in Senegal in the eleventh century, assumed increasing importance, with religious leaders known as marabouts providing spiritual and organizational guidance to their followers, the *talibés*. One of these marabouts, Cheikh Amadou Bamba, attracted a growing number of *talibés*, due to his charismatic personality, his personal virtue, and his close association with Wolof leaders of the resistance to French rule. His growing following and increasingly militant behavior led the French authorities to exile him to Gabon and Mauritania, which only served to boost his reputation and the devotion of his followers. After repeated entreaties by his disciples, Cheikh Amadou Bamba was released and returned to Senegal in 1912.

Following his return, the French established a strategic partnership with the Mourides. Cheikh Amadou Bamba moved to Diourbel in the region of Baol, and his principal disciples were granted large tracts of land for agricultural development. With backing from the French, the Mourides specialized in groundnuts, which became the dominant cash crop in Senegal and The Gambia for the remainder of the century. Meanwhile, Cheikh Amadou Bamba founded the village of Touba, where he was buried and which became the spiritual capital of the Mourides.

Cheikh Amadou Bamba created a tradition of submission by the *talibés* to the leading marabouts and, in turn, an obligation of the marabouts to assist their *talibés*, leading to both a clear hierarchy and a sense of group solidarity within the Mourides. The Mourides continue to revere him as a saint, providing an enduring and powerful symbol of authority and legitimacy to the group. Their shared devotion to his memory is the spiritual foundation for cohesiveness of the group. This allegiance was transferred to his successors.

A monarchic system of succession has been established, with a pyramid hierarchical structure in which the caliph-general is the supreme leader. The caliph-general is the closest living descendant of Cheikh Amadou Bamba. Below the caliph-general are the other caliphs, also descendants of Cheikh Amadou Bamba or of his leading associates. Under the caliphs are sheikhs (marabouts with disciples), with varying degrees of prestige and number of disciples. A certain fragmentation of authority and rivalry among them has diluted the power of the sheikhs, but the basic structure has proven very robust.

A central tenet of Mouride faith is to express devotion to the sheikhs through hard work and self-deprivation. Cheikh Amadou Bamba exhorted his followers to "Go and Work" (O'Brien 1971, 57). A well-known Mouride aphorism reflects the conflation of work and faith: "Pray as if you will die tomorrow and work as if you will live forever" (Bava 2002). In a feudal-like system, the *talibés* contribute produce or money to their sheikhs, which has enabled substantial accumulations of wealth. Mourides donate much greater amounts to their leaders than other Islamic sects. In exchange, the *talibés*, who tend to come mostly from the poor and disenfranchised elements of the population, obtain access to an extended social safety net, in addition to a strong sense of belonging and the promise of paradise. The sheikhs are expected to be generous toward their followers, particularly those who are unable to work due to age or illness. Sheikhs may also provide credit at more favorable terms than traders. The extent of devotion of followers as well as the generosity of the sheikhs varies considerably, but these traditions of mutual obligation are nonetheless pervasive and enduring.

The tight solidarity of the Mourides and their faith enabled them to resist colonial influences and to maintain their group identity, even while engaged in strategic cooperation with the French colonial authorities (Diouf 2000).

Membership in the Mouride brotherhood expanded continually in the twentieth century, with the city of Touba becoming the second largest in Senegal, after Dakar. Touba now has 500,000 inhabitants, up from 5,000 in 1960. Mourides view Touba as their spiritual home no matter where they live. The Great Mosque in Touba, the largest in Sub-Saharan Africa, is the destination of an annual pilgrimage (*magal*) to honor Cheikh Amadou Bamba, attracting hundreds of thousands of Mourides every year. Touba has become a de facto separate city-state within Senegal and is essentially off-limits to the political authorities. In addition to the Great Mosque, contributions by the faithful have financed the construction of a US$10 million hospital, a Mouride cultural center and library, and other monuments and institutes.

Mourides and the Groundnut Economy

The strategic allegiance with the French revolved around groundnut production and trade, with the Mourides increasingly dominating the sector, accounting for two-thirds of production during the colonial era (O'Brien 1971). Until the late 1970s, Mourides remained overwhelmingly rural, continuing to grow groundnuts, which are well suited to Senegal's climate and soils.

Following Senegal's independence in 1960, the Mourides maintained their political influence, transitioning from their close ties to the French to strong connections to the ruling Parti Socialiste. Mourides translated these political connections into economic gains, benefiting from easy access to farm credit (often not reimbursed) for planting groundnuts and substantial de facto control of the groundnut trade and transport, in theory in the hands of the government (Lambert 1996). The clientelistic operation of the groundnut industry contributed to the Senegalese financial crisis of the 1980s and the subsequent period of structural adjustment and trade liberalization.

Mourides developed distinctive forms of social organization around the groundnut trade. Mouride young men are organized into *daras*, which are farming brigades accompanying their religious education.[2] Mouride *daras* were at first isolated and worked under arduous conditions, with no nearby access to water. They served the function of colonizing unoccupied land, thereby extending the domain of the Mourides. Conditions have improved over time, with *daras* now mostly consisting of parcels of a sheikh's estate, but life as a worker on a *dara* remains one of deprivation and hard work in service of the sheikh, with minimal remuneration. After many years on a *dara*, a worker may receive a plot of land of his own (O'Brien 1971; Copans 1980).

Most Mouride peasants are now independent smallholders, but some continue to work on the large estates controlled by sheikhs. Even when not in a *dara*, however, the Mourides benefit from the advantages of membership in a close-knit group, while also meeting their obligation to provide substantial offerings to their leaders. Usually, one day a week is designated to work on the sheikh's fields, called "Wednesday fields" (O'Brien 1971, 210). Their cohesiveness, sense of purpose, and political backing enabled the Mourides to displace other groups and take control of increasing swaths of land for groundnut cultivation.

Mouride farming techniques are not geared toward preserving Senegal's fragile ecosystem, however. Unsustainable cultivation techniques, deforestation, growing population, and droughts have contributed to deteriorating land quality and desertification, reducing the incomes of groundnut farmers. Declining groundnut prices and reduced subsidies to farmers associated with structural adjustment policies have also contributed to lower farmer incomes. These trends spurred an increasing migration of Mourides toward urban areas in the 1970s (O'Brien 1988; Babou 2007).

From Groundnut Farmers to Urban Traders

Mouride migration to the cities occurred in several phases in the twentieth century, with the largest movement beginning in the 1970s. Mourides have long been groundnut traders in the cities of the groundnut region. It was, therefore, natural that Mourides gravitated toward the informal sector and commerce in particular, as they moved to the cities. The fourth caliph-general, Abdou Lahat Mbacke (1968–88), actively promoted the establishment of the Mourides in the cities, unlike his predecessors (Babou 2007). The sprawling open-air informal market of Sandaga in Dakar has become the Mourides' center for informal commerce, paralleling that of Touba for the Mourides' spiritual life. The Okass market in Touba is also a very important distribution center.

The Mourides' rural traditions were adapted with remarkable flexibility and effectiveness to their new urban settings. With family ties and traditional beliefs holding the group together, the Mourides were able to generate a new set of urban connections and economic activities. They congregate in neighborhoods wherever they go, which they rename "Touba" (Diouf 2000).

The *dahira* became the central institution of urban life for the Mourides, in some respects replacing the role of rural *daras* in providing spiritual nurturing and promoting economic success. The *dahira* consists of a weekly reunion of local Mourides for religious singing and discussion, as well as collection of dues. These fees support the local branch of the group as well as the traditional donations sent back to Touba for the general support of the organization. The *dahira* also serves as an informal meeting place for exchanging information and assistance about business opportunities and government relations. Newcomers to the cities are assisted by the more established members of the group, much as the *talibés* are helped by the sheikhs in the countryside (O'Brien 1988). The *dahira* is emblematic of the mixture of central structure and informal collaboration that has proved to be remarkably effective. While the Mourides are linked by their common faith and devotion to the leadership in Touba, there is very little overt central direction, and the *dahiras* function autonomously and compete for influence. *Dahiras* themselves provide umbrellas for individual initiative and networking rather than prescribed relationships.

The peanut farmers' emphasis on hard work and saving has carried over to the cities, with commerce replacing agriculture. The cohesiveness of the Mourides and their deep relations of trust have proven to be extremely valuable in fostering their informal commercial network. Group solidarity and belief in the higher purpose of the brotherhood support the fulfillment of promises and obligations without any formal contracts. Mourides almost never default on loans or commitments to other Mourides, as to do so would be viewed as a breach of religious as well as commercial bonds.

Mourides coming to the cities are often provided with work as street vendors by successful Mouride businessmen. These businessmen mentor young street vendors—often, but not exclusively, Mourides—by providing goods on credit and assistance with housing and food. The street traders work long and arduous hours in the heat and grime of Dakar and other cities, much as the peasants toil on the peanut farms. After a long apprenticeship as a street trader, the more successful and enterprising workers can rise in the hierarchy of trading activities and perhaps start a business of their own, just as workers on *daras* are sometimes allotted plots of land after years of work with minimal remuneration. In their hard work and deprivation, the street traders are sustained by the hope of advancement as well as their faith that honoring Cheikh Amadou Bamba will entitle them to enter paradise. At the same time, the abundant supply of reliable and low-cost workers has enabled urban traders to accumulate substantial fortunes; it also has supported the leadership and central organization of the brotherhood in Touba and, in turn, its ability to assist members, thereby providing funding for a social safety net and information distribution system.

Sandaga market is the center of the Mouride trading activities in Senegal and, indeed, the world. Large wholesalers are at the top of the operation of the mazelike trading networks, with a varied assortment of goods for sale. Ebin (1992) describes the functioning of Sandaga market through an ethnographic study of the Fall family, originally cloth traders from Kaolack who had close ties with a former caliph-general. Cheikh Fall, one of the five Fall brothers, heads the enterprise, due to his business and entrepreneurial acumen. A former street trader, he moved to New York, where he purchased African American cosmetics, which he then sold in Senegal. After eight years in New York, he returned to Senegal and started a factory producing hair extensions, which was highly successful. His brothers then left Kaolack to assist him in his business ventures. The Fall headquarters are in Sandaga, where at the time of Ebin's report, they had three large stores. In addition to the ubiquitous street vendors, major wholesalers such as Fall employ a variety of other intermediaries, including resellers who purchase in bulk, *nyoro* who locate clients and bring them to the store in exchange for a small commission, scouts who find other retailers who might want to purchase merchandise from wholesalers, and spotters who announce the impending arrival of a potential client. Wholesalers are able to diversify risk, lower transaction times, and expand their scale of operations by increasing the number of clients and suppliers, so making contacts and developing relationships are of central importance. Ebin's stories show how successful merchants mentor other traders who go on to start their own businesses and, in turn, become clients and suppliers of their mentor.

In addition to domestic commerce and international trade, Mourides have increasingly dominated other important sectors in the cities of Senegal, notably transport and real estate, all of which operate informally despite their large size. For example, the minivans that serve as the major mode of public transport (*cars rapides*) are often owned by Mourides and frequently colorfully decorated with references to Touba.

The increasing economic role of the Mourides has not been achieved without conflicts, however, and has created tension with other groups. There are also tensions within the Mourides between traders and intellectuals (O'Brien 1988). Nevertheless, the group remains very powerful and effective, thanks to the nearly fanatical devotion, work ethic, group solidarity, and political clout of its members.

Globalization of the Mouride Trading Network

The influx of the Mourides to the urban centers of Senegal and The Gambia was accompanied and fostered by the international migration of Mourides to major cities in Europe and then to the United States, with the brotherhood becoming a highly effective international trading group. The Mourides' global network and business practices have been chronicled by many researchers, including Salem (1981), Fassin (1985), Ebin (1992, 1993), Diouf (2000), Babou (2002), and Tall (2004). The story of the Mourides is one of amazing commercial reach.

In various cities around the world, Mourides congregate in Senegalese neighborhoods and *dahiras*, sharing information and providing mutual support and a springboard to commercial success. The cities are linked by family and kinship networks, headed by a wholesaler usually located in Sandaga. Sheikhs based in Senegal coordinate the travels of their *talibés*, as part of the services they render in exchange for the offerings they receive. The young Senegalese emigrant Mourides live together in cramped quarters, often in dangerous neighborhoods, facing harassment from the authorities and not seeing their families for long periods of time—reminiscent of the hardships of life on the rural *daras*. Ebin (1992) quotes a wholesaler dealing in electronics: "We are used to sleeping on the ground, not eating much, and working until exhaustion. It's what we have always done."

Starting in the 1960s, Mourides migrated to cities in France, where they became street traders. They operated throughout France, particularly in Strasbourg in the north (Salem 1981) and Marseilles in the south (Ebin 1992). Their focus has been on selling trinkets and simple consumer goods to tourists during the summer season, often returning to Senegal in the winter. The Mourides were able to outcompete French merchants through hard work and lower prices, even learning German in Strasbourg to communicate with German tourists, for example. As French immigration policies became more restrictive, the Mourides spread around Europe, in particular to Italy. In the mid-1980s, New York emerged as a major destination, where they also became successful street traders.

Experienced traders travel to New York, Jeddah, and Hong Kong SAR, China, where they purchase large volumes of a wide variety of electronic and cosmetic products, which they sell in Senegal and in other countries. Mouride shipping and financial agents in New York are also in contact with Asian traders, who supply some of the goods such as watches, sunglasses, and cosmetics that are the mainstays of the Mouride value chain. The goods are imported into Senegal through informal mechanisms and end up at Sandaga or other urban markets. In some cases, traders bring back the goods themselves in large trunks and suitcases. Sandaga and other markets are also supplied by contraband imports shipped through The Gambia. As described in more detail in the following chapter, low import duties in The Gambia have provided a major incentive to import officially into The Gambia and then smuggle the goods into Senegal. Goods may also be shipped through the port of Dakar, where customs practices are notoriously discretionary and Mouride traders use their political connections to evade the statutory duties.

Fassin (1985) details how Mourides smuggle and illegally sell pharmaceutical products in Senegal, as also noted in chapter 4. The favored route is through The Gambia; products are brought to Touba via Kaolack, hidden in trucks filled with hay. In addition, unofficial supplies of drugs are obtained from hospitals and the national pharmaceutical importer, Pharmacie Nationale D'Approvisionnement, and sold openly in well-known locations, with the tacit acquiescence of the government.

Ebin (1993) provides a vivid description of a Mouride trading group's operations in Marseilles. Almost all of the members of the group originate from a Mouride town in Senegal, Darou Mousty. Mustapha Sow, the leader of the group, supervises and assists younger traders newly arrived from Senegal, who have been put in contact with him by their sheikhs. Mustapha Sow's operations extend all along the Mediterranean coast, starting from his base in Marseilles. Sow sources from Mouride runners who steadily arrive in Marseilles with products from Spain, Italy, North Africa, and Asia. One of his main suppliers is also from Darou Mousty. Sow himself goes to Paris every Monday morning to replenish his supplies following the weekend sales to tourists. His main supplier in Paris is a Moroccan who employs a Senegalese Mouride, Mamadou Ndiaye, known to the Mourides as the focal point for all information about merchandise and contacts in the Paris region. Ndiaye can supply traders such as Moustapha Sow with a large variety of merchandise or tell him where to obtain it. Sow returns to Marseilles Monday afternoons with his newly purchased stock of goods, which he distributes through a large number of street vendors who operate all around the region, runners who supply other traders, as well as wholesalers heading to Senegal to sell at Sandaga and elsewhere. In short, the Mourides operate in Marseilles much as they do in Dakar.

By the early 1990s, Senegalese Mourides controlled most street trading in New York, selling watches, umbrellas, T-shirts, and hats (Babou 2002). Over time, they invested their savings in other services, mainly shipping, travel, and money transfer services for Senegalese and other African immigrants in the United States. New York increasingly developed into a major hub in the Mouride trading networks. Ebin (1993) describes how Pape Faye, another Mouride from Darou Mousty, served as Moustapha Sow's emissary to New York City. Faye started as a trader in Dakar but left Senegal in 1979 and now travels all around Europe, buying and selling. Ebin (1993) describes Faye's first visit to New York, which was organized by his *sheikh*. At that time, Senegalese from Darou Mousty lived and congregated in an apartment in the Bronx and gathered in the Flatbush neighborhood in a place called the House of Serigne Touba. Currently, Senegalese Mourides are concentrated in Little Senegal, a section of Harlem around West 116th Street (Ebin 2008; Babou 2002). Many Mourides who started as street vendors now own stores in that area. The stores sell a variety of products, including cosmetics, religious objects, compact discs, and digital video discs, and phone cards. The House of Islam is the center for Mourides in the neighborhood, a building purchased under the guidance of one of the grandsons of Cheikh Amadou Bamba. Several loosely cooperating and competing *dahiras* operate in New York City.

Mouride wholesalers such as Cheikh Fall and Mustapha Sow have contacts around the world with whom they can be in instant communication by telephone or Internet. Mouride traders use modern communication and information technologies to advance their commercial transactions, in particular financial transfers (Tall 2004). They know whom to contact when they want to buy or sell particular types of merchandise at the lowest prices and are very nimble in adapting to changing supply and demand. For example, prior to the African Cup of Nations soccer tournament, wholesalers such as Cheikh Fall, anticipating the rise in demand for televisions, may contact a Mouride working in New York who has contacts in China (Ebin 1992). For other products, such as jewelry, wholesalers turn to their networks in Italy.

The strong bonds of solidarity among Mourides enable sophisticated international financial transactions without any contracts or collateral, minimizing transaction costs and detection by the authorities (Tall 2004). Merchants in Sandaga serve as financial intermediaries for fund transfers to and from Senegal. A Mouride residing in the United States or Europe wishing to repatriate funds can remit the funds to a correspondent of a large merchant in Senegal, who, in turn, distributes them to the emigrant's family. These funds are an important source of working capital for traders. Alternatively, an itinerant trader may make transfers home as an advance: the merchant provides funds to the emigrant's family in Senegal, and, on his next trip home, the emigrant repays the merchant with proceeds from the goods he took back for sale in Senegal.

The Kara international money exchange was started in 1991 by a Mouride trader in New York, providing a sophisticated, yet informal, money transfer mechanism for use by merchants traveling between New York and Dakar, allowing them to travel without carrying large sums of money (Tall 2004). Illiterate traders can avail themselves of this system, as little or no documentation is required. Merchants traveling to New York deposit funds with the Kara office in Dakar before they leave Senegal and then have access to the funds when they arrive in the United States. Likewise, a trader in New York transfers money home by bringing cash to the Kara office on Broadway, which remits the funds to the designated beneficiary in Senegal, who can obtain the money without any paperwork. Communication between the Kara offices in New York and Dakar is by fax, and transmission of funds to the recipient is nearly instantaneous and highly secure, despite the lack of formalities. Mouride connections are sufficient to guarantee fulfillment of obligations and deter embezzlement, because a violation would betray the values of the brotherhood and also lead to cutoff of credit.

The Yoruba in Nigeria, Benin, and Togo

Historical Background

The Yoruba are among the most populous and urbanized ethnic groups in Sub-Saharan Africa. Most Yoruba speak a common language, also called Yoruba. Yorubaland, the traditional region of the Yoruba ethnic group, encompasses the central areas of Benin and Togo and the southwestern states of Nigeria, including Lagos, Ogun, Oyo, Osun, Ondo, Ekiti, and Kwara. Historically, Yorubaland was a mix of loosely connected kingdoms. While each kingdom was independent, they all regarded the city of Ile Ife, located in the Nigerian state of Osun, as the common place of origin, *orirun*. The kingdoms operated autonomously but maintained political and economic ties to each other. The hierarchical organization of the group around chiefs is in some ways similar to that of the Mourides and their marabouts.

Barter was likely the earliest form of trade among the Yoruba. One advantage of Yorubaland's fertile soil was that each kingdom was capable of producing slightly more food than required for subsistence. As a result, the minimal surpluses could be bartered among kingdoms to supplement other basic needs, such as clothing and shelter. An extensive societal division of labor, including ruling elites, manufacturers, herbalists, priests, historians, entertainers, and farmers, facilitated barter in a range of goods-for-goods and goods-for-services transactions. Furthermore, as the Yoruba became increasingly sophisticated, they demanded more exotic goods to maintain the elite's extravagant lifestyles and to use in ritual festivals (Falola and Adebayo 2000).

There are many notable examples of barter in the early Yoruba economy. In the agriculture sector, farmers openly traded with each other. For instance, farmers who grew mostly yams tended to exchange yams for millet with farmers who grew primarily millet. Also, farmers exchanged produce for tools with blacksmiths. Priests and herbalists accepted valuable and edible items, often animals and palm oil, for their services. Entertainers were paid with leftover food, expensive costumes, horses, or slaves. Imported goods such as natron (a cleaning substance) and salt were bartered through long-distance trade. It is estimated that, around the fifteenth century, the barter exchanges evolved into monetized trade using cowry shells as currency.

The Yoruba economy eventually expanded into a regional trade network, notably through the trans-Saharan caravan trade (Falola 1991). Extensive long-distance trade routes through West Africa were well established before the arrival of Europeans on the continent. The caravan trade developed systems of credit, transport, information exchange, settlement of business disputes, and insurance among separate peoples without modern institutions to perform these services (Cohen 1969), promoting economic integration among ethnic groups.

Regional trade fostered the Yoruba's interaction with their northern neighbors: the Nupe and the Hausa. The lack of geographic barriers separating these ethnic groups facilitated their cooperation in connecting the region's goods to the major trans-Saharan trade routes (Perani and Wolff 1999). The Hausa, in particular, had long participated in regional trade. The Yoruba provided livestock to the network and received skilled Hausa slaves. They also provided luxury goods, such as salt and natron, to the Egba and Egbado groups to the south. The most northern kingdom of Yorubaland, Oyo, came to dominate regional trade, even operating a cavalry, because of its strategic location. The Oyo controlled trade in Yorubaland and some surrounding areas until the end of the nineteenth century, with a major market at Apomu (Falola and Adebayo 2000; Eades 1993). This lucrative trade was a major source of political power.

Beginning in the sixteenth century, European involvement in the Yoruba economy shifted the focus of regional trade toward the coastal areas, where the Europeans initially operated. The Ijebu increasingly controlled the lucrative trade with the Europeans along the Atlantic coast. While the Oyo lost commercial stature to the Ijebu, the European involvement did not affect the historic inland trade network as much as it did the coastal routes. Europeans sold the Ijebu cowries and manufactured goods in exchange for slaves and cloth. The Yoruba were advantageously located to transport the European goods north. The slave trade made Benin, then called Dahomey, a key location in the international triangle trade and introduced new goods such as tobacco into the regional market.

Many Yoruba traders operated out of Porto Novo and Ouidah in Dahomey at the end of the nineteenth century (Igué and Soule 1992), working with repatriated slaves of Yoruba origin from Brazil. Some traders became very wealthy and famous in the region. France's colonization of Dahomey in 1894 had a profound effect on the Yoruba networks. While the repatriated Brazilian slaves cooperated with the French, local Yoruba people converted to Islam and developed clandestine networks with Nigeria to escape colonial controls and trade barriers.

The Rural Markets System

As of the mid-twentieth century, the Yoruba's historical trade relations remained important despite the effects of colonization and European involvement (Cohen 1969). Trade in Yorubaland and the surrounding region was supported by daily and periodic markets in urban and rural areas, servicing local and long-distance trade routes (Eades 1980). In addition to the markets in rural towns, "rings" were organized outside the larger towns. The "ring" markets operated on four- or eight-day cycles. These markets operated with considerable sophistication. For instance, "forestallers" would wait in the trails a few miles before the markets in an effort to buy the traders' goods for slightly less than the market price and then resell them in the market for a small profit (Hodder 1961).

The Yoruba traded locally produced and imported manufactured goods, notably textiles, as well as local foods and food products (Eades 1980). Manufactured goods were exchanged outward from the major urban centers to rural areas for agricultural goods that moved inward from the rural areas to the urban centers. Women supplied farm produce at the rural markets, including maize, cassava, yams, bananas, kola nuts, tomatoes, okra, and other vegetables, in addition to producing and selling pots, calabashes, palm oil, palm wine, firewood, bundles of leaves, and yam flour (Hodder 1961). Since each woman dealt with only a small quantity of goods, bulking was a central component of the agricultural trade as goods moved toward the cities. In the urban markets, large expatriate and Lebanese firms in Lagos and Ibadan supplied manufactured goods to the system. Since urban Yoruba wholesalers often bought the goods in bulk and distributed them in smaller quantities to retailers, bulk breaking characterized this side of the trade. Nonetheless, the erratic supply of manufactured goods underscored the importance of well-established connections in the trade routes. Raw material shortages, import delays in ports, and price controls all contributed to the unreliable supply of manufactured goods (Eades 1980).

The markets were highly competitive and dominated by large amounts of low-volume transactions, so profitability was low. The numerous middlemen who moved goods from town to town drove profits down to almost nothing for most transactions (Hodder 1961).

Women dominated the low-margin Yoruba retail trade. Eades (1980) estimates that in 1950 women constituted 84 percent of traders in Ibadan and 70 percent in Lagos, reflecting the traditional division of labor in Yoruba society. Men were mostly involved in agriculture, while women were more likely to be involved in processing and selling their husband's produce. If a husband felt that his wife did not trade his produce at a fair price, he was free to sell it to another woman. Many women even sought capital from their husbands to expand their personal enterprises. Hodder (1961, 154) asserts, "To Yoruba women, moreover, marketing, petty trading, or at least attending a market, forms part of their way of life; and their rewards lie as much in the social life offered by the markets as in their cash profits." Despite women's active participation in petty trading, social barriers frequently prevented them from ascending the trade hierarchy. Men could accumulate capital for several years before marriage, enabling them to enter into more lucrative wholesale trade. Meanwhile, women married and had children at younger ages, so their domestic responsibilities significantly limited their trading enterprises. As a result, even though the majority of Yoruba traders were women, the upper echelons were dominated by men (Eades 1980).

Migration

The rural market system and long-distance trade fostered a Yoruba diaspora across West Africa in the twentieth century (Eades 1980). Yoruba migration and trade expanded for several reasons. First, Yoruba laborers and artisans who amassed sufficient capital tended to migrate to impoverished savannah towns to become traders (Eades 1980). Second, in nearby countries, particularly in Ghana and Côte d'Ivoire, large plantations and mining projects created opportunities for migrants as laborers and traders. Third, regional demand for consumer goods increased along with incomes. Yoruba traders sold cloth made in western Nigeria in regions further east, bringing back kola nuts from Ghana to Nigeria (Sudarkasa 1985). Yoruba migrants were particularly active in northern Ghana. This east-west trade increasingly came to include slaves, leather goods, cattle, and Ghanaian textiles. Fourth, the British brought many Yoruba to Accra to fight against the Ashanti. Many of the Yoruba established themselves in Ghana. Fifth, cash crop failures in tobacco and cotton in Nigeria, in conjunction with construction of the Lagos-Kano rail line, increased Yoruba's interest in moving to francophone West Africa (Igué 2003).

By the latter half of the twentieth century, the Yoruba had spread across West Africa into Côte d'Ivoire, Niger, Burkina Faso, and Senegal, although the government of Ghana expelled many Yoruba in 1968. Solidarity among the Yoruba contributed to their successful migration in a wide geographic area. Successful traders brought relatives to assist them with their enterprises, who eventually established their own businesses. This organization was central to the Yoruba's success in international trade, much like the Mourides'.

Modern Trade Networks
The Yoruba remain at the center of a large, informal sector international trade network in West Africa, facilitated by kinship ties, varied market tactics, and hierarchical organizational structure, although the group is less clearly structured than the Mourides (Igué and Soule 1992; Igué 2003). Yoruba tend to transact with other Yoruba traders because of trust, common language, and similar business styles (Sudarkasa 1985). The belief in Islam is a source of solidarity and motivation, as it is for the Mourides. A well-developed informal system of tontines is limited to members of the Yoruba group, fostering economic ties among the group members. The operation of Yoruba supply chains is not well understood, however, due to the secretive nature of smuggling and high illiteracy rates of traders, resulting in poor recordkeeping (Igué 2003).

The Yoruba deal in a large variety of products and sources in various destinations, which have changed over time. They have been particularly dominant in the sales of plastics and medicines. When Ghana restricted imports from Europe in the 1960s, Yoruba traders collected products from Nigeria, Côte d'Ivoire, Sierra Leone, and Burkina Faso to transport clandestinely to Ghana. Starting in the 1970s, Yoruba traders have distributed plastics produced in Côte d'Ivoire throughout the region. Generic medicines are often imported from English-speaking countries of the region where regulations are less stringent. Registered companies in Togo, Benin, Nigeria, and Ghana import certain other goods, such as enamel and cosmetics, from China, which the Yoruba smuggle across the region (Igué 2003). For goods sold in Ghana, Yoruba traders obtain the products wholesale in Kumasi and Accra from Yoruba supply centers.

The structure of migrant trading families is similar to the gender roles in Yorubaland. The head of the family, who is traditionally male, negotiates the supply of a range of goods with domestic and international suppliers. Meanwhile, the wife manages the products and supervises their sale. She may, in turn, redistribute the goods to young female street traders. This structure underscores the importance of migrating in groups. Women constitute the majority of traders and play a key role in the success of Yoruba enterprises. Yoruba women are well known for their resilience and patience at trade. Moreover, the hierarchical organization enables apprentices and other beginner traders to learn the practice before starting their own enterprises (Igué 2003).

The Yoruba have long played a leading role in smuggling between Nigeria and Benin, going back to the colonial era (Flynn 1997). The oil boom in Nigeria and Nigerian protectionism in the 1970s provided a major stimulus to the Yoruba smuggling activities. The Yoruba have been the dominant players in the reexport trade between Nigeria and Benin in most products, aside from rice and wheat (Igué and Soule 1992, 100), as described in detail in the following chapter.

Yoruba traders reach their customers through an array of transactions on the streets and exchanges in market stalls and shops. Street trading is the most informal of the Yoruba's activities. One technique is for groups of young traders to carry products to several villages during a day trip. The groups bring their goods to a village where they display, publicize, and sell them before circulating to another village, reaching many per day. They often operate in open, public spaces so as to attract the attention of the villagers. Another informal technique is for some Yoruba traders, mostly young women, to go through neighboring towns, selling at people's doorsteps. They display their products in small mobile shops and persistently encourage buyers to make a purchase. Igué (2003) outlines specific benefits that the Yoruba obtain from these strategies. First, by not having a permanent shop, traders save the expense and taxes of owning one. Second, they can access remote areas. Third, they can better understand the preferences of their customers and where to distribute each product.

Besides working in the streets, Yoruba traders also occupy a range of positions in urban markets. Like the informality of street trading, stalls in markets also help traders to understand their buyers' tastes. Stalls are small tables that are set up early in the day to display a trader's products and taken down at the end of the day. Since the stalls have low start-up costs, apprentices often maintain them. They are most common in Côte d'Ivoire, where they offer clothing, plastic shoes, watches, and underwear. Profits from stalls are fairly low, limited to around CFAF 1,000 per stall per day (Igué 2003).

Yoruba traders also use market shops for their enterprises. Yoruba shops are known for the plastic goods commonly displayed at the entrance, which are a sign of their monopoly in the plastic trade. The products are often organized so that only the shopkeeper is capable of locating them. The shops also have some advantages for Yoruba traders. The larger the shop, the more the owner can purchase in bulk and store the products. Shops also allow the owners to meet more sophisticated customers who appreciate posted prices, in addition to uneducated customers they reach in village markets (Igué 2003).

The activities of Yoruba shops vary somewhat across countries. In the 1970s, Niger had a small number of Yoruba shops, possibly fewer than 30, all of which were unregistered with the Niger government. These shops fit into three categories: food, clothes, and general. The shops were operated by the owners and their family members and did not employ local people. The value of the transactions at that time was estimated at CFAF 50,000–CFAF 100,000 per shop per day, and the owners were the wealthiest migrants; some even owned nice cars to park in front of their shops. Alternatively, in Côte d'Ivoire, Yoruba shops were more widespread, despite the immigrant expulsion in 1968. Before 1968, the Yoruba accounted for about 70 percent of shops in the country; in 1978, the Yoruba share fell to a still-large 60 percent. After 1968, most shops became much smaller. In addition to making Yoruba traders in Abidjan more cautious, competition from other migrant groups increased after the 1968 expulsions (Igué 2003).

In general, the Yoruba traders are skilled at filling gaps in regional markets. If another ethnic group has a monopoly of supplying a certain good, the Yoruba will not attempt to sell it in that area. As a result, the traders' techniques and choice of products greatly depend on the region in which they are trading. For instance, in Burkina Faso, Yoruba sell cosmetics and spare bike parts. In Niamey, Niger, where people from Gao monopolize cosmetics and the Zarma and Gourmanche control bike parts, the Yoruba sell enamelware, plastics, and ironware. Instead of locating themselves in the central buildings of urban markets, where other groups operate and space is expensive, the Yoruba frequently operate in sheds on the periphery of urban markets (Igué 2003).

In the Dantokpa market of Cotonou, the largest open-air market in West Africa, Yoruba traders are important participants, along with other ethnic groups (Prag 2010). Dantokpa is a center for the regional cross-border trade described in chapters 4 and 9. Large and small informal operators are both prevalent. Dantokpa is similar to Sandaga in Dakar and other sprawling informal markets in West Africa, but no single ethnic group dominates in the ways in which the Mourides dominate in Sandaga. The Chamber of Commerce is dominated by Yoruba traders from Porto Novo. Other ethnic groups with historical trading relations with the Yoruba, such as the Adja and Mina, also play a major role in Dantokpa. Prag (2010) describes the shifting competition and cooperation among various interest groups in Dantokpa and their ethnic dimensions. The government has attempted to assert control over the market and modernize it, with the backing of some market participants, but these efforts have been blocked by an alliance of large and small informal traders.

Traditional Social Networks and the Modern Informal Sector

This section synthesizes the central features of the two groups (Mourides and Yoruba) and relates them to contemporaneous informal sector practices as they emerge from previous chapters of this study.

The social background of informal actors places them in opposition to many Western-style norms. Lack of education is a crucial feature. Most informal entrepreneurs have little or no modern education. Instead, they were trained in *daras* or similar types of apprenticeships. The Mouride *daras* have a strong religious component as well, but this is not always so. Even today, very few young people go through the formal education system imported from the former Western colonial powers. In fact, traditional education remains a strong competitor to modern education (Mbaye 2002; Gérard 1995; Meunier 1995). Surveys in Mali show that 36 percent of parents prefer informal education. Meunier (1995) finds that enrollment in informal schools is growing almost twice as fast as in formal schools. There are a number of key differences between the French education system in francophone Africa and the traditional forms of schooling. The French system was and still is oriented toward preparing students for white-collar jobs, particularly in the civil service. In contrast, African traditional education is much more practical and is well suited for developing entrepreneurial skills. Consequently, many parents and students are more drawn to traditional forms of education, in part explaining the low levels of participation in official schools (Mbaye 2002).

There are many similarities between long-standing traditional practices in African society and informal sector behavior. The role of women in the informal sector parallels that in African villages. This is particularly evident among the Yoruba, where the traditional gender-based division of labor in agriculture extends to informal trading. In agriculture, women do not own land, and men are responsible for cultivation; women's role is to sell the produce in small stalls in the markets. Thus women constitute the majority of traders, but men usually control the business and the capital. Likewise, in the informal sector, women tend to operate small-scale shops and are concentrated in trading activities. The family-centeredness of informal businesses also parallels traditional societies. Large and small informal firms, as discussed in chapters 4 and 5, rely heavily on family ties for loans, staffing, and more, although this tends to diminish as a business grows (Lyons, Dankoco, and Snoxell 2008). Moreover, the sectors in which the informal sector dominates, such as commerce and handicrafts, correspond to the main activities in traditional African economies.

Allegiance to traditional sources of authority, such as the Yoruba chiefs and the Mouride marabouts, is far more binding than the authority of the modern state.

There are both similarities and differences between the Mourides and the Yoruba organization. The Yoruba are an ethnic group based on family, whereas the Mourides are bound together by a form of Islam that encompasses several ethnic groups but is heavily influenced by the traditional Wolof ethnic group. The hierarchical structure is similar. Both groups are supported by belief in the mystical power of their leaders. The chief is the repository of the entire lineage's mystical power and instills both fear and respect such that no one will challenge him. Politicians seek his electoral favor as well as his blessing. The story of Khadim Bousso in chapter 4 illustrates the power of the caliph of the Mourides.

Conclusion

The Mourides' and the Yoruba's trading activities illustrate the continuing importance of informal trading networks operated by kinship networks. These groups originated many centuries prior to European colonization and have adapted to the colonial and postcolonial economic environments. The social and religious bonds linking members of the groups enable complex and flexible trading strategies with property rights and contract enforcement provided by group solidarity rather than formal rules. Adherence to Islam plays a major role in the solidarity of both groups. The Yoruba and Mourides both have hierarchical organizations, although this is much more pronounced and formalized among the Mourides.

The descriptions of the Mourides and the Yoruba presented here bring out the close connection between the informal sector in general and trading in particular. Indeed, to this day, trading is the foremost activity of the informal sector, as seen in chapter 3, involving both domestic and cross-border dimensions. The trading networks of the Mourides extend to Europe, Asia, and North America in addition to Africa. The trading sphere of the Yoruba is confined largely to West Africa. The interplay of historical, cultural, and economic factors is important in understanding the central role of informal trading activities in West African economies.

The structure and operation of these informal networks grow out of traditional African societies. The norms and institutions of the informal sector exert a powerful influence on West African economies, notably how markets are organized, the continued prevalence of traditional forms of education, the role of women, and so forth. Allegiance to religious leaders and traditional chiefs is often much more powerful than allegiance to the modern state.

While group solidarity and mutual trust enable the expansion of commercial activities, the political and economic influence of these groups is not entirely benign. Their main markets, such as Touba and Sandaga in Senegal and Dantokpa in Benin, are largely off-limits to the government, enabling these groups to engage in smuggling and tax evasion in plain view of the authorities.

Notes
1. Lisa Cabral of Swarthmore College assisted in preparing this section, which is partially based on a visit to Touba in October 2007.
2. These groups are unlike *daras* in other sects, which focus exclusively on religious education.

References

Adhikari, Krishna P., and Patricia Goldey. 2009. "Social Capital and Its Downside: The Impact on Sustainability of Community-Based Organizations in Nepal." *World Development* 38 (2): 184–94.

Babou, Cheikh A. 2002. "Brotherhood Solidarity, Education, and Migration: The Role of the Dahiras among the Murid Muslim Community in New York." *African Affairs* 101: 151–70.

———. 2007. "Urbanizing Mystical Islam: Making Murid Space in the Cities of Senegal." *International Journal of African Historical Studies* 40 (2): 197–223.

Barron, Stephen, John Field, and Tom Schuller, eds. 2000. *Social Capital: Critical Issues.* Oxford: Oxford University Press.

Bava, Sophie. 2002. "De la baraka aux affaires: La captation de ressources religieuses comme initiatrices de nouvelles routes migratoires." *Ville-Ecole-Integration Enjeux* 131 (December): 48–63.

Casson, Mark C., Marina D. Guista, and Uma S. Kambhampati. 2009. "Formal and Informal Institutions in Development." *World Development* 38 (2): 137–41.

Cohen, Abner. 1969. *Custom and Politics in Urban Africa: A Study of Hausa Migrants in Yoruba Towns.* Berkeley: University of California Press.

Copans, Jean. 1980. *Les Marabouts de l'arachide: La confrérie mouride et les paysans du Sénégal.* Paris: Le Sycomore.

Diouf, Mamadou. 2000. "The Senegalese Murid Trade Diaspora and the Making of a Vernacular Cosmopolitanism." *Public Culture* 12 (3): 679–702.

Eades, J. S. 1980. *The Yoruba Today.* Cambridge, U.K.: Cambridge University Press.

———. 1993. *Strangers and Traders: Yoruba Migrants, Markets, and the State in Northern Ghana.* Edinburgh: Edinburgh University Press.

Ebin, Victoria. 1992. "À la recherche de nouveaux 'Poissons': Stratégies commerciales Mourides par temps de crise." *Politique Africaine* 45 (March): 86–99.

———. 1993. "Les commerçants mourides à Marseille et à New York: Regards sur les stratégies d'implantation." In *Grands commerçants d'Afrique de l'Ouest: Logiques et pratiques d'un groupe d'hommes d'affaires contemporains,* ed. Grégoire Emmanuel and Pascal Labazée, 101–23. Paris: Karthala-Orstom.

———. 2008. "Little Senegal vs. the New Harlem Renaissance: Senegalese Immigrants and the Gentrification of Harlem." *Asylon Terra* (March). http://terra.rezo.net/rubrique133.html.

Fafchamps, Marcel. 2004. *Market Institutions in Sub-Saharan Africa*. Cambridge, MA: MIT Press.

Falola, Toyin. 1991. "The Yoruba Caravan System of the Nineteenth Century." *International Journal of African Historical Studies* 24 (1): 111–32.

Falola, Toyin, and A. G. Adebayo. 2000. *Culture, Politics, and Money among the Yoruba*. New Brunswick, NJ: Transaction Publishers.

Fassin, Didier. 1985. "Du clandestin a l'officieux: Les reseaux de vente illicite des medicaments au Senegal." *Cahiers d'Études Africaines* 25 (98): 161–77.

Field, John. 2003. *Social Capital*. London: Routledge.

Flynn, D. K. 1997. "'We Are the Border': Identity, Exchange, and the State along the Bénin-Nigeria Border." *American Ethnologist* 24 (2): 311–30.

Gérard, Etienne. 1995. "Jeux et enjeux scolaires au Mali: Le poids des strategies educatives des populations dans le fonctionnement et l'evolution de l'ecole publique." *Cahiers des Sciences Humaines* 31 (3): 585–615.

Hodder, B. W. 1961. "Rural Periodic Day Markets in Part of Yorubaland." *Transactions and Papers* (Institute of British Geographers) 29: 149–59.

Igué, John O. 2003. *The Yoruba in French Speaking West Africa: Essay about a Diaspora*. Paris: Librairie Presence Africaine.

Igué, John O., and Bio G. Soule. 1992. *L'état entrepôt au Benin: Commerce informel ou solution a la crise?* Paris: Editions Karthala.

Lambert, A. 1996. "Les commercants et l'integration regionale." In *Le Senegal et ses voisins*, ed. Momar-Coumba Diop, 81–94. Dakar: Sociétés-Espaces-Temps.

Lyons, Michal, Ibrahima S. Dankoco, and Simon Snoxell. 2008. "Capital social et moyens d'existence durables: Quelle stratégie de survie chez les commerçants urbains du Ghana et du Sénégal." *Revue Ouest Africaine de Science Economique et de Gestion* 1 (1): 12-37.

Mbaye, Ahmoud A. 2002. "Capital humain, compétence et productivité du travail au Sénégal: Une analyse empirique." *Economies et Sociétés* IV (3-4): 567–88.

Meunier, Olivier. 1995. "Enseignement de base: Politique d'éducation et stratégies educatives en milieu haoussa; Le cas de la ville de Maradi (Niger)." *Cahiers des Sciences Humaines* 31 (3): 617–34.

Munshi, Kaivan, and Mark Rosenzweig. 2006. "Traditional Institutions Meet the Modern World: Caste, Gender, and Schooling Choice in a Globalizing Economy." *American Economic Review* 96 (4): 1225–52.

North, Douglass. 1989. "Institutions and Economic Growth: A Historical Introduction." *World Development* 17 (9): 1313–32.

O'Brien, Donald B. C. 1971. *The Mourides of Senegal*. Oxford: Oxford University Press.

———. 1988. "Charisma Comes to Town." In *Charisma and Brotherhood in African Islam*, ed. Donald B. Cruse O'Brien and Christian Coulon. Oxford: Oxford University Press.

Perani, Judith, and Norma H. Wolff. 1999. *Cloth, Dress, and Art Patronage in Africa*. New York: Berg Publishers.

Portes, Alejandro. 1998. "Social Capital: Its Origins and Applications in Modern Sociology." *Annual Review of Modern Sociology* 24: 1–24.

Prag, Ebbe. 2010. "Political Struggles over the Dantokpa Market in Cotonou, Benin." DIIS Working Paper 2010:3, Danish Institute for International Studies, Copenhagen.

Putnam, Robert D. 1995. "Bowling Alone: America's Declining Social Capital." *Journal of Democracy* 6 (1): 65–78.

Rauch, James E. 2001. "Business and Social Networks in International Trade." *Journal of Economic Literature* 49 (4): 1177–203.

Salem, Gérard. 1981. "De la Brousse sénégalaise au Boul'Mich: Le système commercial Mouride en France." *Cahiers d'Études Africaines* 21 (81-83): 267–88.

Sudarkasa, Niara. 1985. "The Role of Yoruba Commercial Migration in West African Development." In *African Migration and National Development,* ed. Beverly Lindsay. University Park, PA: University of Pennsylvania Press.

Tall, Serigne M. 2004. "Senegalese Emigres: New Information and Communication Technologies." *Review of African Political Economy* 31 (99): 31–48.

Chapter **9**

Government Policies, Smuggling, and the Informal Sector

By Stephen Golub

The informal sector in West Africa has become increasingly internationalized in the last few decades. This chapter explores informal cross-border trade—that is, smuggling—in West Africa, focusing on Senegal and Benin. According to official trade data, regional trade flows are minimal despite the West African Economic and Monetary Union (WAEMU) and Economic Community of West African States (ECOWAS) regional trading agreements. In fact, however, smuggling is flourishing in West Africa, reflecting artificial national boundaries imposed in the colonial period, the strong ethnic ties transcending these borders, which are described in chapter 8, the inability to police entry and exit points, and differing economic policies in neighboring countries that create incentives to engage in smuggling.

This chapter illustrates the complex interplay between formal and informal aspects of international trade in West Africa. Much of regional trade is conducted by the large informal firms described in chapter 4. Indeed one of the most important industries controlled by the informal sector, as pointed out in chapter 3, is commerce, which includes cross-border transactions. The demarcation between domestic and foreign trading is very fluid in Africa. Regional exchange in traditional local food staples such as millet predates present national borders. Other bulk foodstuffs consumed in West Africa, such as rice, sugar, and wheat, are largely imported from Asia, Europe, and North America and then distributed around the region. Large informal enterprises are intimately involved throughout the distribution process and interact in complex ways with formal importers and shipping companies such as Balloré, Maersk, and Grimaldi. Cash crops and petroleum extracted in Nigeria are also distributed in West Africa through informal circuits. In short, there are numerous connections between smuggling (illegal trade) and the informal sector (actors

This chapter draws on Golub and Mbaye (2009) and Golub (2008).

operating illegally). This chapter highlights weaknesses in the institutional environment that contribute to the flourishing of informal trade, notably trade policies and customs management. Chapter 6 reviews the institutional weaknesses that foster informality, highlighting the central role of customs. Corruption and bureaucracy at customs open the door to smuggling activities of large informal firms (chapter 4) and kinship networks (chapter 8). Smuggling, in turn, exacerbates the informalization of West African economies directly by serving as an important avenue for entrepreneurship, employment, and income and indirectly by promoting a culture of corruption and tax evasion.

Historical Background

Intra-African trade has been shaped by a long history. Traditional long- and short-distance trading routes predated the colonial era. The colonial powers created artificial borders within regions with long-standing ethnic and cultural ties. Upon independence in the 1950s and 1960s, the new governments often pursued erratic and widely divergent trade and exchange rate policies. Large differences in rates of protection between countries provided an impetus for smuggling, which was facilitated by the weak enforcement abilities of African governments, the cultural and ethnic connections among people in these arbitrarily defined countries, and the trading traditions among them (Berg 1985; Egg and Herrera 1998), as also discussed in chapter 8 of this volume.

The study of smuggling in Africa has focused mostly on whether or not this trade is beneficial. Azam (2007) provides an overview of the literature on the welfare effects of smuggling. In an early contribution, Bhagwati and Hansen (1973) emphasize the waste of resources associated with smuggling activities, but Deardorff and Stolper (1990) point out that smuggling is a response to severe policy distortions and can alleviate those distortions. Relatively few studies have attempted to document the magnitude and determinants of smuggling in Africa.

Prior to the colonial era, states in Africa were not characterized by hard geographic borders, with rulers having only weak control over the territory and movements of people (Herbst 2000, ch. 2). At the Berlin conference of 1884–85, the colonial powers divided up Africa among themselves, creating territorial borders based on their de facto zones of control. These boundaries arbitrarily separated regions with long-standing ethnic ties and often without clear geographic separators (Young 1994).

As illogical and porous as colonial borders were, they remained the basis for national boundaries following the end of colonialism in the early 1960s. Initiatives to consolidate countries into regional unions, including between The

Gambia and Senegal, have failed due to the unwillingness of national political elites to cede authority (Herbst 2000).

Moreover, the newly independent postcolonial nation-states developed their own national economic policies, including monetary and fiscal policies, but, more often than not, these policies were wielded irresponsibly in the first few decades of independence. Trade policies were of particular importance, as they served both to protect local industries and to generate government revenues (Berg 1985). Taxes on international trade have historically provided an unusually large portion of government revenues in Africa, dating back to the colonial period and continuing to the present day. Direct taxes on income and wealth are difficult to enforce in Africa due to lack of state control over much of the population (Herbst 2000, 116). The prevalence of the informal sector also limits the scope for direct taxation, as discussed in chapter 3. In addition, many countries, particularly those pursuing import substitution strategies most vigorously, have adopted very high import barriers, including tariffs and import prohibitions. The high levels of protection have impeded legal trade within Africa and provided large incentives for smuggling.

Regional integration has so far done little to promote legal trade within Africa or to staunch smuggling. There are some 30 regional blocs in Africa, and, on average, each of the 53 countries on the continent is a member of four often-overlapping groups (Yang and Gupta 2005). Yet official intra-African trade flows remain very low. Excluding South Africa, intra-African trade accounts for less than 10 percent of total African exports and imports. Regional integration has failed to promote official trade for several reasons. First, in many regional groups, notably the ECOWAS, effective harmonization of policies has been very limited. Nigeria, in particular, has flouted ECOWAS agreements on harmonizing external tariffs and removing barriers to trade within the group. Second, regional integration has been asymmetric between francophone and anglophone countries. Francophone countries have achieved much deeper integration. The WAEMU countries have formed a customs union, but this agreement is confined to the francophone countries of West Africa, leaving out contiguous anglophone countries, including The Gambia and Nigeria, which are members of ECOWAS but not WAEMU. Consequently, large disparities in trade policies remain the rule between countries sharing porous borders and weak enforcement capabilities. The Gambia—a tiny anglophone country of 1.5 million people completely surrounded by francophone Senegal except for a 60-kilometer border on the Atlantic Ocean—is a case in point. Despite the geographic and cultural ties that link them, political and economic cooperation between Senegal and The Gambia has been minimal. Likewise, Benin and Nigeria have made no efforts to harmonize economic policies despite their long-shared border and long-standing ethnic ties between their people.

Overview of The Gambia-Senegal and Benin-Nigeria Informal Trading

Informal trade activities involve three types of flows (INSAE 2001): smuggling of imports from other continents, usually entering through the port without being recorded, exports and imports of locally produced products within the region, and unofficial reexports of legally imported products. In The Gambia, reexports are the dominant activity, whereas in Benin, informal trade takes all three forms. The focus here is mostly on reexports.

Reexporting involves importing goods and subsequently shipping them to other countries with no additional processing or packaging, except for transport services. The Gambia's reexport activities to Senegal are similar to those of Benin to Nigeria. In the 1960s and 1970s, Senegal and Nigeria developed inefficient import-substituting manufacturing industries behind high import barriers. The Gambia and Benin have never developed a significant industrial base and have evolved into entrepôt economies with development strategies designed to undercut the trade policies of their more protectionist neighbors. The only other significant export industries aside from smuggling in these two countries are declining primary products (groundnuts in The Gambia and cotton in Benin) and tourism. In both countries since the early 1970s, the authorities have sought to maintain trade taxes below those of neighboring countries in a deliberate attempt to foster reexports to their larger neighbors. The Gambia and Benin have become highly dependent on their entrepôt services, especially for government revenues. In both cases, the relationship involves a francophone member and an anglophone nonmember of WAEMU, but the roles are reversed in the two cases (francophone Senegal and anglophone Nigeria are protectionist, while anglophone The Gambia and francophone Benin are more liberal).

The reexport trade straddles the formal and informal sectors in a highly complex and well-organized system that operates quite similarly in different countries. Reexports involve large formal enterprises that import goods through official channels and a sophisticated distribution chain that engages in transshipment through informal mechanisms. Reexports are a major contributor to government revenues in The Gambia and Benin, because imported goods destined for reexport generally pay duties when entering the country before being smuggled out. Consequently, trade taxes are even more important for these two countries than for most other African countries, accounting for about half of both countries' tax revenues.

The commodities involved in reexportation are highly diverse and vary over time, but consist predominantly of imports of basic consumer goods originating from Asia, Europe, or the United States and sold to average African low- or middle-income households. Goods enter through the port of Banjul in The Gambia and Cotonou in Benin before being reexported to Senegal and Nigeria, respectively, as well as to other countries in the region, to a lesser extent. The main products are bulk food items such as rice, sugar, and flour; processed foods such as tomato paste, cooking oil, condensed and canned milk, tea, and soft drinks; fabric of various sorts; used cars; and other basic household items such as batteries, candles, and matches.

Cross-border trade of locally produced goods is also important, especially for Benin. A very large proportion of many agricultural and manufactured goods consumed in Benin are imported from Nigeria, according to fieldwork done by the research institute LARES and reported in INSAE (2001). Petroleum products in particular are imported almost entirely from Nigeria, motivated by the subsidized prices in that country. In some cases, manufactured goods produced in Nigeria are more competitive in neighboring countries such as Benin than imports from Asia, especially since they escape duties when smuggled into Benin. According to our interviewees, however, imports of manufactured products from Nigeria have declined in recent years. There is also substantial unrecorded trade in locally produced agricultural commodities in Benin.

The overall structure of merchandise trade for The Gambia and Benin is shown in table 9.1, which combines official data with estimates of unofficial trade flows, all as a percentage of gross domestic product (GDP). In both countries, official merchandise exports are very small relative to imports, having dropped steadily since the 1970s. These declines in merchandise exports are

Table 9.1 Official Imports, Exports, Reexports, and Transit in The Gambia and Benin, 2004–07
% of GDP

Country and type of trade	2004	2005	2006	2007
The Gambia				
Official exports	2.5	1.7	2.2	2.0
Official reexports	1.6	0.1	—	—
Goods in transit	2.3	1.4	—	—
Official imports	57.1	51.4	50.8	47.4
Estimated unofficial imports for reexport	24.1	18.3	17.1	14.3
Estimated unofficial reexports	32.6	24.7	23.1	19.4
Benin				
Official exports	7.4	5.1	5.0	6.0
Official reexports	0.3	0.5	0.4	0.6
Goods in transit	26.0	30.9	44.3	49.3
Official imports	22.0	20.6	21.3	26.2
Estimated unofficial imports for reexport	22.4	23.6	26.6	32.4
Estimated unofficial reexports	30.2	31.9	35.9	43.7

Sources: Customs and trade statistics for Benin and The Gambia; World Bank 2010.
Note: — = Not available.

partially offset by increases in service exports (not shown in the table), but they also reflect the growth of unrecorded reexports. Official imports as a share of GDP are very high in The Gambia, at more than 50 percent, but are only about half of that in Benin. Benin's official imports as a share of GDP are also far below those of other coastal West African economies such as Senegal, Ghana, and Togo.[1] Benin's low import ratio is inconsistent with its acknowledged role as a regional entrepôt. This contradiction is explained by the failure of official statistics to capture two important dimensions of Benin's trade: (a) a large volume of Benin's imports, particularly petroleum products, are smuggled in from Nigeria, and (b) a large volume of imports are classified as in transit, but in fact much of these goods in transit, mainly used cars, are not substantially different from ordinary imports, insofar as both are diverted to Nigeria and yield significant revenues in the process. Overall, a very large portion of imports in both The Gambia and Benin are not used for domestic consumption but instead are transshipped, mostly to Senegal and Nigeria, respectively.

Operation of Smuggling Networks

A complex and opaque reexport distribution chain operates in both sets of countries in broadly similar ways. Goods are brought into Benin or The Gambia by large importers, in some cases operating in the formal sector, and are then smuggled across the border through various mechanisms. The reexport trade has developed a sophisticated infrastructure, in some respects organized much more efficiently than public infrastructure. Observers in both countries allege that high government officials are aware of these activities and are often involved in organizing and protecting smuggling networks, as they are in much of Africa (Egg and Herrera 1998). As such, these networks operate quite openly and without fear of government crackdowns.

The Gambia and Senegal
Goods are brought into The Gambia by a handful of large wholesale importers, many of whom are Lebanese.[2] The wholesalers then sell much of their merchandise to other traders, often Mauritanians, who have shops all along the border and who, in turn, sell to small-scale traders, typically "market women," from countries in the region—mainly Guinea-Bissau, Guinea, Mali, and, of course, Senegal. These petty traders then smuggle the goods into Senegal either by going through the bush or by paying off customs officials at the official border posts. Alternatively, the wholesalers in Banjul sell directly to Senegalese businessmen who then transport the goods to the frontier in large trucks. Most of the truckers are Senegalese nationals. At the border, the trucks are unloaded, and the goods are smuggled through in smaller quantities, as described above.

Sometimes, the truck crosses the border with the connivance of Senegalese customs officials. Social, religious, and cultural ties among the participants, notably through their frequent affiliation with Mouride Muslim brotherhoods, as described in chapter 8, greatly facilitate these transactions. Goods can also be brought into Senegal by sea using pirogues operating at night. The sprawling informal markets in Dakar, notably Sandaga, and in other cities, are substantially supplied by contraband, much of it flowing from The Gambia, with the tacit acquiescence of the Senegalese authorities.

Traders estimate that about half of the reexports passing through The Gambia are destined for Senegal, with the other half continuing on to Guinea—the destination of about one-quarter of all Gambian reexports—Mali, Guinea-Bissau, and sometimes even Côte d'Ivoire and Sierra Leone.

Benin and Nigeria

The modalities of importation of products intended for reexport to Nigeria vary by the nature of the commodity.[3] Cross-border trade is controlled largely by sophisticated and well-organized networks and the large informal firms described in chapter 4, with many small operators involved on the margins. The trust and connections provided by these informal networks, often ethnic or religious in nature, facilitate market transactions spanning the continents and enable the provision of credit and transfer of funds, as seen in chapter 8.

For bulk items such as rice, wheat, and sugar, importers purchase directly from international brokers with whom they are in regular contact. For some products such as cigarettes, the foreign companies have local representatives in Benin. Importers of second-hand goods such as used cars often travel abroad or have foreign correspondents, providing information about sourcing opportunities. A few large wholesalers dominate the imports of frozen poultry; COMON Company has about 60 percent of the market, employing 470 full-time workers, and CDPA-Agrisatch has some 20 percent of the market, with 150 full-time workers and another 300 part-time workers. Overall, traders display a remarkable flexibility in adapting to changing market opportunities.

A variety of trading networks linked by cultural, ethnic, or commercial ties operate in the reexport trade. These include the Yoruba ethnic group, discussed in the previous chapter, centered in Porto Novo, which operates with a high degree of cohesion, thanks to ethnic and religious affinities, groups of women importers, and middlemen operating in the markets, again mostly women. Foreign traders are also engaged in the reexport business. Most of the descendants of the European trading houses have exited the scene, replaced by Lebanese and other Arabs, some of whom came from Nigeria along with Ibo refugees during the Biafra war, and Indians who began arriving from Ghana and Nigeria starting around 1970.

Unofficial reexports can cross the border by land or water. By land, traders use numerous and ever-changing tracks along the long border with Nigeria.

They also use a complex network of canals, with new canals being dug when customs agents patrol existing routes. Specialized warehouses for various goods destined for reexport are located in Cotonou and along the border. For example, warehouses specializing in wheat, rice, and other products are built and operated by brokers or private traders operating individually or in groups for their own use or are rented out to other traders. A network of markets dots both sides of the Benin-Nigeria border, with sister markets on either side of the frontier.

The parallel trade also runs from Nigeria to Benin. Nigeria has long been a supplier to its francophone neighbors of a large variety of agricultural and manufactured goods, imported from Asia, in the case of items facing low import barriers in Nigeria, or produced locally in Nigeria. The largest unofficial export by far from Nigeria to Benin is petroleum products, which are heavily subsidized in Nigeria, described in detail below. Imports from Nigeria have also been an important source of capital and consumer goods in Benin and other CFA franc zone countries in the region. Products include fertilizer, machinery of various kinds, foodstuffs (corn and millet), plastic goods, spare parts, miscellaneous consumer goods such as dishes, cookware, soaps, school supplies, cosmetics, hardware, toys, scooters, and medicines (Galtier and Tassou 1998). Generic and low-cost pharmaceuticals are produced in Nigeria with minimal regulation, so parallel imports from Nigeria are the source of cheap generic medicines in Benin for people who cannot afford to go to a licensed pharmacy. Some goods move in both directions at different times and places, including bulk food items and textiles, depending on market conditions and Nigeria's trade barriers.

Smuggling from Nigeria into Benin is intricately organized. Transport of goods by truck convoy is permitted under agreements between Beninese importers and high-level customs officials in Nigeria, with a prearranged lump-sum payment per truck estimated to be equivalent to an ad valorem rate of 9–24 percent prior to 1997—well below the statutory import duties and other import taxes (Le Faou 2001). Goods are also shipped to Benin illegally by boats using the complex system of canals described earlier as well as by taxis hired for this purpose on both sides of the border. In February 1997, however, the Beninese authorities abruptly raised the lump-sum charge on trucks by 50 percent, resulting in a sharp reduction in the legal entry of goods in favor of illegal modes of entry.

In recent years, imports of manufactured products into Benin from Nigeria have declined, supplanted by imports into Benin directly from China or indirectly via Dubai. Petroleum imports are also down somewhat, as Nigeria has raised retail prices closer to those in Benin.

The unofficial reexport trade operates in thinly disguised collusion with high government officials in Nigeria. The highly lucrative reexport trade in cigarettes, for example, has been carried out by Nigerian trading groups under the protection of the Nigerian secret service (Hashim and Meagher 1999). In fact, in the case of used clothing and cigarettes, the dominant trading groups can deploy the authorities to crack down on new entrants, preserving their control. Nigerian government involvement is also alleged to be profound in the all-important smuggling of petroleum products out of Nigeria.

More detailed descriptions of cross-border trade in used cars and petroleum products illustrate these mechanisms.

Trade in Used Cars   Used cars have been Benin's most significant reexport since about 2000.[4] Chapter 4 describes the involvement of the large informal sector in this industry in Benin, as it is one of the most important arenas for these firms. Imports of vehicles have risen steeply from 50,000 in 1996 to 200,000 in 2000 and to 250,000 in 2002 and 2003; after a dip in 2004–05 to about 150,000, they rose again to 200,000 in 2006, reaching an all-time high of 300,000 in 2007. Perret (2002) estimates that used cars accounted for as much as 43 percent of all trade flows in 2001, up from 37 percent in 1999. This is confirmed by the fact that in 2001 used cars represented an astounding 45 percent of revenues (fees and taxes) for the port of Cotonou. Indeed the used car trade has become one of Benin's major industries. Huge car parks on the outskirts of Cotonou employ an estimated 10,000 to 15,000 people directly in importing, selling, storing, and driving and several thousand more indirectly. The value added generated by the distribution and handling of used cars was an estimated 9 percent of Benin's GDP in 2001, roughly the same as for cotton.

About 90 percent of used cars imported into Benin are destined for Nigeria, with 5 percent for Niger and 5 percent for the domestic market. The bulk of used cars enter Benin in transit status, officially manifested for Niger or other landlocked countries. For instance, of 230,000 cars declared for shipment to Niger in 2001, only 15,000 ended up there. Almost all the rest wound up in Nigeria. The fact that cars manifested for Niger and other landlocked countries are diverted to Nigeria is not concealed in Benin. There is a well-established set of procedures for obtaining documents from customs authorizing the diversion of cars to Nigeria. The fees and taxes for obtaining the authorizations amount to about CFAF 400,000 per car. This includes a fee for a customs escort to accompany the car to the Nigerian border. With the average cost, insurance, and freight value of a used car of about CFAF 1.0 million to CFAF 1.5 million, the taxes and fees for customs clearance alone amount to about 30 percent of the value of the car.

Used car imports follow an elaborate and well-organized circuit. Importers with connections in developed countries locate, purchase, and arrange for transportation of the cars. In 2001, 65 percent of the cars imported originated in Germany, with most of the rest coming from other European countries. The location of Beninese correspondents and the ease of port operations affect the preferred port of embarkation. The North American share has increased recently, but Europe remains the main source. Some of the importers own their own boats and are affiliated with international shipping companies such as

Grimaldi. Others rent the boats. Customs clearance agents handle all of the paperwork and authorizations. As discussed in chapter 4, there is close cooperation between formal and informal customs clearance agents. Other intermediaries play a role in matching buyers and sellers of cars. After the cars clear the port, they are stored in car parks in Cotonou before being driven to their destination by companies specializing in the delivery of cars to the border, under escort from customs and with police permission. The cars are driven at night in convoys of about 100 cars. They cross the border to Nigeria after paying bribes to both Beninese and Nigerian customs inspectors. The magnitude of the bribes is largely set by precedent, according to the custom clearance agents interviewed. The cars then receive valid license plates in Nigeria. In short, government officials—from the highest to the lowest levels—on both sides of the border facilitate and benefit from this trade.

Competition from Togo is increasing, with Togo charging lower fees for speedier service to offset Benin's geographic advantage. In Togo, the paperwork takes only one day, and Togolese customs charges CFAF 200,000–CFAF 300,000 per car. Competition from Togo was particularly acute around 2003–04, due to problems at the port of Cotonou. Nevertheless, these problems appear to have lessened, and Beninese traders do not seem overly worried about Togo, as the importation of used cars into Benin has picked up strongly since 2005.

The ample supply of aging vehicles in Europe and low incomes in West Africa provide a natural basis for trade in used cars. Imported cars averaged about 16 years of use upon arrival in Benin in 2001, with 95 percent more than 10 years old. Toyota, Mercedes, and Peugeot cars have predominated, but the vehicles of other Japanese and European companies are increasingly prevalent. An accompanying market in spare parts has also flourished.

Nigeria's ineffective attempts to protect its own struggling car industry have diverted this trade to the parallel market. At the end of the 1970s, Nigeria assembled 100,000 cars compared with a mere 10,000 today. In 1994, Nigeria banned imports of vehicles more than eight years old. In 2002, the law was further tightened to ban all cars more than five years old. In 2004, the ban was eased to apply again to cars more than eight years old. Moreover, any imports of cars by land routes, notably from Benin, are banned altogether. These bans have, until recently, proved impervious to the porous border between the two countries, the strong demand for cheap vehicles, and the ambiguous attitudes of the authorities in Nigeria. If Nigeria were either to liberalize its car market or to enforce the ban, as it has sporadically done, most recently in March 2008, this lucrative trade could suffer greatly or even collapse.

Petroleum Product Imports from Nigeria   Like the reexport trade from Benin to Nigeria, smuggling of petroleum products into Benin reflects differential policies combined with the ease of slipping goods across the border and the complicity of the two countries' officials. In this case, however, the main factors are the very large subsidies in Nigeria and partial deregulation of pricing in Benin, which together result in much lower consumer prices in Nigeria than in Benin (Morillon and Afouda 2005). Smuggling of oil products into Benin began around 1980 and increased dramatically in 2000. High-level officials in both Nigeria and Benin are said to be intimately involved.

Nigeria, of course, is one of the world's largest producers of crude oil, with export revenues highly dependent on world market prices, but its domestic consumer prices are largely delinked from world market trends. Nigerian refineries are provided with crude oil at prices far below those of the world market, amounting to a subsidy of 20–30 percent. Due to the poor condition of its refineries, Nigeria imports gasoline, which is also sold at controlled prices. Moreover, Nigeria's taxation of gasoline and diesel fuel is far below that of Benin and other countries in the region. In 2005, the cumulative taxation of gasoline in Benin approached 100 percent, counting import duties, excise taxes, and value added taxes, while taxes on oil products in Nigeria are low.

Benin partially liberalized its petrol sector in 1995 as part of its structural adjustment policies. In 2000, retail prices of gasoline, diesel fuel, and kerosene were raised by about 75 percent and have subsequently been adjusted in line with world oil prices. The 2000 price increase dramatically widened the gap between the official prices of these products in Benin and Nigeria, with prices in Benin more than double those in Nigeria between August 2000 and May 2004, measured at the parallel exchange rate. In the last few years, Nigeria has raised its domestic prices, narrowing the differential between the official prices in Benin and Nigeria. In April 2008, Benin's official price for unleaded gasoline was CFAF 470 per liter, about 50 percent above the price of ₦80 in Nigeria, or about CFAF 300 at the parallel exchange rate. The black market price of gasoline in Cotonou dropped sharply relative to the official price of gasoline following the June 2000 official price increases, whereas in 1997–99 the black market price tended to exceed the official price, reflecting the scarcity of the product in the face of the controlled price. The black market prices of gasoline in Nigeria and Benin are nearly identical, at about 30 percent above Nigeria's official price. In short, black market prices in Benin appear to be determined by a markup on Nigeria's official price and have little connection to Benin's official price. Thus the 2000 official price increases in Benin have had no sustained effect on black market prices (Morillon and Afouda 2005).

Not coincidentally, official imports of gasoline and other petroleum products have dropped dramatically in Benin since 2000, despite continuing increases in the stock of vehicles in use in the country. Morillon and Afouda (2005) consequently estimate that the share of gasoline supplied by informal imports from Nigeria rose from about 10 percent in 1998 and 1999 to about 50 percent in 2000 and 83 percent in 2001 and 2002, tapering off slightly to 72 percent in 2003–04.

In recent years, the share of smuggled petroleum products has declined slightly due to price increases in Nigeria. The share of smuggled gasoline has remained around 60–70 percent of Benin's domestic consumption, but parallel imports of diesel and kerosene have dropped sharply.

Although well above Nigeria's official prices, Benin's official retail petroleum prices are nonetheless considerably below those of other francophone countries in the region. For example, in March 2005, Benin's price for regular gasoline was CFAF 360 per liter, compared to CFAF 415 in Togo, CFAF 470 in Niger, CFAF 522 in Burkina Faso, and CFAF 580 in Mali. Benin consequently also reexports a considerable portion of the gasoline and other petroleum products it imports from Nigeria, with unofficial imports exceeding domestic usage by an undetermined magnitude.

The burgeoning informal market in Benin has been boosted further by the lack of official gas stations, which, in turn, reflects the dominance of the informal market, with the zones bordering Nigeria, in particular, witnessing a decline in the number of operating service stations. In contrast, Nigeria has a very dense network of service stations, which readily supply the informal traders who smuggle gasoline into Benin.

The distribution network in Nigeria includes large wholesalers who have storage depots along the border holding up to 1,000 liters of gasoline. These wholesalers have close political ties to high-level officials in Nigeria. Wholesalers sell to various intermediary distributors of various sizes who sneak gasoline across the border by pirogue, in cars whose gas tanks have been expanded, in small quantities on scooters, or on foot.

The net effect of this massive trade in petroleum products on Benin's economy is complex. It entails a large loss of fiscal revenues but also constitutes a source of employment and income for traders and distributors, accounting in 2005 for 1–2 percent of GDP and 15,000–40,000 jobs, depending on the method of estimation.

Causes of Smuggling: Differences in Import Protection and Other Distortions

Golub and Mbaye (2009) and Oyejide et al. (2008) find large and variable differentials in retail product prices between The Gambia and Senegal and between Benin and Nigeria, confirming the incentive to smuggle. For example, sugar prices are much higher in Senegal than in The Gambia. Differential shipping costs from Europe, North America, or Asia cannot be an explanatory factor, since the distance of shipping to Banjul versus Dakar or Contonou versus Lagos from any point of origin is virtually identical. If anything, shipping to Dakar is cheaper, insofar as Dakar serves as a regional hub for some of the major shippers, and Lagos should benefit from scale economies due to the size of the Nigerian economy.

Differences in national trade policies are widely recognized as a significant factor (Egg and Herrera 1998). The efficiency and probity of trade facilitation, particularly port and customs operations, and the extent of border enforcement are also relevant.

Trade Policies

The Gambia and Senegal   As noted above, The Gambia's relatively liberal trade policies in comparison to those of neighboring countries have undoubtedly contributed to The Gambia's special role as a regional trading hub. The Gambia liberalized earlier and more aggressively than other countries of the region, most notably Senegal. Taxes on international trade in The Gambia and Senegal include customs duties, sales taxes, value added tax (VAT), fees, and special taxes on a few goods such as cigarettes. The import tax differential in the 1970s through the early 1990s between Senegal and The Gambia was very large, with Senegalese import duties alone as high as 100 percent for goods such as textiles, while Gambian duties averaged around 30 percent.

Senegal's Trade Policies   Senegal followed highly restrictive trade and pricing policies during the first decades following its independence in 1960s, with very high tariffs and opaque nontariff barriers. As in much of Africa, Senegal moved toward more market-oriented economic policies as part of its structural adjustment agreements with the International Monetary Fund (IMF) in the late 1980s and in the 1990s, following serious fiscal and financial crises. Import barriers were liberalized somewhat starting in the late 1980s. Following the 1994 devaluation, import restrictions were significantly lowered and simplified, in particular with the elimination of variable levies (*valeurs mercuriales*) and quantitative restrictions, except for a few products, notably sugar. As also discussed in the case studies in chapter 4, the political clout of the Mimran family has resulted in sugar retaining extraordinarily high levels of protection, despite the general liberalization of import barriers in Senegal since the 1980s. The downfall of several of the most powerful large informal entrepreneurs was linked to their alleged smuggling of sugar, a highly lucrative but risky venture. Implementation of the common external tariff (CET) in WAEMU countries in 1998–2000 entailed further declines in trade taxes in Senegal, posing a new challenge for The Gambia's role as an entrepôt and contributing to the impetus for substantial further liberalization. The CET dramatically reduced the infamous complexity and lack of transparency of Senegal's tariff structure by consolidating tariffs into four categories, with the top import duty rate, applicable to consumer goods, being 20 percent.

Gambian Trade Policies   Up to the late 1990s, The Gambia's trade regime was deliberately more liberal than those of its neighbors, particularly Senegal, but still involved considerable complexity and tariff peaks, with rates of up to 90 percent and 27 tariff bands (WTO 2004). In 2000, in response to the implementation of the WAEMU CET, The Gambia simplified its customs duties to five bands, with the highest carrying a rate of 20 percent, the same as the top rate in WAEMU. In 2001, the number of bands was further reduced to four, and the top rate dropped to 18 percent (WTO 2004). In January 2006, Gambian customs duties were aligned with the ECOWAS common external tariff, resulting in an increase in some rates. The maximum rate, applicable to most consumer goods, was raised from 18 to 20 percent. At the same time, the sales tax on imports was increased from 10 to 15 percent, aligning it with the tax rate on domestic goods.

Comparison   Table 9.2 compares import taxes in The Gambia and Senegal as of end-2006 for some of the key goods said to be involved in the reexport trade, aggregating the various taxes listed above. In all cases, Senegal's taxes are higher and sometimes much higher. Not surprising, the greatest differential is for sugar, where the Senegalese composite tax rate is about 80 percent above the Gambian

Table 9.2 Trade Taxes in Senegal and The Gambia, 2007[a]

tax rate (%)

Product	Gambia, The	Senegal	Difference
Flour	22.5	56.6	34.1
Sugar	22.5	103.8	81.3
Rice	16.8	22.7	5.9
Tomato paste	28.3	56.6	28.3
Cigarettes	58.0	97.7	39.7
Soft drinks	39.8	48.2	8.4
Milk (canned liquid)	22.5	44.8	22.3
Condensed milk	22.5	27.1	4.6
Cooking oil	22.5	56.6	34.1
Mayonnaise	39.8	44.8	5.0
Toilet soap	39.8	44.8	5.0
Candles	39.8	44.8	5.0
Matches	39.8	44.8	5.0
Tea	28.3	37.3	9.0
Canned sardines	39.8	44.8	5.0
Shoes	39.8	44.8	5.0
Fabric	39.8	44.8	5.0

Source: Customs data for The Gambia and Senegal; authors' computations.
a. Includes sales taxes, fees, and other special taxes.

tax rate. For flour, tomato paste, cooking oil, and cigarettes, the differential is also quite high (25 to 40 percent). These tax rate differences accord generally well with the price differences for these same items (Golub and Mbaye 2009).

Benin and Nigeria   Differential trade and taxation policies and practices are also the main cause of reexports between Benin and Nigeria, according to the available literature (Igué and Soulé 1992; Soulé 2004; Perret 2002; Morillon and Afouda 2005) and our interviews in the field.

Benin's Trade Policies   As in The Gambia, government revenues in Benin still depend heavily on taxation of international trade to a much greater extent than in other countries in Africa. Trade taxes account for more than half of tax receipts and about half of all government revenue. In 1973, Benin officially adopted trade policies to foster the reexport trade, with the goal of maintaining lower import barriers than Nigeria. Like those of Senegal, Benin's duties and taxes are largely set by WAEMU. Unlike in other WAEMU countries, the CET actually raised tariff rates on average in Benin. Prior to the CET, Benin's tariffs on consumer goods averaged 13.4 percent, far below the 30.0 percent plus rates of most other WAEMU countries, with only Togo somewhat closer to Benin, at 19.0 percent. With implementation of the CET, Benin's overall average tariffs rose slightly from 11.4 to 12.2 percent, whereas average tariffs for all other WAEMU countries fell substantially (World Bank 2005). The CET did little to diminish Benin's reexports, however, given the continued very large differential with Nigeria.

Nigeria's Trade Policies   Nigeria's trade policies have varied widely over time. Nigeria heavily protects some products, particularly those facing strong import competition, while subsidizing others, notably gasoline and other petroleum products. Nigeria's import barriers have been among the highest in the world, as shown in table 9.3, with applied tariffs averaging nearly 30.0 percent in 2003 and a significant number of import prohibitions (IMF 2005; WTO 2005). The Nigerian manufacturing sector is unusually diversified for Africa, but highly inefficient, with capacity utilization rates usually well below 50 percent (IMF 2005). The Nigerian government has sought to protect its struggling, but politically connected, domestic industrial and agricultural industries behind high import barriers.[5] ECOWAS has been moving toward adoption of a common external tariff with the same four-category structure of rates as WAEMU, but Nigeria has so far refused to accept this regime in its entirety. Nigeria also violates ECOWAS's provisions on free trade within West Africa. All imports from West Africa are required to enter Nigeria through the port of Calabar, and there are numerous checkpoints on the roads from Benin into southern Nigeria toward Lagos, 120 kilometers from the border. Nigeria's import bans are applied to imports from Benin, even if the products are produced in Benin.

Table 9.3 Selected Import Barriers in Nigeria, 1995–2007
tariff rates (%) or bans

Product	1995	1997	1999	2001	2003	2005	2007
Edible oil	Banned	Banned	55	40	Banned	Banned	Banned
Poultry meat	Banned	Banned	55	75	Banned	Banned	Banned
Beer	Banned	Banned	100	100	100	Banned	Banned
Wine	100	100	100	100	100	20	20
Milk products	55	55	50	50	100	20	20
Tomato preserves	45	45	45	45	45	20	20
Used clothes	Banned	Banned	Banned	Banned	Banned	Banned	Banned
Tires	Banned	Banned	Banned	Banned	Banned	Banned	Banned
Wheat dough	Banned	Banned	Banned	Banned	Banned	Banned	Banned
Used cars[a]	Banned	Banned	Banned	Banned	Banned	Banned	Banned
Sugar	10	10	10	40	100	50	50
Cloth and apparel	Banned	50	65	55	100	Banned	Banned
Tobacco and cigarettes	90	90	80	80	100	50	50
Rice	100	50	50	75	110	50	50

Source: Soulé 2004; Nigerian customs data provided by the World Bank.
a. Defined as more than eight years old in 1994–2002, more than five years old in 2002–04, and more than eight years old since 2004.

Table 9.3 presents the recent evolution of Nigeria's trade barriers on some of the key products involved in the reexport trade, illustrating the very high levels and variability of restrictions on imports. A long list of banned products varies from year to year. The extent to which these bans are enforced, however, also varies, and exemptions can be granted with the approval of the president. In short, Nigerian trade policy operates with an enormous complexity and opacity above and beyond the very high import barriers.

Trade Facilitation and Other Factors
Trade barriers can explain much, but not all, of the differences observed in wholesale prices. This section considers other factors, including trade facilitation, enforcement of border crossings, and currency exchange.

The Gambia and Senegal

Port Efficiency and Customs Practices   Customs practices are as important as statutory customs duties. These practices include customs valuation procedures and the speed and ease at which goods are cleared through the port and beyond. In Senegal, customs is said to engage in highly discretionary valuation practices. Senegalese customs apparently still applies reference pricing mechanisms to protect "sensitive goods," such as matches, that are produced domestically, similar to, but less blatant than, the reference price maintained though the variable levy on sugar. The Gambia's customs services are relatively efficient in comparison to the more complex and bureaucratic procedures in Senegal.

Another factor is the unusually efficient port of Banjul. Unlike other African countries, including Senegal, the port of Banjul is known for its rapid and efficient clearance of goods. While merchandise can languish for days or even weeks in most African ports, including Dakar, clearance usually occurs within 24 hours in Banjul.

The Overall Business Climate   Both Senegal and The Gambia benefit from social harmony and relative political stability. But while Senegal suffers from the legacy of a French-style highly bureaucratized system, The Gambia's more laissez-faire tradition has contributed to the development of trading establishments in Banjul. Ease of access to foreign exchange through the banking system in particular is a plus for The Gambia. In all of these areas, however, other countries are narrowing the gap with The Gambia. In some cases, The Gambia is at a disadvantage. For example, the tax rate on profits is 35 percent in The Gambia, while it has been lowered to 25 percent in Senegal.

Relations with Senegal   Senegal inevitably looms large in the Gambian reexport business, given the country's near-total enclosure within Senegal. For the same reason, economic relations with Senegal are critical. Yet relations with Senegal have not always been smooth, as noted in the introduction. Border disputes with Senegal can severely disrupt reexport trade. According to wholesalers, every significant border conflict with Senegal leads to a substantial drop in reexports, and the subsequent recovery is always incomplete. The border dispute following an increase in Gambian ferry fees in August 2005, when Senegalese truckers blockaded the border crossings in retaliation, contributed to the decline in reexports in 2006–07. While traders are, to some extent, able to avoid the official border crossings and slip across the frontier through the bush, the reexport trade was severely disrupted until the issue was resolved in October 2005, when The Gambia rescinded the fee increases.

Currency Movements   Depreciation of the Gambian dalasi vis-à-vis the CFA franc also affects the attractiveness of reexporting. Although the prices of imported goods are set in euros or U.S. dollars, and, therefore, free on board import prices are unaffected by fluctuations in the bilateral dalasi-CFA franc, the competitiveness of the transport services sector in The Gambia improves when the dalasi depreciates. The real depreciation of the dalasi in 2001–03 may explain some of the increase in reexports since 2001. According to traders, substantial exchange rate volatility is inimical to the reexport trade, as it makes arbitraging between markets more risky.

Benin and Nigeria

Business Climate and Trade Facilitation   Although far from perfect, Benin offers a much friendlier climate for business and trade than Nigeria, where insecurity and crime are rampant, including at the ports. The port of Cotonou suffers from significant problems of corruption and weak infrastructure, but is superior to the ports in Nigeria. Clearance of goods is much faster, cheaper, and easier in Cotonou than in Nigerian ports. According to shippers, however, ports in Nigeria are improving, so this factor may become less significant.

Border Enforcement   Benin has long had complex economic and political ties to Nigeria. Nigeria has made sporadic efforts and threats to close down cross-border trade with Benin and has occasionally done so. The borders have sometimes been closed due to other political tensions between the two countries. From February 1984 to February 1986, Nigeria shut down the border with Benin in an effort to curb smuggling of petroleum products out of Nigeria. During this time, Nigeria closed down all service stations within 10 kilometers of the border with Benin in a futile attempt to curb smuggling. In 1996, President Abacha of Nigeria closed the border in a political dispute with Benin's President Soglo related to the latter's military cooperation with the United States, which Abacha viewed as a threat. The resulting dislocations in Benin, notably gasoline shortages, contributed to Soglo's defeat in the 1996 presidential elections. In August 2003, the border was closed for a week following a confrontation between the Nigerian and Beninese government precipitated by the harboring of a Nigerian suspected criminal in Cotonou.[6] Another brief, but disruptive, border closing occurred in 2005. In March 2008, Nigeria reportedly initiated a crackdown on imports of used cars, holding up car convoys at the usual crossing points such a Krake and Igolo.[7]

Notwithstanding these occasional border closings and frequent threats from Nigeria, the reexport trade has always recovered as the enforcement of border controls reverts to its normal laxity. Nevertheless, Benin clearly is highly vulnerable to the vagaries of economic policy in Nigeria and could face serious difficulties if Nigeria adopts less-restrictive trade barriers or makes a serious effort to crack down on parallel trade.

Exchange Rates and Convertibility   Exchange rate changes themselves should not much alter the relative prices of importable goods from Asia or Europe in Benin versus Nigeria, since these prices are set in world markets and a change in the CFA franc–naira exchange rate should be reflected in corresponding movements of local currency prices in Benin and Nigeria. It can, however, affect the competitiveness of locally produced goods. In any event, the devaluation of the CFA franc in 1994 had little effect on the reexport trade beyond the short-run disruptions it entailed. For a few months immediately following the 1994 devaluation, reexports dropped, but they recovered rapidly, and no clear change in the volume of reexports occurred between 1993 and 1994 (Galtier and Tassou 1998, 129; Hashim and Meagher 1999). The effect of the devaluation of the CFA franc may also have been obscured by the subsequent sharp depreciation of the naira in the parallel market and the rapid increase of Nigerian inflation.

The greater stability and liquidity of the CFA franc relative to the Nigerian naira has played a role in boosting Benin's role as a trading center. Unlike the CFA franc, which is pegged to the euro and freely convertible into foreign currency within the CFA zone, the naira is highly volatile and subject to strict exchange controls, with a large black market. In 1993, however, when the CFA franc was made temporarily inconvertible outside of the franc zone, it had no lasting negative effect on the reexport trade.

Estimates of Unofficial Cross-Border Trade

Official bilateral trade statistics from both The Gambia and Senegal report a tiny volume of bilateral trade between the two countries. According to these official statistics, The Gambia's bilateral exports and imports with Senegal each accounted for only about 3.5 percent of The Gambia's total exports and imports, respectively, over 2002–05, with Senegal having a bilateral surplus. Likewise, Benin's trade data indicate that only about 15 percent of Benin's exports and imports in recent years are with other members of the regional groups WAEMU and ECOWAS. In particular, Benin's recorded exports to, and imports from, Nigeria are very low, averaging about 5 percent of its total official exports and imports between 2000 and 2005.

The official statistics, therefore, seem at variance with reality. By all accounts, there is a very large volume of reexports from The Gambia to Senegal and from Benin to Nigeria. But there are no reliable estimates of the volume of this trade. This situation is consistent with the findings of Berg (1985), who concludes that the anomalies of African trade statistics are due mostly to smuggling.

Although there are no available data on unofficial trade, estimates of the magnitude of reexports can be garnered by examining the pattern of imports of goods subject to large price distortions, under the assumption that these imports are recorded correctly at the port. One strategy is to compare imports to domestic consumption, but it is difficult to estimate the latter.

The IMF estimates of reexports in The Gambia amount to about four times the domestically produced exports or 80 percent of total exports, figures that are in line with the estimates of knowledgeable observers interviewed and Elhadj's (2000) qualitative discussion. Golub and Mbaye's (2009) findings are similar for average levels of reexports, but show greater variation than the IMF estimates.

Reexport products from Benin to Nigeria are dominated by a limited number of goods that are highly protected or banned in Nigeria, including those listed in table 9.4: bulk food items (rice, wheat, sugar), processed foods (tomato paste, condensed milk), frozen poultry, cigarettes, textiles and clothing, and used goods (cars, tires, and clothes). Most of these products have been mainstays of the reexport trade since at least the 1970s, although variations have occurred in their relative importance in response to fluctuations in the severity of Nigeria's import restrictions.

Table 9.4 presents the values of imports over 2004–07 on 14 of the most important goods of Benin's reexport trade. Importers in Benin estimate that 70–90 percent of these goods are reexported illegally to Nigeria. Overall, table 9.4 suggests that the reexport trade is very significant relative to recorded imports, GDP, and government revenues. Imports of these 14 goods alone are greater than all officially recorded imports reported in IMF and World Bank databases, largely because these databases exclude imported goods labeled as in transit. Duties collected on these 14 goods alone amounted to about 30 percent of total government tax revenues over 2004–07. These figures are considerably above those suggested in much of the previous literature, such Galtier and

Table 9.4 Imports in Benin, by Selected Reexport Items, 2004–07[a]
CFAF, billions

Product	2004	2005	2006	2007
Used cars	150.5	178.7	264.2	327.7
Rice	50.4	90.9	104.4	151.7
Textiles	44.7	60.1	57.0	82.9
Used clothes	27.8	32.7	41.9	48.9
Palm oil	9.1	9.0	27.1	44.4
Frozen poultry	29.7	26.0	23.6	38.5
Batteries	20.4	23.5	29.6	34.5
Furniture	4.7	6.6	14.5	28.6
Sugar	8.0	9.8	13.2	13.4
Clothing	4.1	10.7	2.3	8.8
Cigarettes	1.9	3.8	5.7	8.8
Prepared tomatoes	0.7	0.7	2.4	4.6
Used tires	3.5	4.2	4.2	4.5
Cardboard	4.3	4.2	3.7	3.1
Subtotal	359.7	460.9	593.9	800.2
Share of GDP (%)	22.4	23.6	26.6	32.4

Source: Customs data for Benin; authors' calculations.
a. Includes goods imported in transit status.

Tassou (1998). According to Igué and Soulé (1992), however, reexports have at various earlier times amounted to more than half of recorded imports, for example, in the late 1970s and early 1980s.

Significance of Informal Cross-Border Trade

The contribution of the reexport trade to the economies of Benin and The Gambia is difficult to measure, but is certainly large. Reexports account for about 80 percent of total exports for The Gambia. Net reexports (after deducting imports intended for reexport) contribute about 20 percent of foreign exchange earnings and 7 percent of GDP, below the contribution of tourism, but above that of groundnuts.[8] Large numbers of people are employed in the handling, storage, and transport of goods.

In Benin, reexports may be even more important. Perret (2002) estimates that trade in used cars alone accounts for 9 percent of Benin's GDP—the same magnitude as for cotton. Given that used cars contribute about half of total unofficial reexports, unofficial trade generates perhaps 20 percent of Benin's GDP. Its contribution to employment is less than its contribution to GDP, given that much of the latter consists of profits of importers and tax revenues, but it is still substantial, involving perhaps 50,000 people directly, of which about 15,000 are in the used car market (Perret 2002).

The most important contribution of the reexport trade is to government revenues. Indeed, as noted earlier, Benin's and The Gambia's trade policies have revolved around maximizing the income from reexports by taxing goods when they enter Benin at a rate well below those of their more protectionist neighbors. Taxes on international trade represent about half of government revenues in both countries, with taxes on imports intended for reexport accounting for half or more of trade tax revenues.

Harmonization of trade policies within WAEMU and ECOWAS poses a threat to the reexport business. The effect of the WAEMU CET in raising tariffs on consumer goods reduced Benin's competitive advantage vis-à-vis Togo, and the prospect of Nigeria's agreeing to lower its trade barriers is a major threat to the continued viability of smuggling. To counter the disincentive effects of trade liberalization by their neighbors, it is alleged that Beninese and Gambian customs officials have at times endeavored to offset the rate increases by lowering the declared taxable value of some merchandise. Essentially, a preferential regime is in effect for reexports relative to goods for local use.

While Benin and The Gambia reap substantial revenue gains from reexports, a lot of smuggling almost completely escapes taxation. Moreover, these benefits are fragile, because reexports are subject to the vagaries of neighbors' trade policies and the effectiveness of border controls.

It could be argued that smuggling serves a positive social function by undermining and circumventing distortions. The sustainability of trade strategies that prey on the distorted policies of neighbors is highly questionable, however. More generally, smuggling contributes to an acceptance of and even admiration for tax evasion and corruption in West Africa.

Conclusion

This chapter has examined cross-border smuggling between Senegal and The Gambia and between Benin and Nigeria. The volume of unrecorded and untaxed trade between neighboring countries in West Africa is very large. The causes of this trade are varied, but the main drivers are policy distortions that create price differentials across borders, combined with long-standing ethnic and religious ties that transcend national borders, as described in chapter 8, long porous borders, weak enforcement, and the involvement of influential political actors. The large informal firms described in chapter 4 are actively involved in cross-border trade.

As in other areas relating to the informal sector covered in chapter 6, reducing smuggling requires policy reforms that diminish the incentives promoting illegal behavior (in this case, further tariff harmonization in the region), along with stronger state institutions (in particular, customs administration) that deter opportunistic behavior.

Notes
1. Togo also engages in reexport to Nigeria.
2. This description is based on Lambert (1994), Boone (1989), and Rice (1967) as well as our interviews with traders and customs officials in both The Gambia and Senegal in 2005.
3. This description is based on Igué and Soulé (1992) as well as interviews in Benin.
4. This discussion of the used car market is based on Perret (2002) and interviews with traders and businesses involved in the import and sale of used cars.
5. For example, it is alleged that the ban on poultry imports is related to former president Obasanjo's chicken farming business.
6. The case involved the killing of one of the nieces of then Nigerian president Obasanjo in a carjacking in Lagos. The carjacking ring stole cars in Nigeria and took them to Cotonou. The head of the carjacking ring, Tidjani Hamani, a Niger national, was based in Cotonou, where he was arrested and later released by the Benin judiciary.
7. "Difficultés commerciales entre le Bénin et Le Nigeria: Embargo sur les véhicules d'occasion venues de Cotonou," Le Matinal (Benin), March 14, 2008.
8. IMF (2005). The contribution to GDP is based on the IMF's estimate of "the margins added to the cost of imports to account for services provided by enterprises based in The Gambia."

References

Azam, Jean Paul. 2007. *Trade, Exchange Rate, and Growth in Sub-Saharan Africa.* New York: Cambridge University Press.

Berg, Elliot. 1985. *Intra-African Trade and Economic Integration.* Washington, DC: Development Alternatives.

Bhagwati, Jagdish, and Bent Hansen. 1973. "A Theoretical Analysis of Smuggling." *Quarterly Journal of Economics* 87 (4): 172–87.

Boone, Catherine. 1989. *Merchant Capital and the Roots of State Power in Senegal, 1930–1985.* New York: Cambridge University Press.

Deardorff, Alan, and Wolfgang Stolper. 1990. "Effects of Smuggling under African Conditions: A Factual, Institutional, and Analytic Discussion." *Weltwirtchaftliches Archiv* 126 (1): 116–41.

Egg, Johnny, and Javier Herrera, eds. 1998. *Échanges transfrontaliers et intégration régionale en Afrique subsaharienne.* Paris: Autrepart.

Elhadj, Charbel. 2000. "Improving the Competitiveness and Efficiency of the Trading Sector, with Particular Reference to the Reexport Trade." Paper presented at the public-private sector forum, Banjul, The Gambia, November 29–30.

Galtier, Franck, and Zakari Tassou. 1998. "La reexportation: Vice ou vertu? Le commerce du Bénin vers le Nigeria." In *Échanges transfrontaliers et intégration en Afrique subsaharienne,* ed. Johnny Egg and Javier Herrera. Orstrom: IRD Editions.

Golub, Stephen S. 2008. "Benin's Reexport Trade." Background paper for the Benin Country Economic Memorandum. World Bank, Washington, DC.

Golub, Stephen S., and Ahmadou A. Mbaye. 2009. "National Trade Policies and Smuggling in Africa: The Case of The Gambia and Senegal." *World Development* 37 (3, March): 595–606.

Hashim, Yahaya, and Kate Meagher. 1999. "Cross-Border Trade and the Parallel Currency Market: Trade and Finance in the Context of Structural Adjustment." Research Report 113, Nordiska Afrakainstitutet, Uppsala.

Herbst, Jeffrey. 2000. *States and Power in Africa.* Princeton, NJ: Princeton University Press.

Igué, John O., and Bio G. Soulé. 1992. *L'état entrepôt au Bénin: Commerce informel ou réponse à la crise?* Paris: Karthala.

IMF (International Monetary Fund). 2005. "Nigeria: Selected Issues and Statistical Appendix." Country Report 05/203, IMF, Washington, DC, August.

INSAE (Institut National de la Statistique et de l'Analyse Economique). 2001. "Estimation du commerce extérieur non-enregistré au Benin." INSAE, Bénin, October.

Lambert, Agnés. 1994. "Les commerçants et l'intégration régionale." In *Le Sénégal et ses voisins,* ed. Momar-Coumba Diop. Dakar: Sociétés-Espaces-Temps.

Le Faou, Steven. 2001. "Les exportations de produits manufacturés du Nigeria vers le Bénin." *Economie Régionale* (LARES).

Morillon, Virginie, and Servais Afouda. 2005. "Le trafic illicite des produits pétroliers entre le Bénin et Nigeria." *Economie Régionale* (LARES), September.

Oyejide, T., E. Ademola, Olawale Ogunkola, Abiodun S. Bankole, and Adeolu O. Adwuyi. 2008. "Study of Trade Policy and Nigerian Wholesale Prices." Report prepared for the World Bank, Washington, DC.

Perret, Christophe. 2002. "Le commerce de véhicules d'occasion au Bénin: Problématique régionale et aspects nationaux." *Economie Régionale* (LARES), November.

Rice, Berkeley. 1967. *Enter Gambia: The Birth of an Improbable Nation.* Boston: Houghton-Mifflin.

Soulé, Bio. G. 2004. "La dynamique régionale." *Economie Régionale* (LARES), April.

World Bank. 2005. *Benin Diagnostic Trade Integration Study [DTIS].* Washington, DC: World Bank.

———. 2010. *World Development Indicators.* Washington, DC: World Bank.

WTO (World Trade Organization). 2004. *The Gambia Trade Policy Review.* Geneva: WTO.

———. 2005. *Nigeria Trade Policy Review.* Geneva: WTO.

Yang, Yongzheng, and Sanjeev Gupta. 2005. "Regional Trade Arrangements in Africa: Past Performance and the Way Forward." Working Paper 05/36, IMF, Washington, DC, February.

Young, Crawford. 1994. *The African Colonial State in Comparative Perspective.* New Haven, CT: Yale University Press.

Index

Boxes, figures, maps, notes, and tables are indicated by b, f, m, n, and t, respectively, following the page numbers.

ECO-AUDIT
Environmental Benefits Statement

The World Bank is committed to preserving endangered forests and natural resources. The Office of the Publisher has chosen to print *The Informal Sector in Francophone Africa* on recycled paper with 50 percent post-consumer waste, in accordance with the recommended standards for paper usage set by the Green Press Initiative, a nonprofit program supporting publishers in using fiber that is not sourced from endangered forests. For more information, visit www.greenpressinitiative.org.

Saved:
- 3 trees
- 1 million British thermal units of total energy
- 230 pounds of net greenhouse gases (CO_2 equivalent)
- 1,036 gallons of waste water
- 65 pounds of solid waste

green
press
INITIATIVE

www.ingramcontent.com/pod-product-compliance
Lightning Source LLC
Chambersburg PA
CBHW061149220326
41599CB00025B/4418